海派文化英译
系列丛书

丛书总主编／冯奇

主编　张欢

副主编　邱玉情　卢倩男

审校　冯军

生态旅游翻译教程

——以上海崇明岛为例

WUHAN UNIVERSITY PRESS
武汉大学出版社

图书在版编目(CIP)数据

生态旅游翻译教程：以上海崇明岛为例：英文、汉文／张欢主编．武汉：武汉大学出版社，2025.4. -- 海派文化英译系列丛书／冯奇主编． -- ISBN 978-7-307-24592-1

Ⅰ.F590.75

中国国家版本馆 CIP 数据核字第 2024P828J1 号

责任编辑:邓　喆　　　责任校对:杨　欢　　　版式设计:韩闻锦

出版发行：**武汉大学出版社**　（430072　武昌　珞珈山）

（电子邮箱：cbs22@ whu.edu.cn　网址：www.wdp.com.cn）

印刷:武汉邮科印务有限公司

开本:787×1092　1/16　印张:14.25　字数:291 千字　插页:1

版次:2025 年 4 月第 1 版　　2025 年 4 月第 1 次印刷

ISBN 978-7-307-24592-1　　定价:69.00 元

前　　言

在全球生态环保理念的推动下，生态旅游逐渐成为人们旅行的新选择。然而，要获得生态旅游的更深层次体验，我们需要对旅游地的自然环境、历史文化、生态特色有深入的了解。因此，将生态旅游与翻译教学相结合，既可以提高我们的语言能力，又可以增进我们对生态旅游的认识。在此背景下，我们编写了这本《生态旅游翻译教程》。

本书围绕崇明岛的生态旅游展开，内容涵盖了崇明岛的地理位置、气候特点、自然环境、生态特色、历史文化背景等方面。全书共分为九章，从地理、湿地、农园、民宿、民俗、美食、交通、教育、政策和建筑等方面，为读者真实呈现了崇明岛的生态旅游资源。

本书有三个特点。首先，本书结合了翻译教学和生态旅游的知识，使得学习过程富有趣味性，同时也具备很强的实用性。其次，本书以崇明岛的实际案例为基础，结合了大量的实地考察和采访，使得内容真实、准确、生动。最后，本书在介绍崇明岛的过程中，深入浅出地解释了许多生态和旅游的专业术语，对于读者来说，既是一本实用的翻译教程，又是一本生态旅游的知识读本。

本书读者对象群主要包括翻译专业的学生、教师，以及对生态旅游有兴趣的广大读者。对于翻译专业的学生和教师来说，本书不仅可以提高他们的翻译能力、拓宽知识视野，还可以提升他们的生态文化素养。对于对生态旅游有兴趣的读者来说，本书可以帮助他们更全面、深入地了解崇明岛的生态旅游资源，从而优化他们的生态旅游体验。

阅读本书的好处主要有三点。首先，通过阅读本书，读者可以熟悉和掌握大量关于生态旅游和翻译的专业知识，这对于提高他们的专业素养和综合素质具有重要的意义。其次，读者可以进一步了解崇明岛的生态旅游资源，这对于他们进行生态旅游活动，或开展相关的研究工作具有重要的参考价值。最后，读者可以提升语言能力和文化素养，这对于他们的职业发展和个人成长都具有重要的促进作用。

总体而言，本教程是一本将翻译教学、生态旅游与文化研究融为一体的多功能教程。我们相信，无论是翻译专业的学生、教师，还是对生态旅游感兴趣的游客和广大读者，都能从本书中获得一个更宽广、更有深度的视角，从而更好地洞察生态旅游的新趋势以及语言景观建设的新路径。

冯　奇

2024 年 8 月

目　　录

第一章　崇明生态岛屿

一、崇明岛的地理位置和气候特点

翻译简介

本文的译文整体上准确度较高，语言风格较为正式。在翻译原文时，第一大难点就是数字的翻译，如经纬度、土地面积、降水量、温度、时间等。第二大难点是地理、物种术语的翻译，如"河口冲积岛""淤积""亚热带季风型气候""柿子""橘子""崇明水杉（落羽杉）""樟树""柳树""旱柳""池杉""中山杉""重阳木"等。而多数物种术语又同时存在英文名和拉丁名，一般翻译多以英文名为主，拉丁名为辅。第三大难点是衔接地理位置描述中零散的句型结构，如"岛屿总面积约为 1269.1 平方公里，横贯长江口，东临东海，南靠上海本土，形成了独特的地理环境"。总体来说，本文的译文体现了灵活的句子衔接技巧、术语选择和数字译法。

词汇表

崇明岛：Chongming Island

河口冲积岛：estuarine alluvial island

地理坐标：geographical coordinates

东经：east longitude

北纬：north latitude

总面积：total area

平方公里：square kilometer

长江口：the mouth of the Yangtze River

上海本土：the mainland of Shanghai

经济发展：economic development

生态建设：ecological construction

生态屏障：ecological shield

候鸟保护区：bird sanctuary

气候特点：climate characteristics

泥沙淤积：sedimentation

地势平坦：flat terrain

海拔：elevation

亚热带季风型气候：subtropical monsoon climate

四季分明：distinct seasons

雨量充沛：abundant rainfall

气温适中：moderate temperatures

年平均气温：annual average temperature

年总降水量：total annual precipitation

降水量：precipitation

原文

崇明岛的地理位置和气候特点

崇明岛的地理位置

崇明岛位于中国东海沿岸，上海市东北部，是中国仅次于台湾岛、海南岛的第三大岛屿，是世界上最大的河口冲积岛。地理坐标介于东经 121°09′30″ 至 121°54′00″，北纬 31°27′00″ 至 31°51′15″。岛屿总面积约为 1269.1 平方公里，横贯长江口，东临东海，南靠上海本土，形成了独特的地理环境。

作为上海市辖区的一部分，崇明岛对上海的经济发展和生态建设具有重要意义。此外，崇明岛还是长江口的重要生态屏障和候鸟保护区，对于长江、黄浦江的水质保护具有重要作用。

崇明岛气候特点

崇明岛建立在泥沙淤积上，岛屿地势平坦，海拔较低，仅有 3.5—4.5 米。崇明岛属于亚热带季风型气候，具有四季分明、雨量充沛、气温适中的特点。年平均气温约为

16.9℃，年总降水量为1283.6毫米，日最大降水量为68.6毫米(7月2日)。春季温暖舒适，夏季炎热多雨，秋季凉爽宜人，冬季寒冷干燥。

春季

春季气温逐渐回升，3月份平均气温在10℃至16℃，昼夜温差较大；4月份平均气温约为14℃至20℃；5月份平均气温在18℃至25℃。春季降水逐月增加，3月份的平均降水量大约为80毫米，4月份的平均降水量大约为100毫米，5月份的平均降水量大约为120毫米。春季是崇明岛植物生长的开始，花儿竞相开放，吸引了大量游客前来观赏。

夏季

夏季是崇明岛最炎热的季节，6月份的平均气温在22℃至28℃，7月份的平均气温在26℃至32℃，8月份的平均气温在26℃至31℃。夏季降水量丰富，尤其是2021年7月份，平均降水量达到了220毫米，占全年降水量的近20%。此外，夏季还有台风侵袭，需注意防范。夏季是崇明岛农作物生长的关键时期，岛上的水稻、棉花等农作物拥有良好的生长条件。

秋季

秋季崇明岛气温逐渐下降，9月份的平均气温在21℃至27℃，10月份的平均气温在16℃至22℃，11月份的平均气温在11℃至17℃。降水量逐月减少，9月份的平均降水量大约为85毫米，10月份的平均降水量大约为70毫米，11月份的平均降水量大约为50毫米。秋季是崇明岛最宜人的季节，气候凉爽，适合户外活动。此时正是水果丰收的季节，崇明岛的柿子、葡萄、橘子等水果口感鲜美，吸引了大量游客。

冬季

冬季是崇明岛最寒冷的季节，12月份的平均气温在6℃至12℃，1月份的平均气温在3℃至8℃，2月份的平均气温在3℃至9℃。2022年12月份总降水量约为31毫米；2023年1月份总降水量约为34毫米；同年2月份总降水量约为101毫米。冬季气候寒冷干燥，此时崇明岛的景色也显得宁静、素雅。

崇明岛的生态环境和旅游资源

崇明岛的气候条件和地理位置为其生态环境提供了得天独厚的条件。崇明岛森林覆盖率达到23%，拥有丰富的植物资源，如崇明水杉(落羽杉)、樟树、柳树、旱柳、池杉、中山杉、重阳木等。此外，崇明岛还有世界著名的东平国家森林公园，是长江口地区最大的湿地，拥有丰富的水鸟资源，吸引了成千上万的候鸟前来栖息。

崇明岛旅游资源丰富，拥有独特的生态、农业、历史文化等旅游资源。如著名的崇明东滩鸟类国家级自然保护区、陈家宅园、崇明学宫等景点，吸引了大量游客前来游玩。

崇明岛地处长江口，地理位置独特，气候条件优越。四季分明的气候为岛上的生态环境和农业发展提供了良好条件，同时也为游客提供了宜人的旅游环境。作为上海市的重要组成部分，崇明岛在经济、生态和旅游等方面都具有举足轻重的地位，值得我们深入了解和大力保护。

译文

Geographical Location and Climate Characteristics of Chongming Island

Geographical Location of Chongming Island

Chongming Island is located on the coast of the East China Sea, in the northeast of Shanghai, China. It is the third largest island in China, following Taiwan Island and Hainan Island, and the largest estuarine alluvial island in the world. Its geographical coordinates range from 121°09′30″ to 121°54′00″ east longitude and 31°27′00″ to 31°51′15″ north latitude. With a total area of approximately 1,269.1 square kilometers, the island spans the mouth of the Yangtze River, borders the East China Sea to the east, and is adjacent to the mainland of Shanghai, creating a unique geographical environment.

As part of Shanghai municipality, Chongming Island plays a significant role in the economic development and ecological construction of Shanghai. Furthermore, it serves as an important ecological shield and bird sanctuary at the mouth of the Yangtze River, contributing to the protection of water quality of the Yangtze River and Huangpu River.

Climate Characteristics of Chongming Island

Built on sedimentation, Chongming Island has a flat terrain with a low elevation ranging from 3.5 to 4.5 meters. It belongs to a subtropical monsoon climate zone, characterized by distinct seasons, abundant rainfall, and moderate temperatures. The annual average temperature is around 16.9℃, with a total annual precipitation of 1283.6 millimeters. The maximum daily precipitation recorded was 68.6 millimeters on July 2nd. Spring is warm and comfortable; summer is hot and rainy; autumn is cool and pleasant; and winter is cold and dry.

Spring

During spring, temperatures gradually rise. The average temperature in March ranges from around 10℃ to 16℃, with significant temperature differences between day and night. In April, the average temperature is approximately 14℃ to 20℃, and in May, it ranges from 18℃ to 25℃. Precipitation increases month by month during spring. The average monthly precipitation in March is about 80 millimeters, while in April it's around 100 millimeters, and in May it's approximately 120 millimeters. Spring marks the beginning of plant growth on Chongming Island, with flowers blooming and attracting a large number of visitors for flower appreciation.

Summer

Summer is the hottest season on Chongming Island. The average temperature in June ranges from around 22℃ to 28℃. In July it's approximately 26℃ to 32℃, and in August it's around 26℃ to 31℃. Summer is characterized by abundant rainfall, especially in July 2021 when the average precipitation reached 220 millimeters, accounting for nearly 20% of the annual rainfall. Additionally, typhoons can occur during summer, so precautions should be taken. It is the critical season for crop growth on the island, providing favorable conditions for rice, cotton, and other crops.

Autumn

During autumn, temperatures gradually decrease. The average temperature in September ranges from around 21℃ to 27℃, while in October it's approximately 16℃ to 22℃, and in November it's around 11℃ to 17℃. Precipitation decreases month by month, with an average of around 85 millimeters in September, 70 millimeters in October, and 50 millimeters in November. Autumn is the most pleasant season on Chongming Island, with a cool climate that is suitable for outdoor activities. It is also the harvest season for fruits such as persimmons, grapes, and oranges, attracting a large number of tourists.

Winter

Winter is the coldest season on Chongming Island. The average temperature in December ranges from around 6℃ to 12℃, while in January it's approximately 3℃ to 8℃, and in February it's around 3℃ to 9℃. The total precipitation in December 2022 was about 31 millimeters, while in January 2023 it was around 34 millimeters, and in February 2023 it was approximately 101 millimeters. The winter is cold and dry, and the scenery on Chongming Island appears tranquil and elegant.

Ecological Environment and Tourism Resources of Chongming Island

The climate conditions and geographical location of Chongming Island provide unique advantages for its ecological environment. The island has a forest coverage rate of 23% and abundant plant resources, including *Metasequoia glyptostroboides*, camphor tree, willow, *Salix matsudana Koidz*, *Taxodium distichum*, *Taxodium hybrid*, and *Bischofia polycarpa*. Additionally, Chongming Island is home to the world-renowned Dongping National Forest Park, the largest wetland in the Yangtze River estuary region, with rich waterbird resources that attract thousands of migratory birds.

Chongming Island boasts abundant tourism resources, including unique ecological tourism, agricultural tourism, and historical and cultural tourism. Popular attractions include the famous Chongming Dongtan National Nature Reserve, Chenjia Village Garden, and Chongming Academy, attracting a large number of visitors.

Located at the mouth of the Yangtze River, Chongming Island possesses a unique geographical location and favorable climate conditions. Its distinct four seasons provide favorable conditions for the island's ecological environment and agricultural development, while offering a pleasant tourism environment for visitors. As an important part of Shanghai, Chongming Island holds a significant position in terms of economy, ecology, and tourism, deserving our in-depth understanding and protection.

例句赏析

例 1：

原文：地理坐标介于东经 121°09′30″至 121°54′00″，北纬 31°27′00″至 31°51′15″。岛屿总面积约为 1269.1 平方公里，横贯长江口，东临东海，南靠上海本土，形成了独特的地理环境。

译文：Its geographical coordinates range from 121°09′30″ to 121°54′00″ east longitude and 31°27′00″ to 31°51′15″ north latitude. With a total area of approximately 1,269.1 square kilometers, the island spans the mouth of the Yangtze River, borders the East China Sea to the east, and is adjacent to the mainland of Shanghai, creating a unique geographical environment.

赏析：对原文的翻译存在的难点为地理数字、地理方位的叙述和长难句的衔接。其中的"坐标"为复数，说明指多种坐标，指坐标的范围，而非具体某一坐标点。在翻译该数字单位时，中文单位"东经""北纬"在数字左侧，而译文则相反。第二句的翻译难点在于零散句型的衔接，原文的逻辑主语为"岛屿"，其谓语则包括"约为""横贯""东临""南靠""形成了"，分别被灵活地处理为"with"伴随状语、动词、"doing"伴随状语。

例2：

原文：崇明岛属于亚热带季风型气候，具有四季分明、雨量充沛、气温适中的特点。年平均气温约为 16.9℃，年总降水量为 1283.6 毫米，日最大降水量为 68.6 毫米（7月2日）。

译文：It belongs to a subtropical monsoon climate zone, characterized by distinct seasons, abundant rainfall, and moderate temperatures. The annual average temperature is around 16.9℃, with a total annual precipitation of 1283.6 millimeters. The maximum daily precipitation recorded was 68.6 millimeters on July 2nd.

赏析：原文介绍了崇明岛的气候特点，从全年、四季、某天的气候特点出发，由大到小地介绍了温度、降水等气候特点。翻译难点为零散的句型结构、气候术语。原文第一句介绍了崇明岛全年的三个气候特点，各特点以顿号隔开，而译文采用代词 it 作主语，以避免用词重复，并采取"characterized by"和名词化的技巧，灵活地保留了气候特点的并列结构。译文将"四季分明""雨量充沛""气温适中"的结构，调整为"分明的四季""充沛的雨量""适中的气温"，通过名词的并列，使译文句型简单化。

例3：

原文：春季气温逐渐回升，3月份平均气温在 10℃ 至 16℃，昼夜温差较大；4月份平均气温约为 14℃ 至 20℃；5月份平均气温在 18℃ 至 25℃。

译文：During spring, temperatures gradually rise. The average temperature in March ranges from around 10℃ to 16℃, with significant temperature differences between day and night. In April, the average temperature is approximately 14℃ to 20℃, and in May, it ranges from 18℃ to 25℃.

赏析：原文介绍了崇明岛春季不同月份的气温变化情况。在译文中，"气温"被翻译成复数形式"temperatures"，以对应不同月份的气温。数字翻译也以符号的形式呈现。句型上，原文每个分句的篇幅较短，以分号隔开，而译文篇幅较长，以句号隔开。译文的月份时间状语和原文一致，都位于句首，利于顺句驱动。译文还体现了避免用词重复的原则，如描述模糊数字的高频词组"……至……"的通常译法为"range from… to…"或"be…

to…"；在最后一个分句里，"average temperature"被简化为代词"it"，以避免用词重复。

例4：

原文：崇明岛森林覆盖率达到23%，拥有丰富的植物资源，如崇明水杉(落羽杉)、樟树、柳树、旱柳、池杉、中山杉、重阳木等。

译文：The island has a forest coverage rate of 23% and abundant plant resources, including *Metasequoia glyptostroboides*, camphor tree, willow, *Salix matsudana Koidz*, *Taxodium distichum*, *Taxodium hybrid*, and *Bischofia polycarpa*.

赏析：原文介绍了崇明岛的植被特点，以"总体特点+具体例子"的结构来描述。原文的谓语"达到""拥有"在译文中被合并为"has"，体现了篇幅的精简性。例子的衔接词"如"被处理为"including"。译文的最大难点为术语翻译，尤其是一些特有的树种名称既包含拉丁文又包含英文。因英文名比拉丁文更具有通俗性，所以首选英文名称来翻译树种术语，但有些树种只有拉丁文名称。专业术语是翻译的一大障碍，译者需要掌握、组建翻译软件的术语库，以减少查电子词典的时间。

☞ **练习**

（一）将下列短语翻译成英文。

1. 世界上最大的河口冲积岛
2. 游客的理想目的地
3. 可持续发展的关键方面
4. 多样而充满活力的生态系统
5. 中国第三大岛屿

（二）将下列句子翻译成英文。

1. 崇明岛以其独特的地理环境而闻名，形成了其生态屏障。
2. 该岛明显的季节变化和春秋季节的适宜气温吸引了许多游客。
3. 环境保护在崇明岛的可持续发展中起着至关重要的作用。
4. 该岛丰富的降水量支持着各种植物和鸟类物种。
5. 崇明岛位于长江口和杭州湾之间，这有助于其生态多样性的形成。

（三）将下面段落翻译成英文。

崇明岛是中国第三大岛屿，也是世界上最大的河口冲积岛。它以其独特的地理环境而闻名，形成了其生态屏障。岛屿位于长江口和杭州湾之间，拥有丰富的降水量，创造了多样而充满活力的生态系统。崇明岛有明显的季节变化，春季和秋季气温适中，是游客的理想目的地。该岛致力于可持续发展，并高度重视环境保护。

☞ **参考答案**

（一）

1. The largest estuarine alluvial island in the world

2. Ideal destination for tourists

3. Key aspect of sustainable development

4. Diverse and vibrant ecosystem

5. The third-largest island in China

（二）

1. Chongming Island is renowned for its unique geographical environment, which forms its ecological shield.

2. The island's distinct seasonal changes and pleasant temperatures in spring and autumn attract many tourists.

3. Environmental protection plays a crucial role in the sustainable development of Chongming Island.

4. The abundant rainfall on the island supports a variety of plant and bird species.

5. Chongming Island's location between the mouth of the Yangtze River and Hangzhou Bay contributes to its ecological diversity.

（三）

Chongming Island is the third-largest island in China and the largest estuarine alluvial island in the world. It is renowned for its unique geographical environment, forming its ecological barrier. Located between the mouth of the Yangtze River and Hangzhou Bay, the island receives abundant rainfall, creating a diverse and vibrant ecosystem. Chongming Island experiences noticeable seasonal changes, with moderate temperatures in spring and autumn, making it an ideal destination for tourists. The island is committed to sustainable development and places great emphasis on environmental protection.

二、崇明岛的历史和文化背景

翻译简介

本文讲述了崇明岛的历史和文化背景，本文的译文整体上做到了内容准确、语言简洁、句型结构流畅、术语翻译恰当。译文对原文内容进行了准确的翻译，没有遗漏或误解原文中的信息和意思。译文的语言风格简洁明了，尽量重现原文的句子结构和内容顺序。难点在于文化词、地理术语，例如景点地名、佛教建筑、民间艺术、器具、地理现象等的翻译。由于个别的景点名称没有现有的译文，所以译者通常要在音译和意译间进行斟酌。音译利于游客根据地名来问路，而意译则利于游客领略景点的内涵。另外，地名有时也容易造成歧义，如"园"的译文有时候不是"garden"而是"park"，具体译法取决于景点的介绍和实际场景规模。

词汇表

崇明岛：Chongming Island

沃土：fertile land

考古学家：archaeologist

历史学家：historian

地理学家：geographer

唐初：early Tang Dynasty

北宋晚期：late Northern Song Dynasty

沙洲：sandbar

明末：late Ming Dynasty

泥沙：sediment

潮汐：tides

长江入海口：the estuary of the Yangtze River

蛋形岛：oval-shaped island

灶文化博物馆：Stove Culture Museum

灶：stove

文化遗产：cultural heritage

古迹：cultural relics

广福寺：Guangfu Temple

佛教：Buddhism

唐朝：the Tang Dynasty

建筑风格：architectural style

严谨：rigorous

代表：representative

南方：southern

山门楼：mountain gate tower

香客楼：guesthouse

念佛堂：chanting hall

斋堂：dining hall

客堂：guest hall

生活楼：living quarters

佛学院教学楼：Buddhist teaching buildings

学生宿舍楼：student dormitories

佛像：Buddha statue

壁画：mural

精湛的：exquisite

博物馆：museum

火炉：stove

灶文化：culture of stoves

灶神：stove god

灶花：stove painting

炉灶：hearth

火盆：fire pan

火塘：fire pit

文化内涵：cultural significance

学宫博物馆：Academy Museum

传统教育文化：traditional Chinese educational culture

祭祀：worship

孔子：Confucius

寿安寺：Shou'an Temple

四大古刹：four ancient temples

大雄宝殿：Great Buddha Hall

天王殿：Hall of Heavenly Kings

三圣殿：Hall of the Three Saints

地藏殿：Hall of Ksitigarbha

财神殿：Hall of Wealth Gods

祖师殿：Ancestral Hall

问心亭：Pavilion of Self-Reflection

钟楼：Bell Tower

鼓楼：Drum Tower

唐一岑墓：Tang Yicen's Tomb

烈士：martyr

明朝：the Ming Dynasty

反倭寇：fight against Japanese pirates

澹园：Danyuan Garden

典型的：typical

江南园林：Jiangnan-style garden

寒山寺：Hanshan Temple

禅宗：Zen Buddhism

历史悠久：long-standing

古迹：ancient sites

博大精深：profoundness

地域文化：regional culture

原文

崇明岛自古以来就是一块沃土，有着悠久的历史和灿烂的文化。据考古、历史、地理学家的研究发现，自崇明岛形成以来，距今已有 1380 多年的历史。从那时起，崇明岛就逐渐成为长江下游地区的重要居民点。

崇明岛的发展历程可以划分为以下几个阶段。从唐初到北宋晚期（公元 7—11 世纪），崇明地区形成了若干沙洲。到唐武德年间（公元 618—627 年），长江入海口处出现了东、西两片沙洲，它们构成了日后崇明岛的雏形。到了五代十国时期，静海都镇遏使姚彦洪于杨吴天祚三年（公元 937 年）在西沙建立了崇明镇，自此，"崇明"这一名称正式出现，开启了它后续的发展篇章。从北宋晚期到明末（公元 12—16 世纪），由于潮汐作用带来的北海沿岸泥沙沉积，崇明岛及其沙洲经历了显著的扩张。从 17 世纪至今，崇明岛逐渐发展成为一个大型的蛋形岛，并且仍在持续扩大。

崇明岛的历史文化底蕴深厚，古迹众多，有丰富的民间艺术，如崇明灶文化、土布、竹编等，充分展示了崇明岛深厚的历史底蕴和独特的地域文化。

崇明岛有着丰厚的民俗文化底蕴和文化古迹。其中最有名的是灶文化博物馆，这个博物馆是全国唯一一个以"灶"为主题的博物馆，展示了中国灶文化的历史和发展。在这里，游客可以了解到灶神、灶花、灶台美食和各种不同类型的灶具，包括炉灶、火盆、火塘、火炉，等等。此外，博物馆还展示了制作灶具的工具和材料，以及灶具在生活中的应用和文化内涵。

广福寺是一座历史悠久的佛教寺庙，始建于唐朝。广福寺建筑风格独特，结构严谨，是中国南方佛教建筑的代表之一。寺庙内的建筑包括大雄宝殿（伽蓝殿）、山门楼、香客楼、念佛堂、斋堂、客堂、生活楼及佛学院教学楼、学僧宿舍楼等。在这里，游客可以欣赏到精美的佛像和壁画，感受到佛教文化的博大精深。

此外，崇明岛还有学宫博物馆、寿安寺、唐一岑墓、澹园、寒山寺等文化古迹。学宫博物馆是一座展示中国传统教育文化的博物馆，是祭祀孔子的地方；寿安寺是一座历史悠久的佛教寺庙，为崇明岛四大古刹之一，寺内有大雄宝殿、天王殿、三圣殿、地藏殿、财神殿、祖师殿、问心亭、钟楼、鼓楼等建筑；唐一岑墓是明朝抗倭烈士唐一岑的墓葬；澹园是一座典型的江南园林；寒山寺则是一座历史悠久的禅宗寺庙。

总的来说，崇明岛是一个既有着悠久历史，又有着独特文化的地方。它的历史文化遗产丰富，岛上的古迹众多，民间艺术也十分精湛。这里不仅有历史的厚重感，还有独特的地域文化，让人们可以从中领略到中华文化的博大精深。希望更多的人能够走进崇明岛，了解这里的历史和文化，感受它的独特魅力。

译文

Chongming Island has been a fertile land with a long history and splendid culture since ancient times. According to the research of archaeologists, historians, and geographers, Chongming Island has a history of over 1,380 years. Since its formation, Chongming Island gradually became an important settlement in the downstream area of the Yangtze River.

The development of Chongming Island can be divided into several stages. From the early Tang Dynasty to the late Northern Song Dynasty (7th to 11th century AD), the Chongming area formed a few sandbars. During the Wude Period of the Tang Dynasty (618–627 AD), two sandbars, the East Sandbar and the West Sandbar, emerged at the estuary of the Yangtze River. These were the predecessors of Chongming Island. During the Five Dynasties and Ten Kingdoms Period, Yao Yanhong, the commander of Jinghai Du Town, established Chongming Town on the West Sandbar in the third year of Tianzuo of the Yang Wu Regime (937 AD). Since then, the name "Chongming" has come into existence. From the late Northern Song Dynasty to the late Ming Dynasty (12th to 16th century AD), due to the deposition of sediment from the northern coastal area carried by tides, Chongming Island and its sandbars experienced significant expansion. Since the 17th century to the present, Chongming Island has gradually formed a large oval-shaped island and continues to expand.

Chongming Island has a rich historical and cultural heritage with numerous cultural relics, and boasts a wealth of folk arts, such as Stove Culture, homespun cloth, and bamboo weaving, fully showcasing the island's profound historical heritage and unique regional culture.

Chongming Island has a rich historical and cultural heritage with many famous cultural relics. The most renowned is the Stove Culture Museum, which is the only museum in the country dedicated to the culture of stoves, showcasing the history and development of Chinese stove culture. Here, visitors can learn about the Stove God, stove painting, delicious food prepared on stoves, and various types of stoves including hearths, fire pans, fire pits, and stoves. The museum also exhibits the tools and materials used in stove making, as well as the application and cultural significance of stoves in daily life.

Guangfu Temple is an ancient Buddhist temple that was built during the Tang Dynasty. It has a unique architectural style and rigorous structure. It is one of the representatives of southern Chinese Buddhist architecture. The temple complex includes the Great Buddha Hall (Qielan Hall), mountain gate tower, guesthouse, chanting hall, dining hall, guest hall, living quarters, Buddhist teaching buildings, and student dormitories. Here, visitors can admire exquisite Buddha statues and murals, experiencing the profoundness of Buddhist culture.

In addition, Chongming Island is home to the Academy Museum, Shou'an Temple, Tang Yicen's Tomb, Danyuan Garden, and Hanshan Temple, among other cultural relics. The Academy Museum is a museum showcasing traditional Chinese educational culture and serves as a place of worship for Confucius. Shou'an Temple is a long-standing Buddhist temple and one of the four ancient temples on Chongming Island. It features buildings such as the Great Buddha Hall, Hall of Heavenly Kings, Hall of the Three Saints, Hall of Ksitigarbha, Hall of Wealth Gods, Ancestral Hall, Pavilion of Self-Reflection, Bell Tower, and Drum Tower. Tang Yicen's Tomb is the burial site of Tang Yicen, a martyr who fought against Japanese pirates during the Ming Dynasty. Danyuan Garden is a typical Jiangnan-style garden, and Hanshan Temple is a long-standing Zen Buddhist temple.

In conclusion, Chongming Island is a place with a rich history and unique culture. It possesses abundant historical and cultural heritage, numerous ancient sites, and exquisite folk arts. It not only carries a sense of historical weight, but also showcases the unique regional culture, allowing people to appreciate the profoundness of Chinese culture. We hope that more people can visit Chongming Island, understand its history and culture, and experience its unique charm.

例句赏析

例1:

原文:崇明岛的发展历程可以划分为以下几个阶段。从唐初到北宋晚期(公元 7—11 世纪),崇明地区形成了若干沙洲。到唐武德年间(公元 618—627 年),长江入海口处出现了东、西两片沙洲,它们构成了日后崇明岛的雏形。到了五代十国时期,静海都镇遏使姚彦洪于杨吴天祚三年(公元 937 年)在西沙建立了崇明镇,自此,"崇明"这一名称正式出现,开启了它后续的发展篇章。从北宋晚期到明末(公元 12—16 世纪),由于潮汐作用带来的北海沿岸泥沙沉积,崇明岛及其沙洲经历了显著的扩张。从 17 世纪至今,崇明岛逐渐发展成为一个大型的蛋形岛,并且仍在持续扩大。

译文:The development of Chongming Island can be divided into several stages. From the early Tang Dynasty to the late Northern Song Dynasty (7th to 11th century AD), the Chongming area formed a few sandbars. During the Wude Period of the Tang Dynasty (618–627 AD), two sandbars, the East Sandbar and the West Sandbar, emerged at the estuary of the Yangtze River. These were the predecessors of Chongming Island. During the Five Dynasties and Ten Kingdoms Period, Yao Yanhong, the commander of Jinghai Du Town, established Chongming Town on the West Sandbar in the third year of Tianzuo of the Yang Wu Regime (937 AD). Since then, the name "Chongming" has come into existence. From the late Northern Song Dynasty to the late Ming Dynasty (12th to 16th century AD), due to the deposition of sediment from the northern coastal area carried by tides, Chongming Island and its sandbars experienced significant expansion. Since the 17th century to the present, Chongming Island has gradually formed a large oval-shaped island and continues to expand.

赏析:这个长句子为"总—分"结构,涵盖了崇明岛历史发展的不同时间段。原文的三个时间段均采用"从……到"的表达方式,译文则使用了一些较为简单直接的表达,例如,"from...to"和"since...to"。一般来说,中文习惯将状语放在句子的开头、中间位置,而英文通常置于句子末尾。但在上面例子中,译者则尽量顺句驱动,让译文的时间、原因状语从句与原文的位置一致。该策略利于减少句型转换所耗费的脑力,提高翻译效率。

例2:

原文:崇明岛的历史文化底蕴深厚,古迹众多,有丰富的民间艺术,如崇明灶文化、土布、竹编等，充分展示了崇明岛深厚的历史底蕴和独特的地域文化。

译文：Chongming Island has a rich historical and cultural heritage with numerous cultural relics, and boasts a wealth of folk arts, such as Stove Culture, homespun cloth, and bamboo weaving, fully showcasing the island's profound historical heritage and unique regional culture.

赏析：(1)关于"崇明灶文化"的英文表达："崇明"是特定地名，应直接使用拼音"Chongming"表示。"灶"对应的英文是"stove"，在这里指的是与炉灶相关的文化。"文化"用"culture"来表达。在英文中，表达特定地域的某种文化时，通常采用"地名 + 文化主题词 + Culture"的结构，因此"崇明灶文化"应翻译为"Chongming Stove Culture"。(2)关于"土布"的英文表达："homespun"有"家里织的、手织的"的意思，强调这种布是在家庭环境中通过手工纺织而成，符合土布的传统生产方式。"handwoven"则更直接地表示"手工编织的"，突出了土布靠手工织造的特点。"cloth"即"布"的意思。因此，"土布"可以用"homespun cloth"或"handwoven cloth"来表达，这两个翻译都能准确传达"土布"的概念。虽然在一些资料中也会见到"native cloth"的说法，但它更多强调本土的、本地的布，没有很好地体现"手工织造"这一关键特征。(3)关于"竹编"的英文表达："bamboo"表示"竹子"，"weaving"和"plaiting"都有"编织"的意思。在描述用竹子进行编织这种手工艺时，这两个词都很常用。例如，在介绍中国传统手工艺的英文资料中，提到竹编大多会使用"bamboo weaving"或者"bamboo plaiting"，像"竹编制品"就可以说"bamboo woven products"或者"bamboo plaited products"。此外，"wickerwork"也有"柳条编制品；竹编制品"的意思，但相对来说没有前两者那么常用，也没有那么直接地体现竹子这一材料。

例3：

原文：在这里，游客可以了解到灶神、灶花、灶台美食和各种不同类型的灶具，包括炉灶、火盆、火塘、火炉，等等。

译文：Here, visitors can learn about the Stove God, stove painting, delicious food prepared on stoves, and various types of stoves including hearths, fire pans, fire pits, and stoves.

赏析：原文是对灶文化博物馆内部展品的罗列，涉及与厨房有关的文化、艺术、器具等。"灶花"通"灶画"，具体指灶台上绘制的图案，因此译为stove painting。"火盆""火塘"分别指以盆、坑洞为容器所点燃的火堆，用于户外、野营时烹饪食物。然而，"火盆"为什么不译为fire basin？这是因为basin的容量比pan更深，远大于烹饪时用的锅，因此pan更符合"火盆"的实际尺寸。"火塘"的译文fire pits则与英语对火坑的习惯叫法对应。"火盆"的译法源自逻辑，而"火塘"的译法则源自约定俗成。

例4：

原文：寺庙内的建筑包括大雄宝殿（伽蓝殿）、山门楼、香客楼、念佛堂、斋堂、客堂、生活楼及佛学院教学楼、学僧宿舍楼等。

译文：The temple complex includes the Great Buddha Hall (Qielan Hall), mountain gate tower, guesthouse, chanting hall, dining hall, guest hall, living quarters, Buddhist teaching buildings, and student dormitories.

赏析：原文是对景点内建筑名称的罗列，这类术语通常包含建筑的规模和功能，少数佛教建筑甚至有多种汉语叫法。例如，"大雄宝殿"和"伽蓝殿"分别是同一建筑的汉语和梵文叫法，是佛教寺庙中最为重要的建筑之一，佛教最高领袖释迦牟尼佛就被供奉在其中。"大雄"指的是释迦牟尼佛，象征佛的广博、恒久和坚不可摧的灵魂与道心。其英文翻译使用"the Great Buddha Hall"，更具通用性，更易于理解和记忆。其余建筑的译文主要体现其功能，唯独"山门楼"的译文则侧重于体现其位于寺庙大门的位置。

☞ **练习**

（一）将下列短语翻译成英文。

1. 崇明地区

2. 沙洲

3. 潮汐作用带来的北海沿岸泥沙的沉积

4. 蛋形岛

5. 稀有濒危物种

（二）将下列句子翻译成英文。

1. 这里的湿地也是许多稀有濒危物种，如黑面琵鹭和白鹭的栖息地。

2. 在这里，你可以乘坐环岛旅游公交车，感受崇明岛的自然风光和民俗风情。

3. 这里还有丰富的文化遗产，包括灶文化、崇明船民的民俗和传统手工艺，等等。

（三）将下面段落翻译成英文。

崇明岛的发展历程可以划分为以下几个阶段。从唐初到北宋晚期（公元7—11世纪），崇明地区形成了若干沙洲。到唐武德年间（公元618—627年），长江入海口处出现了东、西两片沙洲，它们构成了日后崇明岛的雏形。到了五代十国时期，静海都镇遏使姚彦洪于杨吴天祚三年（公元937年）在西沙建立了崇明镇，自此，"崇明"这一名称正式出现，开启了它后续的发展篇章。从北宋晚期到明末（公元12—16世纪），由于潮汐作用带来的北海沿岸泥沙沉积，崇明岛及其沙洲经历了显著的扩张。从17世纪至今，崇明岛逐渐发展成为一个大型的蛋形岛，并且仍在持续扩大。

☞ **参考答案**

（一）

1. Chongming area

2. sandbars

3. the deposition of sediment from the northern coastal area carried by tides

4. oval-shaped island

5. rare and endangered species

（二）

1. The wetland also provides a habitat for many rare and endangered species, such as the black-faced spoonbill and the Chinese egret.

2. Here, you can take the circular tourist bus to experience the natural scenery and folklore of Chongming Island.

3. There is also a wealth of cultural heritage here, including stove culture, the customs of Chongming boatmen, and traditional handicrafts.

（三）

The development of Chongming Island can be divided into several stages. From the early Tang Dynasty to the late Northern Song Dynasty (7th to 11th century AD), the Chongming area formed a few sandbars. During the Wude Period of the Tang Dynasty (618−627 AD), two sandbars, the East Sandbar and the West Sandbar, emerged at the estuary of the Yangtze River. These were the predecessors of Chongming Island. During the Five Dynasties and Ten Kingdoms Period, Yao Yanhong, the commander of Jinghai Du Town, established Chongming Town on the West Sandbar in the third year of Tianzuo of the Yang Wu Regime (937 AD). Since then, the name "Chongming" has come into existence. From the late Northern Song Dynasty to the late Ming Dynasty (12th to 16th century AD), due to the deposition of sediment from the northern coastal area carried by tides, Chongming Island and its sandbars experienced significant expansion. Since the 17th century to the present, Chongming Island has gradually formed a large oval-shaped island and continues to expand.

三、崇明岛的自然环境和生态特色

翻译简介

本文的译文比较准确地表达了原文的意思，句型结构和内容的呈现顺序基本与原文一致，体现了顺句驱动的翻译策略。译文恰当地表达了崇明岛的自然条件、生态资源、生态环境、农作物种类、珍稀动植物资源、生态岛等重要信息。译文的语言风格简洁明了，用词得当、生动，整体上比较易读易懂。例如，在表达崇明岛拥有某个旅游资源时，译文将"有"译为 boast，而非 have，以表达崇明岛因具有某个旅游资源而感到自豪。在翻译数字方面，译文巧妙地衔接了从多个角度描述崇明岛地理参数的句子，如面积、跨度、地势、地貌。在处理包含多个分句的长难句时，译文将并列结构的分句切分为 doing 从句、with 从句、主句，将并列结构转化为主从结构，并尽量不改变原文的顺序。

词汇表

县级市：county-level city

上海市辖区：under the jurisdiction of Shanghai

长江口东北部：northeast of the Yangtze River estuary

长江口湿地：Yangtze River estuary wetland

形似卧蚕：resembling a silkworm

自然条件优越：superior natural conditions

生态资源丰富：abundant ecological resources

生态环境优美：beautiful ecological environment

湿地：wetlands

农作物：crops

粮食生产基地：grain production base

环保城市：eco-friendly city

风景优美：beautiful scenery

珍稀动植物资源：rare plant and animal resources

国家森林公园：national forest park

日出景色：sunrise view

芦苇沼泽：reed marshes

潮汐变化：tidal movements

河流分叉：river bifurcations

浑浊区域：turbid zones

盐水入侵：saltwater intrusion

鸟类迁徙：bird migration

生态岛：ecological island

协调发展：coordinated development

绿色产业发展：development of green industries

原文

崇明岛是上海市辖区中唯一的县级市，位于长江口东北部，是长江口湿地的重要组成部分。崇明岛地势较低且平坦，全岛面积为 1269.1 平方公里，东西长约 80 公里，南北宽13 至 18 公里，形似卧蚕。崇明岛的自然条件优越，生态资源丰富，是一个生态环境优美的绿色岛屿。

崇明岛拥有广袤的湿地、肥沃的土地、清新的空气和优美的风景。岛上著名的湿地包括东滩和西沙湿地，是国家级湿地保护区，保护了珍贵的湿地生态系统和生物多样性。崇明岛的土地肥沃，适宜种植谷类作物、豆类作物、瓜类作物、叶菜类，如水稻、玉米、大豆、花生、棉花、卷心菜、花菜、大白菜、西瓜、冬瓜、西兰花、大葱，是上海市的重要粮食生产基地。此外，崇明岛的空气清新，是上海市的"绿肺"，也是国家级环保城市。岛上的风景优美，有着独特的自然风光和人文景观，吸引着众多游客前来观光旅游。

在崇明岛上，有许多珍稀动植物资源。其中最著名的是东平国家森林公园，这里是世界上最大的人工林区之一，拥有众多珍稀植物和野生动物。此外，崇明岛还有长江口、长兴岛湿地公园、横沙岛湿地等重要湿地保护区，为众多候鸟和水生生物提供了重要的栖息地。崇明岛还有很多独特的自然景观，如东滩日出、芦苇荡、潮汐运动、大河分流、混浊带景观、盐水入侵、候鸟迁徙等，吸引了大量游客前来观赏。

崇明岛建设生态岛的目标，是充分挖掘和利用生态资源，实现经济、社会与生态的协调发展。崇明岛建设生态岛的重要举措有：推进绿色产业发展，大力发展生态农业、绿色旅游等产业；强化生态环境保护，加大治理力度，实现生态系统修复；推动绿色生活方式，增强人民群众的生态文明意识。近年来，崇明岛建设生态岛取得了显著成果。绿色产业和生态旅游成为崇明岛的支柱产业，生态环境得到有效改善，人民群众生活水平不断提高，最为典型的示范地为瀛东度假村。

通过生态岛的建设，崇明岛正在实现经济、社会和生态的协调发展，成为一个生态宜居、经济繁荣、人文荟萃的绿色岛屿。未来，崇明岛将继续积极推进生态文明建设，加强生态环境保护和修复，促进经济、社会和生态的可持续发展。同时，崇明岛还将加强科学研究和技术创新，推动生态文明建设不断深入发展，为全国的生态建设作出更大的贡献。

崇明岛建设生态岛，展示了人类与自然环境和谐共生的美好愿景。这里既有悠久的历史文化，又有丰富的生态资源。在未来的建设中，崇明岛将继续坚持生态优先、绿色发展的理念，努力实现经济、社会与生态的和谐发展。

译文

Chongming Island is the only county-level city under the jurisdiction of Shanghai, located in the northeast of the Yangtze River estuary and an important part of the Yangtze River estuary wetland. With a relatively low and flat terrain, the island covers a total area of 1,269.1 square kilometers, stretching about 80 kilometers from east to west and 13 to 18 kilometers from north to south, resembling a silkworm. Chongming Island boasts superior natural conditions and abundant ecological resources, making it a green island with beautiful ecological environment.

On Chongming Island, there are vast wetlands, fertile land, fresh air, and beautiful scenery. The well-known wetlands on Chongming Island include Dongtan and Xisha Wetlands, which are national-level wetland reserves, protecting a large number of precious wetland ecosystems and biodiversity. The fertile land of Chongming Island is suitable for cultivating cereal crops, leguminous crops, melon crops, leafy vegetable crops, etc. The main agricultural crops include rice, corn, soybeans, peanuts, cotton, cabbages, cauliflowers, Chinese cabbages, watermelons, wax gourds, broccoli, scallions, etc., making it an important grain production base in Shanghai. The island enjoys fresh air and is known as the "green lung" of Shanghai, being a nationally recognized eco-friendly city. With its picturesque landscapes, Chongming Island attracts numerous tourists who come to enjoy its unique natural beauty and cultural attractions.

Chongming Island is home to many rare plant and animal resources. Among them, the most famous is Dongping National Forest Park, one of the world's largest artificial forest areas, housing numerous rare plants and wildlife. Additionally, Chongming Island has important wetland reserves such as the Yangtze River Estuary, Changxing Island Wetland Park and Hengsha Island Wetland, providing crucial habitats for migratory birds and aquatic organisms. Chongming Island also boasts unique natural landscapes, including sunrise at Dongtan, reed marshes, tidal movements, river bifurcations, turbid zones, saltwater intrusion, and bird migration, attracting a large number of visitors.

The goal of building Chongming as an ecological island is to fully tap and utilize its ecological resources, achieving coordinated development of economy, society, and ecology. Key measures for building the ecological island of Chongming include promoting the development of green industries, vigorously developing eco-agriculture and green tourism;

strengthening ecological environment protection, intensifying governance efforts, and implementing ecosystem restoration; promoting a green lifestyle and raising public awareness of ecological civilization. In recent years, remarkable achievements have been made in building Chongming as an ecological island. Green industries and eco-tourism have become pillar industries, while the ecological environment has been effectively improved, and the living standards of the people have continuously improved. The most typical demonstration site is Yingdong Resort.

Through the construction of an ecological island, Chongming Island is achieving coordinated development of economy, society, and ecology, and becoming an eco-friendly and livable green island with flourishing economy and rich cultural heritage. In the future, Chongming Island will continue to actively promote the construction of ecological civilization, strengthen ecological environment protection and restoration, and promote sustainable development of economy, society, and ecology. At the same time, Chongming Island will enhance scientific research and technological innovation, continuously promote the construction of ecological civilization, and make greater contributions to the ecological construction of the whole country.

The construction of Chongming Island as an ecological island showcases the beautiful vision of harmonious coexistence between humans and the natural environment. There are both a long history and rich cultural heritage, as well as abundant ecological resources. In future development, Chongming Island will continue to adhere to the concept of ecological priority and green development, striving to achieve harmonious development of economy, society, and ecology.

例句赏析

例1:

原文: 崇明岛地势较低且平坦，全岛面积为1269.1平方公里，东西长约80公里，南北宽13至18公里，形似卧蚕。

译文: With a relatively low and flat terrain, the island covers a total area of 1,269.1 square kilometers, stretching about 80 kilometers from east to west and 13 to 18 kilometers from north to south, resembling a silkworm.

赏析: 原文描述了崇明岛的地形、地势、面积、地貌，译文比较准确地表达了原文的意思。译文中的"relatively low"准确地表达了"较低"这一语义，用词恰当。另外，原文由五个分句组成，翻译时句子衔接的难度较大。译文分别用"with 状语"、有动词"covers"的主句、"stretching"和"resembling"伴随状语衔接，基本上实现了顺句驱动，内容呈现的顺序与原文一致。

例 2：

原文：崇明岛还有很多独特的自然景观，如东滩日出、芦苇荡、潮汐运动、大河分流、混浊带景观、盐水入侵、候鸟迁徙等，吸引了大量游客前来观赏。

译文：Chongming Island also boasts unique natural landscapes, including sunrise at Dongtan, reed marshes, tidal movements, river bifurcations, turbid zones, saltwater intrusion, and bird migration, attracting a large number of visitors.

赏析：原文主要为崇明岛自然景观的罗列，包含大量术语，词汇密度和信息量较大。原文中的"有"被译成"boast"，而非我们通常想到的"have"，这是因为"boast"可以表示自豪地拥有或展示某些东西，与"have"类似，但更强调自豪感和炫耀。在这个句子里，"boast"强调了崇明岛自然景观的独特性和吸引力，表达了一种自豪和炫耀的语气，更符合原文的意思；同时，"boast"又更加生动、形象，更能够吸引读者的注意力。因此，将"有"翻译成"boast"是一种比较恰当的选择。

例 3：

原文：崇明岛建设生态岛的重要举措有：推进绿色产业发展，大力发展生态农业、绿色旅游等产业；强化生态环境保护，加大治理力度，实现生态系统修复；推动绿色生活方式，增强人民群众的生态文明意识。

译文：Key measures for building the ecological island of Chongming include promoting the development of green industries, vigorously developing eco-agriculture and green tourism; strengthening ecological environment protection, intensifying governance efforts, and implementing ecosystem restoration; promoting a green lifestyle and raising public awareness of ecological civilization.

赏析：原文为崇明岛建设生态岛的具体措施，罗列了三个宏观措施，并以分号隔开。句型结构上，原文句子较长，分句较多，各分句以动词开头，其译文的衔接难度较大。译文保留了原文的分号，各个分句均以"doing"开头，以罗列信息为主。分号象征三大举措，各逗号隔开的从句则为各大举措的具体措施。然而，原文中的许多动词，其实在本质上概念一致，如"推进""大力发展""强化""加大""实现""推动""提高"，都是促进某事物的发展，但动词的多样化能够进一步体现各个举措和用词的多样性。不过，在翻译时，我们应追求语言精简，尽量删除多样的动词，仅保留原文的核心意义。

例 4：

原文：通过生态岛的建设，崇明岛正在实现经济、社会和生态的协调发展，成为一个生态宜居、经济繁荣、人文荟萃的绿色岛屿。

译文：Through the construction of an ecological island, Chongming Island is achieving coordinated development of economy, society, and ecology, and becoming an eco-friendly and livable green island with flourishing economy and rich cultural heritage.

赏析：原文介绍了崇明岛的生态发展现状。原文的句型结构包含一个方式状语、一个主句和两个谓语。主句的定语较长，如"经济、社会和生态的"和"生态宜居、经济繁荣、人文荟萃的"。译文巧用形容词、介词和连词，将"经济繁荣、人文荟萃的"分别用 with 和 and 置于"生态宜居的""绿色岛屿"之后。"正在实现"和"成为"分别采用现在进行体，说明"成为"的状态仍然在实现的过程中，而非完成。

☞ **练习**

(一)将下列短语翻译成英文。

1. 崇明岛

2. 生态资源

3. 珍稀动植物资源

4. 鸟类迁徙

5. 绿色产业发展

(二)将下列句子翻译成英文。

1. 崇明岛地势较低且平坦，全岛面积为 1269.1 平方公里，东西长约 80 公里，南北宽 13 至 18 公里，形似卧蚕。

2. 崇明岛的自然条件优越，生态资源丰富，是一个生态环境优美的绿色岛屿。

3. 崇明岛是中国最大的淡水鱼产区之一，也是重要的农作物种植基地之一。

4. 崇明岛珍稀动植物资源丰富，是鸟类迁徙和水生生物的重要栖息地。

5. 崇明岛的发展重点是协调发展和绿色产业发展。

(三)将下面段落翻译成英文。

崇明岛位于长江口东北部，是上海市辖区，县级市。全岛面积 1269.1 平方公里，东西长约 80 公里，南北宽 13 至 18 公里，形似卧蚕。崇明岛地势较低且平坦，自然条件优越、生态资源丰富，是一个生态环境优美的绿色岛屿。岛上拥有大片湿地和农田，是中国最大的淡水鱼产区之一，也是重要的农作物种植基地之一。此外，崇明岛珍稀动植物资源丰富，是鸟类迁徙和水生生物的重要栖息地。岛上的风景优美，有日出景色、芦苇沼泽、潮汐变化、河流分叉、浑浊区域等特色景观。然而，崇明岛也面临着盐水入侵、生态环境破坏等问题。为了实现协调发展和绿色产业发展，崇明岛正在努力打造生态岛和环保城市，发展旅游业和现代农业等绿色产业。

☞ **参考答案**

（一）

1. Chongming Island

2. ecological resources

3. rare plant and animal resources

4. bird migration

5. development of green industries

（二）

1. With a relatively low and flat terrain, the island covers a total area of 1,269. 1 square kilometers, stretching about 80 kilometers from east to west and 13 to 18 kilometers from north to south, resembling a silkworm.

2. Chongming Island boasts superior natural conditions and abundant ecological resources, making it a green island with beautiful ecological environment.

3. Chongming Island is one of the largest freshwater fish production areas in China and also an important base for crop cultivation.

4. With abundant rare plant and animal resources, Chongming Island is a crucial habitat for migratory birds and aquatic organisms.

5. The focus of Chongming Island's development is on coordinated development and the development of green industries.

（三）

Chongming Island is located in the northeast of the Yangtze River estuary, under the jurisdiction of Shanghai as a county-level city. With a total area of 1,269. 1 square kilometers, stretching about 80 kilometers from east to west and 13 to 18 kilometers from north to south, resembling a silkworm. The island boasts superior natural conditions and abundant ecological resources, making it a green island with beautiful ecological environment. The island has large wetlands and farmland, which makes it one of the largest freshwater fish production areas in China and an important base for crop cultivation. In addition, Chongming Island has abundant rare plant and animal resources, making it a crucial habitat for migratory birds and aquatic organisms. The island has beautiful scenery, such as sunrise view, reed marshes, tidal movements, river bifurcations, turbid zones and other unique landscapes. However, Chongming

Island also faces problems such as saltwater intrusion and environmental degradation. In order to achieve coordinated development and the development of green industries, Chongming Island is striving to build an ecological island and an eco-friendly city, as well as developing green industries such as tourism and modern agriculture.

第二章　崇明生态湿地

一、崇明湿地公园的概况和特点

翻译简介

本文介绍了崇明区湿地公园的动植物种类、对生态环境保护的意义、公园建设的生态理念和生态修复的措施。原文翻译的难点在于多义性、语境、术语翻译、双主语句、无主句以及一主多谓句型。例如，"五一劳动节"有多种译法，其中"May Day"就不适合，因为它容易使游客联想到空难的求救信号。在翻译包含较多术语的段落时，如动植物术语，通常会碰到拉丁文和英文两种名称并存的情况，而英文名更具通俗性。句型上，原文存在典型的双主语、一主多谓、无主句。在翻译的过程中，译文分别采用断句、并列分句主次化、语境推导主语等翻译技巧，较为恰当地表达了崇明湿地的生态特点。

词汇表

崇明湿地公园：Chongming's wetland parks
东滩湿地公园：Dongtan Wetland Park
西沙湿地公园：Xisha Wetland Park
长江：Yangtze River
生态资源：ecological resources
地理环境：geographical environments
自然观光：nature sightseeing
家庭户外休闲度假：outdoor family leisure vacations
生态系统：ecosystems
沙洲湿地：sandbar wetlands

沼泽湿地：marsh wetlands

芦苇沼泽：reed marshes

植物和动物：flora and fauna

攀援植物：bulbous flowers

芳香植物：aromatic plants

鸟类友好植物：bird-friendly plants

大白鹭：great egret

绿头鸭：mallard duck

黑喉莺雀：*Amplhispiza bilineate*

鹳类：stork

黑鹳：black stork

丹顶鹤：red crowned crane

白尾海雕：*Haliaeetus albicilla*

两栖动物：amphibians

爬行动物：reptiles

黑鼬：black mink

刺猬：hedgehog

中华鲟：*Acipenser sinensis*

长江江豚：Yangtze River dolphin

长江白鳍豚：*Lipotes vexilliper*

独特的地貌：unique landforms

鸟类迁徙路线：migratory bird flyways

和谐共存：harmonious coexistence

建设和管理：construction and management

生态环境：ecological environment

观测平台：observation platforms

木板路：boardwalks

令人惊叹的景色：breathtaking views

生态保护：ecological conservation

生态恢复工程：ecological restoration projects

土壤保护：soil conservation

生态承载能力：ecological carrying capacity

旅游吸引力：tourism appeal

发展理念：development philosophy

生态质量：ecological quality

旅游产品：tourism products

观光和探索：sightseeing and exploration

湿地保护组织：wetland conservation organizations

湿地研究：wetland research

全球湿地保护：global wetland conservation

生态旅游目的地：ecological tourist destination

和谐共存的模范：model for harmonious coexistence

原文

崇明的湿地公园主要是东滩湿地公园和西沙湿地公园，分别位于长江口崇明岛的东西侧。这些湿地公园拥有丰富的生态资源和独特的地理环境，是一个理想的自然观光、科研教育、户外亲子休闲度假之地。本文将详细介绍崇明湿地公园的概况，以及其独特的生态特点。

丰富的生态资源

崇明湿地公园有多种生态系统，包括沙洲湿地、沼泽湿地、芦苇荡等。这些生态系统为不同的动植物提供了生存空间。据统计，崇明湿地公园内有植物198种，可分类为乔木、球根花卉、芳香植物、鸟嗜植物。动物资源也十分丰富，公园内记录到的鸟类有26种，其中常见的有大白鹭、绿头鸭、震旦雅雀等。此外，湿地公园内还有国家一级保护的鸟类：东方白鹳、黑鹳、白头鹤、白尾海雕。

崇明湿地公园有着丰富的动物资源。两栖类有泽蛙、虎纹蛙、大鲵；爬行类有水蛇、石龙子、中华草龟；鱼类有鲢鱼、草鱼、泥鳅、鲈鱼等。这些多样的动物资源共同构建起崇明湿地公园的生态网络。

独特的地理环境

崇明湿地公园位于长江口的河口三角洲地区，是长江水系与东海交汇的地带。这里地理位置独特，环境优美，充满生机。由于长江口水系的冲击与沉积，使得崇明湿地公园形成了独特的地貌。公园内的湿地土壤肥沃，适宜各类生物生长。此外，崇明湿地公园所处的地理位置，使其成为世界上著名的候鸟迁徙通道之一，每年春秋两季，大量的候鸟在此歇脚、繁衍后代。

人与自然和谐共生

崇明湿地公园的建设和管理充分体现了人与自然和谐共生的理念。在公园的规划建设中，坚持生态优先，尊重自然、保护生态环境，力求实现人与自然的和谐共生。通过保护生态环境、改善生态景观，提升人们的生活品质。崇明湿地公园的建设，为当地居民提供了美丽的生活环境，同时也为游客提供了休闲度假的好去处。

公园内设置了多个观景台和栈道，方便游客观赏湿地风光和动植物资源。在游览过程中，游客可以欣赏到美丽的湿地风光，同时也可以了解到湿地生态系统的重要性和保护意义。此外，公园还开展了丰富的科普教育活动，让游客在欣赏美景的同时，增长知识，增强生态保护意识。

崇明湿地公园还积极开展生态修复工程，对五一劳动节期间因游客数量激增而受损的湿地生态系统进行恢复。例如，通过植树造林、水土保持等措施，有效改善水土流失问题；同时，对于退化的湿地进行生态修复，提高湿地的生态承载能力。这些举措不仅有利于保护生态环境，还有助于提高公园的旅游吸引力。

未来的发展

未来，崇明湿地公园将继续秉承"生态优先、和谐共生"的发展理念，着力提升公园的生态品质和旅游服务水平。在保护生态资源的基础上，进一步丰富旅游产品，吸引更多的游客前来观光游览。同时，崇明湿地公园将加强与国内外湿地保护机构的合作，积极开展湿地科研、教育等工作，为推动全球湿地保护事业贡献中国智慧和力量。通过不断努力，使崇明湿地公园成为国内外著名的生态旅游胜地，成为人与自然和谐共生的典范。

小结

崇明湿地公园以其丰富的生态资源、独特的地理环境和人与自然和谐共生的理念，成为一个理想的自然观光、科研教育、休闲度假之地。在未来的发展中，崇明湿地公园将继续秉持生态优先、和谐共生的发展理念，努力提升公园的生态品质和旅游服务水平，为推动全球湿地保护事业贡献中国智慧和力量。

译文

Chongming's Wetland Park consists of Dongtan Wetland Park and Xisha Wetland Park, located on the eastern and western sides of Chongming Island at the mouth of the Yangtze River. These wetland parks possess abundant ecological resources and unique geographical environments, making them an ideal destination for nature sightseeing, scientific research, and outdoor family leisure vacations. This text will provide a detailed overview of Chongming Wetland Park and its unique ecological features.

Abundant Ecological Resources

Chongming Wetland Park encompasses various ecosystems, including sandbar wetlands, marsh wetlands, and reed marshes. These ecosystems provide habitats for diverse flora and fauna. According to statistics, there are 198 plant species in Chongming Wetland Park, classified as trees, bulbous flowers, aromatic plants, and bird-friendly plants. The park is also rich in animal resources, with 26 recorded bird species, including common ones such as the great egret, mallard duck, and *Amphispiza bilineate*. Additionally, the wetland park is home to China's first-class protected birds: Asian white stork, black stork, hooded crane, and *Haliaeetus albicilla*.

Chongming Wetland Park is rich in animal resources. Among amphibians, there are *Rana limnocharis*, *Hoplobatrachus rugulosus*, and *Andrias davidianus*. Reptiles include water snakes, *Eumeces chinensis*, and Chinese pond turtles. Fishes consist of silver carp, grass carp, loach, and perch. These diverse animal resources jointly construct the ecological network of Chongming Wetland Park.

Unique Geographical Environment

Chongming Wetland Park is situated in the Yangtze River estuary delta region, where the Yangtze River system meets the East China Sea. Its geographical location is distinctive, with a beautiful and vibrant environment. Due to the impact and sedimentation of the Yangtze River system, Chongming Wetland Park has formed unique landforms. The wetland soil in the park is fertile and conducive to the growth of various organisms. Furthermore, the park's geographical position has made it one of the world's renowned migratory bird flyways. During the spring and autumn seasons, a large number of migratory birds rest and reproduce here.

Harmonious Coexistence of Humans and Nature

The construction and management of Chongming Wetland Park fully embody the concept of harmonious coexistence between humans and nature. During the planning and development of the park, ecological environment is prioritized, respected and protected, with the aim of achieving harmonious coexistence between humans and nature. By preserving the ecological environment and improving the landscape, the park enhances the quality of life for people. The construction of Chongming Wetland Park provides local residents with a beautiful living environment while offering visitors a great destination for leisure and vacations.

The park features multiple observation platforms and boardwalks, making it convenient for visitors to enjoy the wetland scenery and observe the flora and fauna. During the visit, tourists can appreciate the beautiful wetland landscapes while gaining an understanding of the importance and significance of wetland ecosystems. Additionally, the park conducts various educational activities to increase visitors' knowledge and raise awareness of ecological conservation, allowing them to learn while enjoying the breathtaking views.

Chongming Wetland Park actively carries out ecological restoration projects to restore the damaged wetland ecosystems caused by the surge in visitor numbers during the International Worker's Day. Measures such as afforestation and soil conservation effectively address soil erosion issues. Simultaneously, degraded wetlands are restored to enhance their ecological carrying capacity. These efforts not only contribute to the protection of the ecological environment but also enhance the park's tourism appeal.

Future Development

In the future, Chongming Wetland Park will continue to adhere to the development philosophy of "ecological priority and harmonious coexistence" and strive to improve the park's ecological quality and tourism services. Based on the protection of ecological resources, the park will further enrich its tourism products to attract more visitors for sightseeing and exploration. Additionally, Chongming Wetland Park will strengthen cooperation with domestic and international wetland conservation organizations, actively engage in wetland research, education, and contribute China's wisdom and efforts to promote global wetland conservation. Through continuous efforts, Chongming Wetland Park aims to become a renowned ecological tourist destination both domestically and internationally, serving as a model for harmonious coexistence between humans and nature.

Conclusion

With its abundant ecological resources, unique geographical environment, and the concept of harmonious coexistence between humans and nature, Chongming Wetland Park has become an ideal destination for nature sightseeing, scientific research, and leisure vacations. In its future development, the park will uphold the principles of ecological priority and harmonious coexistence, striving to enhance its ecological quality and tourism services, and contribute China's wisdom and efforts to the global wetland conservation cause.

例句赏析

例1：

原文：据统计，崇明湿地公园内有植物 198 种，可分类为乔木、球根花卉、芳香植物、鸟嗜植物。动物资源也十分丰富，公园内记录到的鸟类有 26 种，其中常见的有大白鹭、绿头鸭、震旦雅雀等。此外，湿地公园内还有国家一级保护的鸟类：东方白鹳、黑鹳、白头鹤、白尾海雕。

译文：According to statistics, there are 198 plant species in Chongming Wetland Park, classified as trees, bulbous flowers, aromatic plants, and bird-friendly plants. The park is also rich in animal resources, with 26 recorded bird species, including common ones such as the great egret, mallard duck, and *Amphispiza bilineate*. Additionally, the wetland park is home to China's first-class protected birds: Asian white stork, black stork, hooded crane, and *Haliaeetus albicilla*.

赏析：原文为崇明湿地公园内动植物物种的罗列和分类。原文的翻译难点主要在于密集的专业术语，而术语的查找、鉴别、筛选有许多时间成本。动植物的术语可在百科、CNKI 学术词典、专业术语词典等查询。然而，同一术语可能会有多种译法，例如一些植物、鸟类的名称有拉丁文和英文两种名称，有些则只有拉丁文。拉丁文更具学术性，英文名则更具有通俗性，因此在取舍时首选英文名。术语的数量和词汇的密度是衡量翻译文章难度的一个重要的标准，尤其在翻译词汇密度大的文章、书籍时，译者要及时构建翻译软件的术语库，以减少查询重复出现的术语所带来的工作量，并利用好翻译软件的记忆功能。

例2：

原文：此外，崇明湿地公园所处的地理位置，使得其成为世界上著名的候鸟迁徙通道之一，每年春秋两季，大量的候鸟在此歇脚、繁衍后代。

译文：Furthermore, the park's geographical position has made it one of the world's renowned migratory bird flyways. During the spring and autumn seasons, a large number of migratory birds rest and reproduce here.

赏析：原文介绍了崇明区湿地公园对于候鸟迁徙的意义。原文的翻译难点在于各分句的衔接。原文虽然为一个长句，但有两个主语，即"崇明湿地公园所处的地理位置"和"大量的候鸟"，而英文的句型逻辑性强，习惯一个句子只能用一个主语。译文将原文断成两句话，并用句号隔开。动词"歇脚、繁衍"指候鸟周而复始的习惯，而习惯是过去、现在、将来一直发生的动作，因此译文用一般现在时来指习惯、规律、真理性的事物。

例3：

原文：在公园的规划建设中，坚持生态优先，尊重自然、保护生态环境，力求实现人与自然的和谐共生。通过保护生态环境、改善生态景观，提升人们的生活品质。

译文：During the planning and development of the park, ecological environment is prioritized, respected and protected, with the aim of achieving harmonious coexistence between humans and nature. By preserving the ecological environment and improving the landscape, the park enhances the quality of life for people.

赏析：原文为崇明区湿地公园建设中的生态理念。原文的两个句子为汉语里典型的"无主句"，即没有主语的句子。表面上，虽然两句没有形式上的主语，但在深层里语境会告诉我们其逻辑上的主语，即公园的环境或公园本身。原文翻译的另一个难点在于谓语动词过多。英文的句型风格不习惯这种对谓语的简单罗列，而是各从句的主次分明。原文的谓语动词包括坚持、尊重、保护、力求、改善、提升，为并列关系。译文将这种并列关系主次化，分别处理为主句，"with the aim of"目的状语，或是"by doing"方式状语。

例4：

原文：崇明湿地公园还积极开展生态修复工程，对五一劳动节期间因游客数量激增而受损的湿地生态系统进行恢复。

译文：Chongming Wetland Park actively carries out ecological restoration projects to restore the damaged wetland ecosystems caused by the surge in visitor numbers during the International Worker's Day.

赏析：原文记叙了崇明湿地公园的生态修复措施。原文的句型结构为"一主两谓"，即一个主语"崇明湿地公园"和两个谓语"积极开展"和"进行恢复"。然而，第二个宾语的定语从句过长，如"五一劳动节期间因游客数量激增而受损的"，包含了时间、原因信息。译文则巧妙地将第二个谓语处理为"to do"目的状语从句，并将原因、时间状语从句后置到句尾。"五一劳动节"的译法也有好几个，"May Day"为其一，然而该译法容易让游客联想到空难的求救语，因此在旅游的语境中不宜使用，所以采用较为正式的"International Worker's Day"。

☞ **练习**

（一）将下列短语翻译成英文。

1. 生态系统的建设和管理

2. 野生动物的栖息地

3. 木板路

4. 生态恢复工程

5. 湿地保护组织

(二)将下列句子翻译成英文。

1. 湿地是野生动物的栖息地。

2. 观测平台和木板路为游客提供了欣赏湿地美景的便利。

3. 生态恢复工程是保护和提高生态系统承载能力的重要手段。

(三)将下面段落翻译成英文。

湿地是生态系统中不可或缺的一部分，对于维护生态平衡和保护生物多样性具有重要作用。湿地可以为野生动物提供栖息地，是鸟类、鱼类等生物的栖息地和繁殖地。同时，湿地还可以净化水质、缓解洪涝灾害、保护海岸线等。因此，湿地保护和恢复是非常必要的工作。

☞ 参考答案

(一)

1. construction and management of ecosystems

2. habitat for wildlife

3. boardwalk

4. ecological restoration project

5. wetland conservation organization

(二)

1. Wetlands are habitats for wildlife.

2. Observation platforms and boardwalks provide visitors with convenient access to enjoy the beauty of the wetlands.

3. Ecological restoration projects are important means to protect and improve the ecological carrying capacity of ecosystems.

(三)

Wetlands are an essential part of the ecosystem and play an important role in maintaining ecological balance and protecting biodiversity. Wetlands provide habitats for wildlife, serving as habitats and breeding grounds for birds, fish, and other organisms. Additionally, wetlands can purify water, alleviate floods, and protect coastlines. Therefore, wetland conservation and restoration are necessary tasks.

二、崇明湿地公园的生态系统和物种资源

翻译简介

本文主要介绍了崇明湿地公园的动植物种类和生态资源，涉及许多物种术语、百科知识、数字单位、复杂句型。一些物种术语专业性较强，不具有通俗性，仅有拉丁译文，无英文名。译文在解释部分术语时会溯源其谐音命名来历，为了让外国游客领略该命名过程的乐趣，翻译时需要增译命名的拼音、字面义。数字翻译上，一些中国制的土地面积单位，例如"亩"大约为 666.667 平方米，其译法在保留中国特色和方便外国读者理解之间存在博弈。因旅游翻译更注重体现中国文化的特色，"亩"可译为 mu；若兼顾外国游客的理解，可括号注解其国际单位的数量。在句型的处理上，本译文多采用断句法、并列句的主从句化、举例结构等技巧，实现了复杂句的衔接。

词汇表

崇明湿地公园：Chongming Wetland Park

人工湿地公园：artificial wetland park

植物资源：plant resources

种子植物：seed plants

沉水植物：submerged plants

挺水植物：emergent plants

芦苇：reeds

野茭白：*Zizania latifolia*

荩草：*Arthraxon hispidus*

马兰：*Kalimeris indica*

糙叶苔草：*Carex scabrifolia Steud*

狐尾藻：*Myriophyllum verticillatum*

狭叶香蒲：*Typha angustifolia*

旱柳：*Salix matsudana Koidz*

落羽杉：*Taxodium distichum*

植被类型：vegetation type

动物：animals

水鸟：water birds

筑巢和栖息环境：nesting and habitat environments

净化水质：purify water quality

生态平衡：ecological balance

鸟类资源：bird resources

白头鹤：hooded crane

黑脸琵鹭：black-faced spoonbill

黑嘴鸥：Saunders gull

东方白鹳：Asian white stork

芦苇荡：reed marshes

多年生草本植物：perennial herbaceous plant

蔬菜：vegetables

膳食纤维：dietary fiber

维生素：vitamins

矿物质：minerals

汤：soup

炒菜：stir-fries

原文

崇明湿地公园位于中国上海市崇明区，是中国最大的人工湿地公园。公园内有丰富的植物资源和珍稀动物，为游客提供了观察和了解自然的机会。本文将详细介绍崇明湿地公园的生态系统和物种资源。

植物资源

崇明湿地公园内有植物 198 种，其中包括种子植物、沉水植物、挺水植物。具体植物包括芦苇、野茭白、苊草、马兰、糙叶苔草、狐尾藻、狭叶香蒲等，以及旱柳、落羽杉等陆生植物。这些植物构成了丰富多样的植被类型，为动物提供了食物和栖息地。

芦苇：芦苇是湿地公园内最常见的水生植物，它们生长在水边，具有较强的适应性和生长速度。芦苇的茎秆粗壮，可以用来制造编织品、纸张、建筑材料等。芦苇不仅是很多水鸟的食物来源，还能为鸟类提供优良的筑巢和栖息环境。此外，芦苇还有净化水质、维持生态平衡的作用，例如芦苇荡。

野茭白：野茭白是一种多年生草本植物，生长在水田、河岸和湖泊等潮湿环境中。野茭白的嫩茎和嫩叶可以作为蔬菜食用，富含多种营养物质，如膳食纤维、维生素和矿物质等，对人体健康有很多好处。野茭白的烹饪方法也非常多样化，可以做成凉拌、炒、煮汤等多种美味佳肴。因为野茭白生长在自然环境中，所以它没有受到任何化学农药和化肥的污染，是一种天然绿色食品，备受人们的喜爱。

荩草：荩草是一种多年生草本植物，生长在水边、河岸和湖泊等潮湿环境中。荩草的茎秆柔软而有弹性，可以用来编织篮子、帽子等工艺品。此外，荩草枝叶可煮成棉、毛、丝的黄色染料，并入药以驱寒定喘。

马兰：马兰是一种多年生草本植物，生长在河岸、山坡和田野等环境中。马兰植物喜欢温暖的气候，最适宜的生长温度为20℃—30℃，过低或过高的温度都会影响其正常生长。马兰全草都有药用价值，有清热解毒、散瘀止血之效。幼叶通常作蔬菜食用，可用于作汤、炒菜等。传说中，马兰植物生长在田间地头，其多汁的嫩叶常常吸引着贪吃的马儿前来啃食。由于马儿吃得太多，总是停留在原地不肯挪步，于是人们就把这种植物命名为"马拦头"。

糙叶苔草：糙叶苔草是一种莎草科植物，属于薹草属（苔草属）。它的根状茎具地下匍匐茎，秆常2~3株簇生于匍匐茎节上，高30~60厘米，较细，三棱形，平滑，产于辽宁、河北、山东、江苏、浙江、福建、台湾。糙叶苔草生于海滩沙地或沿海地区的湿地与田边，植株纤维韧性强可制成绳索。目前尚未由人工引种栽培。

鸟类资源

崇明东滩湿地公园是众多候鸟迁徙的重要栖息地，共记录着超过300种鸟类在这里繁衍生息，包括国家一级保护动物：白头鹤、黑脸琵鹭、黑嘴鸥、东方白鹳等。其中，国家二级保护动物有大滨鹬、小天鹅、鸳鸯、大杓鹬、白腰杓鹬等。最具有代表性的迁徙鸟类包括鸻鹬类、雁鸭类、鹭类、鸥类、鹤类鸟。在冬季的东滩湿地公园，你能看到万鸟过境和遮天蔽日的候鸟迁徙景观。

白头鹤：白头鹤是一种高大优雅的鸟类，以其独特的外貌和优雅的飞行姿态而闻名。它的头部、颈部和胸部呈现出纯白色，身体为石板灰色，羽毛柔软而丰满。白头鹤的双腿修长，适应于在湿地和沼泽地等水域环境中觅食。它们主要以鱼类、两栖动物和昆虫为食，捕食时展现出独特的猎食技巧。白头鹤在许多文化中被视为吉祥和神圣的象征，是人们喜爱的观赏鸟类之一。

黑脸琵鹭：黑脸琵鹭是一种小型鹭鸟，以其黑色的面部和白色的羽毛而得名。它的身体相对较小，嘴长而直，黑色，上下扁平呈琵琶状。黑脸琵鹭主要栖息在沿海地区、河口和湖泊等水域和沼泽环境中，生性机警避于人，常常筑巢于水边崖壁或水中小岛上。它们以鱼类、甲壳类动物和昆虫为食，常常在浅水中觅食。

黑嘴鸥：黑嘴鸥是一种中等大小的海鸟，以其黑色的喙、头而得名。它们的腹部羽毛主要呈现出白色，背部和翅膀上为石板灰色，脚为红色。黑嘴鸥主要栖息在海岸线、河口和湖泊等水域环境中。它们以沙蚕、鱼类、虾类动物和底栖生物为食，常常在空中盘旋觅食，然后俯冲下水捕捉猎物。黑嘴鸥具有良好的适应能力，可以在各种气候条件下生存，冬季则常见于港湾、海岛、码头等处。

东方白鹳：东方白鹳是一种高大的鹳类鸟类，以其纯白色的羽毛和长长的喙而著名。它们的身体修长而优雅，有长而粗壮黑色嘴，深红的双腿细长，身体羽毛为纯白色，飞羽则为黑色。东方白鹳主要栖息在湿地、沼泽和稻田等水域环境中，筑巢于高大乔木或建筑物上。它们以小鱼、蛙、昆虫为食，常常在浅水中觅食。东方白鹳在繁殖季节会形成大规模的繁殖群落，它们的巢由大量的树枝和草构建而成。东方白鹳在许多文化中被视为吉祥和幸福的象征，是受人们喜爱的观赏鸟类之一。

其他动物资源

除了鸟类之外，崇明湿地公园还有其他珍稀动物，如白鱀豚和中华鲟等，以及大闸蟹、鳗苗、泥螺、日本沼虾、海瓜子等经济性价值的动物。这些动物不仅对生态系统具有重要价值，还是游客观赏的亮点。

总之，崇明湿地公园拥有丰富的生态系统和物种资源，为游客提供了难得的自然观察和生态体验的机会。通过对这些植物和动物的了解和保护，我们可以更好地认识生态系统的平衡与和谐，同时也为地球上的生物多样性作出贡献。

译文

Chongming Wetland Park is located in Chongming District, Shanghai, China, and is the largest artificial wetland park in China. The park is home to abundant plant resources and rare animals, providing visitors with opportunities to observe and understand nature. This text will provide a detailed introduction to the ecosystem and species resources of Chongming Wetland Park.

Plant Resources

There are 198 plant species in Chongming Wetland Park, including seed plants, submerged plants, and emergent plants. Specific plants include reeds, *Zizania latifolia*, *Arthraxon hispidus*, *Kalimeris indica*, *Carex scabrifolia Steud*, *Myriophyllum verticillatum*, *Typha angustifolia*, as well as *Salix matsudana Koidz* and *Taxodium distichum*. These plants constitute a diverse vegetation type, providing food and habitats for animals.

Reeds: Reeds are the most common aquatic plants in the wetland park, growing along the water's edge with strong adaptability and rapid growth. The sturdy stems of reeds can be used to make woven products, paper, and construction materials. Reeds not only serve as a food source for many water birds but also provide excellent nesting and habitat environments for birds. Additionally, reeds play a role in purifying water quality and maintaining ecological balance, such as in reed marshes.

Zizania latifolia: It is a perennial herbaceous plant that grows in wet environments such as paddy fields, riverbanks, and lakes. The tender stems and leaves of it can be used as a vegetable, rich in various nutrients such as dietary fiber, vitamins, and minerals, which are beneficial to human health. It can be prepared in various ways, such as cold dishes, stir-fries, and soups, creating a variety of delicious dishes. As it grows in a natural environment, it is not contaminated by any chemical pesticides or fertilizers, making it a natural and popular green food.

Arthraxon hispidus: It is a perennial herbaceous plant that grows in wet environments such as water edges, riverbanks, and lakes. The stems are soft and elastic, suitable for weaving baskets, hats, and other handicrafts. Additionally, the branches and leaves of it can be boiled to produce yellow dyes for cotton, wool, and silk, and can be used medicinally to dispel cold and relieve asthma.

Kalimeris indica: It is a perennial herbaceous plant that grows in environments such as riverbanks, slopes, and fields. It prefers warm climates, with the optimal growth temperature ranging from 20 to 30 degrees Celsius. Extremely low or high temperatures can affect its normal growth. The entire horseweed plant has medicinal value, with effects such as clearing heat, detoxicating, promoting blood circulation and stopping bleeding. The young leaves are usually used as vegetables and can be used for making soups and stir-fried dishes. According to legend, it grows in the fields, and its' juicy young leaves often attract greedy horses to come and graze. Because the horses eat too much and refuse to move, people named this plant "马拦头" (mǎ lán tóu), which means "stopping horses".

Carex scabrifolia Steud: *Carex scabrifolia Steud* is a plant of the sedge family and belongs to the genus Carex. It has underground rhizomes and stems that often cluster on the rhizome nodes, reaching a height of 30-60 centimeters. The stems are slender, triangular, smooth, and found in Liaoning, Hebei, Shandong, Jiangsu, Zhejiang, Fujian, and Taiwan. *Carex scabrifolia Steud* grows in beach sandy areas or wetlands and field edges along the coast. The plant has strong and fibrous stems that can be used to make ropes. Currently, it has not been artificially cultivated.

Avian Resources

Chongming Dongtan Wetland Park is an important habitat for numerous migratory birds. It has recorded over 300 bird species that breed and inhabit here, including national first-level protected animals such as the hooded crane, black-faced spoonbill, black-headed gull, and Asian white stork. Among them, national second-level protected animals include the great knot, tundra swan, mandarin duck, Far Eastern curlew, and Eurasian curlew. Representative migratory bird species include plovers, geese and ducks, herons, gulls, and cranes. In the winter, the wetland park offers the spectacular sight of countless migratory birds in transit, creating a breathtaking scene.

Hooded crane: The hooded crane is a tall and graceful bird known for its unique appearance and elegant flying posture. Its head, neck, and chest are pure white, while its body is slate gray, and its feathers are soft and full. Hooded cranes have long and slender legs adapted for foraging in water environments such as wetlands and marshes. They mainly feed on fish, amphibians, and insects, displaying unique hunting skills. Hooded cranes are considered auspicious and sacred symbols in many cultures and are beloved as a bird species for observation.

Black-faced Spoonbill: The Black-faced Spoonbill is a small species of heron, named for its black facial skin and white feathers. It has a relatively small body with a long, straight, black beak that is flat and spoon-shaped. Black-faced Spoonbills primarily inhabit coastal areas, river mouths, lakes, and marshes, and they are wary of humans, often nesting on cliffs or small islands in the water. They feed on fish, crustaceans, and insects, often foraging in shallow water.

Black-headed gull: The Black-headed gull is a medium-sized seabird, named for its black bill and head. Its belly feathers are predominantly white, while its back and wings are slate gray, and its feet are red. Black-headed gulls mainly inhabit coastal areas, river mouths, lakes, and other water environments. They feed on sandworms, fish, shrimp, and benthic organisms, often hovering in the air and then diving into the water to catch prey. Black-headed gulls possess good adaptability and can survive in various climatic conditions. They are commonly seen in harbors, islands, and docks during winter.

Asian white stork：The Oriental Stork is a tall species of stork known for its pure white feathers and long beak. They have a slender and elegant body with a long and sturdy black beak, deep red slender legs, white body feathers, and black flight feathers. Oriental Storks mainly inhabit wetlands, marshes, and rice fields, and they nest on tall trees or buildings. They feed on small fish, frogs, and insects, often foraging in shallow water. During the breeding season, Oriental Storks form large breeding colonies, and their nests are constructed with a large number of twigs and grass. Oriental Storks are considered symbols of auspiciousness and happiness in many cultures and are beloved birds for observation.

Other Animal Resources

In addition to birds, Chongming Wetland Park is home to other rare animals such as the *Lipotes vexilliter* and *Acipenser sinensis*, as well as economically valuable animals like Chinese mitten crabs, eel larvae, mud snails, *Macrobrachium nipponense*, and *Musculus senhousei*. These animals not only have important ecological value but also serve as highlights for visitors to observe.

In conclusion, Chongming Wetland Park boasts a rich ecosystem and species resources, providing visitors with rare opportunities for nature observation and ecological experiences. Through understanding and protecting these plants and animals, we can better comprehend the balance and harmony of ecosystems and contribute to biodiversity on Earth.

例句赏析

例1：

原文：崇明湿地公园内有植物 198 种，其中包括种子植物、沉水植物、挺水植物。具体植物包括芦苇、野茭白、苫草、马兰、糙叶苔草、狐尾藻、狭叶香蒲等，以及旱柳、落羽杉等陆生植物。这些植物构成了丰富多样的植被类型，为动物提供了食物和栖息地。

译文：There are 198 plant species in Chongming Wetland Park, including seed plants, submerged plants, and emergent plants. Specific plants include reeds, *Zizania latifolia*, *Arthraxon hispidus*, *Kalimeris indica*, *Carex scabrifolia Steud*, *Myriophyllum verticillatum*, *Typha angustifolia*, as well as *Salix matsudana Koidz* and *Taxodium distichum*. These plants constitute a diverse vegetation type, providing food and habitats for animals.

赏析：原文为崇明湿地公园内植物种类的分类、罗列。原文的翻译难点在于术语的罗列，由于多数是生活中不常见的植物，而且许多植物没有英文名，只有拉丁文，拉丁文术语译文多以-us、-ia、-um 为后缀，为学术性用语风格，易造成理解困难。好在全文为"总—分"结构，为术语的罗列展开与解释作好了铺垫，对游客的术语理解起到了辅助作用。

例2：

原文：芦苇不仅是很多水鸟的食物来源，还能为鸟类提供优良的筑巢和栖息环境。此外，芦苇还有净化水质、维持生态平衡的作用，例如芦苇荡。

译文：Reeds not only serve as a food source for many water birds but also provide excellent nesting and habitat environments for birds. Additionally, reeds play a role in purifying water quality and maintaining ecological balance, such as in reed marshes.

赏析：原文介绍了芦苇对生态环境的作用。该句为复合句，包含三个并列句。翻译时，译者将原文的"不仅……还能"翻译为"not only……but also"，使句子结构更加清晰。由于三个分句都是介绍芦苇的生态功能，内容和句子结构上都为并列关系，所以在译文中难以转化为主句和从句结构，因此译文采用了断句法以减少句型转换的难度。此外，"有……的作用"在许多领域的翻译中出现频率较高，译者采用了 have the function of，类似的情况如 play a role of，contribute to，have an effect on，help to 等。

例3：

原文：马兰植物喜欢温暖的气候，最适宜的生长温度为20℃~30℃，过低或过高的温度都会影响其正常生长。马兰全草都有药用价值，有清热解毒、散瘀止血之效。

译文：It prefers warm climates, with the optimal growth temperature ranging from 20 to 30 degrees Celsius. Extremely low or high temperatures can affect its normal growth. The entire horseweed plant has medicinal value, with effects such as clearing heat, detoxicating, promoting blood circulation and stopping bleeding.

赏析：原文介绍了马兰植物的生存环境和药用价值。原文的分句较多，结构零散，给翻译带来了句型衔接的难度。译文对第一句的分句，分别采用 with 短语结构、ranging 从句、断句的技巧来衔接。第二个句子则采用举例结构，如 such as+doing，以对应原文的"评价+举例"的内容结构。"清热解毒、散瘀止血"虽然为两个四字词，但包含的功效却有四个，即清热、解毒、散瘀、止血，为中医术语。因此，译文将其转化成四个并列的 doing 短语。

例4：

原文：由于马儿吃得太多，总是停留在原地不肯挪步，于是人们就把这种植物命名为"马拦头"。

译文：Because the horses eat too much and refuse to move, people named this plant "马拦头"（mǎ lán tóu），which means "stopping horses".

赏析： 原文为马兰植物的命名来历，生动形象。"马拦头"为马兰植物的谐音，而这种命名的方式难以在译文中体现。对于非中文学习者，"马拦头"的字面义、发音都不好理解。要想让外国游客领略到这一谐音命名的过程，感受到语言的乐趣，译文需要采用增译法，增加"马拦头"的字面义、发音信息。本文译文就是通过添加拼音、定语从句，达到了让外国游客理解这一谐音命名理据的目的。

☞ **练习**

（一）将以下短语翻译成英文。

1. 湿地公园

2. 珍稀动物

3. 植被类型

4. 优良的筑巢和栖息环境

5. 生态平衡

（二）将以下句子翻译成英文。

1. 崇明湿地公园是中国最大的人工湿地公园，位于上海市崇明区。

2. 芦苇是湿地公园内最常见的水生植物，它们生长在水边，具有较强的适应性和生长速度。

3. 野茭白是一种多年生草本植物，生长在湿地环境中，可以作为野菜和蔬菜食用。

4. 崇明湿地公园内有超过 300 种的鸟类在这里繁衍生息，包括国家一级保护动物：白头鹤、黑脸琵鹭、黑嘴鸥、东方白鹳等。

5. 芦苇不仅是很多水鸟的食物来源，还能为鸟类提供优良的筑巢和栖息环境，同时还有净化水质、维持生态平衡的作用。

（三）将下面段落翻译成英文。

本文介绍了中国上海市崇明区的崇明湿地公园，是中国最大的人工湿地公园。公园内有丰富的植物资源和珍稀动物，为游客提供了观察和了解自然的机会。文章详细介绍了崇明湿地公园的生态系统和物种资源，包括植物资源和鸟类资源。其中，芦苇、野茭白、苔草、马兰、糙叶苔草等植物构成了丰富多样的植被类型，为动物提供了食物和栖息地。而鸟类资源中有超过 300 种鸟类在这里繁衍生息，包括国家一级保护动物：白头鹤、黑脸琵鹭、黑嘴鸥、东方白鹳等。

☞ **参考答案**

（一）

1. wetland park

2. rare animals

3. vegetation type

4. excellent nesting and habitat environments

5. ecological balance

（二）

1. Chongming Wetland Park is the largest artificial wetland park in China, located in Chongming District, Shanghai.

2. Reeds are the most common aquatic plants in the wetland park. They grow by the water and have strong adaptability and growth rate.

3. Zizania latifolia is a perennial herbaceous plant that grows in wetland environments and can be used as wild vegetables and vegetables.

4. There are more than 300 species of birds breeding in Chongming Wetland Park, including national first-class protected animals such as Siberian crane, black-faced spoonbill, black-headed gull, Oriental stork, and so on.

5. Reeds not only serve as a food source for many water birds but also provide excellent nesting and habitat environments for birds. They also have the function of purifying water quality and maintaining ecological balance.

（三）

This article introduces Chongming Wetland Park in Chongming District, Shanghai, China. The park covers an area of 20, 000 mu and is the largest artificial wetland park in China. It has rich plant resources, including seed plants, submerged plants, and emergent plants such as reeds, *Zizania latifolia*, *Arthraxon hispidus*, *Kalimeris indica*, *Carex scabrifolia Steud*, *Myriophyllum verticillatum*, *Typha angustifolia*, *Salix matsudana Koidz*, *Taxodium distichum*, *etc*. The vegetation types in the park are diverse and well-preserved, providing an excellent habitat for animals, especially water birds. The park has excellent nesting and habitat environments for birds, which helps to maintain ecological balance. In addition to its ecological value, the park also provides wild vegetables and vegetables with high nutrients such as dietary fiber, vitamins, minerals, etc. , as well as various dishes such as cold dishes, stir-fries, soup, etc. The park also has a variety of handicrafts for visitors to enjoy.

三、崇明湿地公园的旅游项目和活动

翻译简介

  本文为崇明区湿地公园内鸟类、景点、游玩项目、自然景观的罗列与介绍。翻译的难点涉及具体地点名称的翻译、篇幅的精简、单复数的推断、英汉定语衔接词的差异。一般来说景区的中文具体地点名称强调文化特色和意象，而景区英文地点名称更强调介绍地点的功能，如"观海楼"，中文强调了观海的场景，但实际上英文指的是景区的饭店，因此翻译时需呈现 restaurant（饭店），否则 Seascape Pavilion（观海楼）无法让外国游客理解该处地点的功能。篇幅的精简指的是缩减、合并重复的信息。名词单复数的运用是英汉语言中较为明显的一种差异现象，汉语依赖语境，而英文则需明确标记复数后缀。英汉定语衔接词差异较大，汉语定语衔接词以"……的"为主，但英文则需依据逻辑作具体细分，常常会把汉语"……的"翻译成 over，in，of 引导的短语。

词汇表

生态保护：ecological conservation

科普教育：science education

综合性公园：comprehensive park

生态资源：ecological resources

旅游项目：tourism programs

观鸟活动：birdwatching

鸟类栖息地：bird habitats

迁徙通道：migration routes

观鸟阁：birdwatching tower

鸟类国家自然保护区：Bird National Nature Reserve

候鸟迁徙：migratory birds

观鹭台：Heron Observation Platform

雀鸣渡：Queming Ferry

芳草地：Fragrant Grassland

观海楼：Seascape Pavilion

生态游览：ecological tour

沙洲湿地：sandbar wetlands

沼泽湿地：marsh wetlands

芦苇荡：reed marshes

环保意识：environmental protection awareness

展品：exhibits

互动设施：interactive facilities

导游的语音讲解：tour guide voice explanations

亲水活动：water-related activities

原文

崇明岛的湿地公园是集生态保护、科普教育、旅游观光、休闲度假为一体的综合性公园。西沙和东滩湿地公园内拥有丰富的生态资源和多样的旅游项目，能够满足不同游客的需求。以下是公园推荐的部分旅游项目和活动：

观鸟活动

游客可以参加专业的观鸟活动，观察和了解公园内的各种鸟类。这既是一种休闲方式，也是一种生态教育活动。崇明湿地公园是鸟类栖息地和迁徙通道的重要站点，每年都有大量的候鸟在这里栖息和过境，是中国东部最重要的候鸟栖息地之一。游客可以在观鸟活动中，近距离地观察到丰富的鸟类种类，同时了解到鸟类的生态习性和保护知识。在西沙国家湿地公园的观鸟阁和东滩湿地公园的东滩鸟类国家自然保护区，游客们都能在每年的11月到次年的3月，观看到壮丽的国内和世界性的候鸟迁徙。游客们可以在东滩湿地公园内的观鹭台、雀鸣渡、芳草地、观海楼欣赏这一自然景观，并观察鸟类的外形、姿态、数量、取食方式、饮食结构、繁衍、迁徙的特点，并鉴别鸟的种类。

生态游览

游客可以参观湿地公园内的各种生态系统，如沙洲湿地、沼泽湿地、芦苇荡等。游客能在一望无际的芦苇滩涂中亲身感受大自然的魅力，欣赏秋冬大片稻花的开放、候鸟的迁徙，还能增加对生态环境的认识和保护意识。崇明湿地公园拥有独特的自然景观和生态系统，游客可以在生态游览中，领略到不同季节、不同气候下的湿地美景，同时了解湿地生态系统的形成和演化过程。

科普教育

西沙和东滩湿地公园内设有生态科普教育区，通过展示和讲解，让游客了解湿地生态系统的知识，提高环保意识。科普教育区有丰富的展品和互动设施，能够让游客更加深入地了解湿地的形成、生态系统的运作机制以及湿地生物的特点和分类。此外，自驾游的游客还能在地图导航上听到导游的语音讲解，为我们介绍路上所看到的风景。

亲水活动

在崇明的西沙和东滩湿地公园，游客可以尽情地与水亲近，体验划船、观赏水生动植物、钓虾、钓螃蟹、抓蛏子、摸鱼等亲水活动，感受水的乐趣。崇明湿地公园是一个典型的水乡景区，有着丰富的水生生物资源和独特的水乡文化。游客可以在亲水活动中，近距离地感受到水乡文化和生态环境的魅力。

自然摄影

崇明岛的西沙和东滩湿地公园的美丽景色和丰富的生态资源为摄影爱好者提供了极佳的拍摄素材。在这里，游客可以捕捉到生动的自然画面，留下珍贵的记忆。公园内有很多拍摄点，如观鸟塔、芦苇荡、沙洲湿地等，能够为摄影爱好者提供多样的拍摄体验和角度。可拍摄的大自然特写镜头包括飞跃在稻田间的白鹭和大雁，东滩湿地的海平面日出和日落，芦苇荡间的渔船，名贵鸟类的觅食行为等。

休闲度假

西沙和东滩湿地公园内和周边设有生态度假村，游客可以在此休息，感受自然的宁静与美好。游客们不仅能享受到多种舒适的客房，还能品尝到当地特色的崇明本土菜，享受最新鲜的食材。游客们还能在整面书墙的边上安静地阅读，同时还能让思绪在安静的落地飘窗旁随风摇曳。公园内的驿站，还能提供不同类型的自行车，供游客骑行游览田园风光。度假村内还提供了有关崇明湿地公园的介绍和导览服务，方便游客了解和参观。度假村的建设和运营，也体现了公园的可持续发展理念和对生态环境的保护。

崇明岛的生态露营项目为游客提供了一种与自然深度接触的独特体验。露营区通常选址在湿地公园边缘或森林保护区附近，周围环绕着茂密的树林、清澈的湖泊和广阔的芦苇荡，夜晚可聆听蛙鸣鸟叫，清晨可欣赏日出晨雾。露营区配备了完善的设施，包括多种帐篷选择、干净的洗手间和淋浴间、自助烧烤区以及安全保障服务。游客可以参与夜间观星、湿地探索、篝火晚会和生态手工坊等活动，感受自然的魅力与乡土文化的氛围。此外，露营项目始终坚持环保理念，倡导垃圾分类、节能减排和无痕露营，并通过生态教育增强游客的环保意识。无论是家庭出游、朋友聚会还是独自旅行，崇明岛的生态露营都能为游客带来难忘的自然体验。

总之，崇明湿地公园凭借其丰富的生态资源和多样的旅游项目，成为越来越多游客的旅游首选。在公园内，游客可以尽情地探索大自然的奥秘，享受生态旅游的乐趣，增强对环保的认识和责任感。同时，崇明湿地公园也在不断地推进可持续发展和生态保护工作，希望能够得到更多游客和社会各界的支持和关注，共同守护这个重要的自然宝库。

译文

The wetland parks in Chongming Island are a comprehensive park that combines ecological conservation, science education, tourism, and leisure. The Xisha and Dongtan Wetland Parks have rich ecological resources and diverse tourism programs to meet the needs of different tourists. The following are some recommended tourist programs and activities:

Birdwatching

Tourists can participate in professional birdwatching activities to observe and understand various bird species in the park. This is both a leisure activity and an ecological education. Chongming Wetland Park is an important site for bird habitats and migration routes, and one of the most important wintering bird habitats in eastern China. During birdwatching activities at the Xisha National Wetland Park's birdwatching tower and Dongtan Wetland Park's Dongtan Bird National Nature Reserve, visitors can watch magnificent domestic and world-class migratory birds from November to March of the following year. Visitors can appreciate this natural landscape from the Heron Observation Platform, Queming Ferry, Fragrant Grassland, and Seascape Pavilion within Dongtan Wetland Park, and observe the appearance, posture, quantity, feeding habits, dietary structure, reproduction, migration characteristics of birds, and identify bird species.

Ecological Tour

Tourists can visit various ecosystems in the wetland park, such as sandbar wetlands, marsh wetlands, and reed marshes. Tourists can experience the charm of nature in the vast reed beaches, enjoy the opening of large areas of rice flowers in autumn and winter, the migration of birds, and increase their awareness of ecological environment protection. Chongming Wetland Park has unique natural scenery and ecosystems. Through ecological tours, tourists can appreciate wetland landscapes in different seasons and weather conditions, and understand the formation and evolution of wetland ecosystems.

Science Education

The Xisha and Dongtan Wetland Parks have ecological science education areas that allow tourists to learn about wetland ecosystem knowledge through exhibits and explanations, and improve their environmental awareness. The science education area has rich exhibits and interactive facilities that allow tourists to gain a deeper understanding of wetland formation, ecosystem operation mechanisms, wetland biological characteristics, and classification. In addition, self-driving tourists can hear tour guide voice explanations on map navigation to introduce the scenery along the way.

Water-related Activities

In the Xisha and Dongtan Wetland Parks in Chongming, tourists can get close to water and experience water-related activities such as boating, viewing aquatic plants and animals, fishing shrimp, crab, clam, and fish. Chongming Wetland Park is a typical water town scenic area with rich aquatic biological resources and unique water town culture. Through water-related activities, tourists can experience the charm of water town culture and ecological environment up close.

Nature Photography

The beautiful scenery and rich ecological resources of the Xisha and Dongtan Wetland Parks in Chongming Island provide excellent shooting conditions for photography enthusiasts. Here, tourists can capture vivid natural images and leave precious memories. There are many shooting spots in the park, such as birdwatching towers, reed marshes, sandbar wetlands, etc., which can provide photographers with diverse shooting experiences and angles. Close-up shots of nature include white egrets and geese leaping between rice fields, sunrises and sunsets over the sea level at Dongtan Wetland, fishing boats in reed marshes, hunting behaviors of rare birds, etc.

Leisure Vacation

Ecological resorts are located within and around the Xisha and Dongtan Wetland Parks where tourists can relax and enjoy the tranquility and beauty of nature. Tourists can not only enjoy various comfortable rooms but also taste local specialties of Chongming's local cuisine with fresh ingredients. Tourists can also quietly read by the entire wall of books while letting their thoughts sway by the quiet floor-to-ceiling window. The post stations in the park also provide different types of bicycles for tourists to ride around the countryside. The resort also provides introduction and guided tours of Chongming Wetland Park for tourists' convenience. The construction and operation of the resort also reflect the park's concept of sustainable development and environmental protection.

Chongming Island's eco-camping project offers visitors a unique opportunity to immerse themselves in nature. The camping areas are typically located near the edges of wetland parks or forest reserves, surrounded by dense woods, clear lakes, and vast reed marshes. At night, visitors can listen to the sounds of frogs and birds, while in the morning, they can enjoy the beauty of sunrise and morning mist. The camping areas are equipped with comprehensive facilities, including various tent options, clean restrooms and showers, self-service barbecue areas, and security services. Visitors can participate in activities such as stargazing, wetland exploration, bonfire parties, and eco-craft workshops, experiencing the charm of nature and the atmosphere of local culture. Additionally, the camping project adheres to environmental protection principles, promoting waste sorting, energy conservation, and "leave-no-trace" camping, while enhancing visitors' environmental awareness through ecological education. Whether for family trips, friend gatherings, or solo travel, Chongming Island's eco-camping provides an unforgettable natural experience.

In summary, with its rich ecological resources and diverse tourism programs, Chongming Wetland Park has become the first choice for more and more tourists. In the park, tourists can explore the mysteries of nature to their hearts' content, enjoy the fun of ecotourism, while enhancing their awareness and sense of responsibility for environmental protection. At the same time, Chongming Wetland Park is also constantly promoting sustainable development and ecological protection work, hoping to receive more support and attention from tourists and society to jointly protect this important natural treasure trove.

例句赏析

例1：
原文： 游客们可以在东滩湿地公园内的观鹭台、雀鸣渡、芳草地、观海楼欣赏这一自然景观，并观察鸟类的外形、姿态、数量、取食方式、饮食结构、繁衍、迁徙的特点，并鉴别鸟的种类。

译文：Visitors can appreciate this natural landscape from the Heron Observation Platform, Queming Ferry, Fragrant Grassland, and Seascape Pavilion within Dongtan Wetland Park, and observe the appearance, posture, quantity, feeding habits, dietary structure, reproduction, migration characteristics of birds, and identify bird species.

赏析：原文为东滩湿地公园内具体景点、鸟类观赏的罗列。具体景点名称的翻译有音译和意译两种，音译的好处在于方便外国游客和中国人交流时对地点定位，利于外国游客问路，但是无法让外国游客理解地名的中文内涵和象征意义。意译有利于外国游客理解地名的中文内涵，保留文化特色，但不利于外国游客对地点的定位和问路。旅游景区更注重的是游客能迅速理解景点的旅游特色和功能，所以更注重保留地名的文化特点和意象。因此，该译文中的多数地名基本还原了地点的功能和呈现的意象，为"地名意象+地点功能"结构。观海楼(Seascape Pavilion)为景区现用译文，但实际上观海楼是公园内的一家饭店，该译文无法使外国游客理解其地点功能，因此"Seascape Restaurant"更符合实际需要。

例2：

原文：崇明湿地公园拥有独特的自然景观和生态系统，游客可以在生态游览中，领略到不同季节、不同气候下的湿地美景，同时了解湿地生态系统的形成和演化过程。

译文：Chongming Wetland Park has unique natural scenery and ecosystems. Through ecological tours, tourists can appreciate wetland landscapes in different seasons and weather conditions, and understand the formation and evolution of wetland ecosystems.

赏析：原文介绍了崇明区湿地公园的生态特点和游客体验。原文的长难句包含两个主句，主语分别为"崇明湿地公园"和"游客"，第二个主句因包含两个谓语而篇幅较长。英文句子习惯一个句子只包含一个主语，如果难以做到主句主从化，译者一般会采用断句法，以避免因译文过长而导致阅读不便。

例3：

原文：在崇明的西沙和东滩湿地公园，游客可以尽情地与水亲近，体验划船、观赏水生动植物、钓虾、钓螃蟹、抓蛏子、摸鱼等亲水活动，感受水的乐趣。

译文：In the Xisha and Dongtan Wetland Parks in Chongming, tourists can get close to water and experience water-related activities such as boating, viewing aquatic plants and animals, fishing shrimp, crab, clam, and fish.

赏析：原文为崇明两大湿地公园游玩项目的罗列。原文的谓语动词较多，如"体验""观赏""钓""抓""摸""感受"，呈现的是"评价+举例"结构，为此译文以"such as"引出罗列的成分。汉语举例时，习惯用"动词+名词"结构，但译文如果采用此结构，容易拉长篇幅并显得用词重复，因此"钓""抓""摸"在译文中被合并为"fishing"。

例 4：

原文：可拍摄的大自然特写镜头包括飞跃在稻田间的白鹭和大雁，东滩湿地的海平面日出和日落，芦苇荡间的渔船，名贵鸟类的觅食行为等。

译文：Close-up shots of nature include white egrets and geese leaping between rice fields, sunrises and sunsets over the sea level at Dongtan Wetland, fishing boats in reed marshes, hunting behaviors of rare birds, etc.

赏析：原文为湿地公园摄影爱好者可拍摄的镜头罗列。汉语和英语的一大差异在于单复数形式，汉语无复数后缀，单复数同形，复数含义需要根据语境推理，为此"白鹭和大雁"分别被译为"egrets and geese"，运用复数以呈现稻田间多只鸟的数量。原文特写镜头的罗列采用"定语+名词"结构，而译文则为"名词+定语"结构，并以介词"over""in""of"短语连接名词和定语，而汉语只需单一地用"……的"连接，体现了英汉在定语衔接上的用词差异。

☞ **练习**

(一)将下列短语翻译成英文。

1. 生态保护

2. 旅游观光

3. 观鸟活动

4. 候鸟迁徙

5. 观鸟阁

(二)将下列句子翻译成英文。

1. 游客可以在观鸟活动中，近距离观察到丰富的鸟类种类。

2. 这既是一种休闲方式，又是一种生态教育活动。

3. 每年都有大量的候鸟在这里栖息和过境。

4. 游客可以在东滩湿地公园内的观鹭台、雀鸣渡、芳草地、观海楼欣赏这一自然景观。

5. 游客可以通过生态旅游，欣赏不同季节和不同气候条件下的湿地景观。

(三)将下面段落翻译成英文。

崇明岛的湿地公园是集生态保护、科普教育、旅游观光、休闲度假为一体的综合性公园。西沙和东滩湿地公园内拥有丰富的生态资源和多样的旅游项目，能够满足不同游客的需求。以下是公园推荐的部分旅游项目和活动：观鸟活动、生态旅游、科普教育、亲水活动等。游客可以通过参加这些活动，了解湿地生态环境，增强环保意识，同时享受自然风光带来的愉悦和放松。

☞ **参考答案**

（一）

1. ecological conservation

2. tourism

3. birdwatching

4. migratory birds

5. birdwatching tower

（二）

1. Tourists can observe a variety of bird species up close during birdwatching activities.

2. This is an activity that is both a leisurely pursuit and an ecological education.

3. Every year, a large number of migratory birds come here to rest and pass through.

4. Visitors can appreciate this natural landscape from the Heron Observation Platform, Queming Ferry, Fragrant Grassland, and Seascape Pavilion within Dongtan Wetland Park.

5. Through ecological tours, tourists can appreciate wetland landscapes in different seasons and weather conditions.

（三）

Chongming Island's wetland park is a comprehensive park that combines ecological conservation, science education, tourism, and leisure. The Xisha and Dongtan Wetland Parks have rich ecological resources and diverse tourism programs to meet the needs of different tourists. The following are some recommended tourist programs and activities: birdwatching, ecological tours, science education, water-related activities, etc. Through participating in these activities, tourists can learn about wetland ecology, enhance their environmental awareness, and enjoy the pleasure and relaxation brought by natural scenery.

第三章　崇明生态农园

一、崇明生态农业的发展历程和现状

翻译简介

本文介绍了崇明岛生态农业的发展历程与现状，罗列和介绍了上海市政府的一系列发展崇明生态农业、旅游资源的重要举措和农业特色。本篇的翻译难点在于一些组织机构、产业区、特产的名称，以及篇幅的精简和战略术语的理解与通俗化。一些农业示范区在崇明岛设立了好几个点，因此翻译时不能特指某地，其译文名应小写，但特指的"光明集团的崇明农垦部"，则应大写。许多特产名带有地区名称，翻译时，应保留特产名中的地名以凸显其地域特点。在句型的转换上，译文较为灵活，尤其是状语从句可以不与原文一致，但这并不影响句意的表达效果。

词汇表

崇明岛：Chongming Island
生态环境：ecological environment
文化底蕴：cultural heritage
生态农业：ecological agriculture
发展历程：development history
绿色农业：green agriculture
创新发展：innovative development
转型升级：transformation and upgrading
生态岛：ecological island
发展战略：development strategy

主阵地：main base

示范区：demonstration zone

绿色产业园区：green industrial park

技术：technology

低碳：low-carbon

环保：environmentally friendly

可持续发展：sustainable development

有机农业：organic agriculture

生态养殖：ecological breeding

绿色种植：green planting

土壤保护：soil protection

生态平衡：ecological balance

生物防治方法：biological control methods

化学农药和化肥：chemical pesticides and fertilizers

动物福利：animal welfare

环境保护：environmental protection

科学种植技术：scientific planting techniques

品质和安全性：quality and safety

农产品：agricultural products

农业产业转型升级：transformation and upgrading of the agricultural industry

农业示范区：agriculture demonstration zone

原文

崇明岛是中国东海沿岸的一座岛屿，它以其独特的生态环境和丰富的文化底蕴，成为中国生态农业发展的重要示范区之一。本文将为读者介绍崇明生态农业的发展历程和现状。

崇明生态农业的发展历程

崇明生态农业的发展历程可追溯至 20 世纪 90 年代。当时，崇明区开始着手实施绿色农业和生态农业的创新发展，以促进农业转型升级。在 21 世纪初，崇明区政府提出了建设"生态岛"的发展战略，将生态农业作为一项重要的发展任务。随着国家对生态环境的重视，2010 年，上海市政府明确崇明为上海生态岛建设的主阵地，并将生态农业发展纳入国家战略。此后，崇明生态农业逐步壮大，生态农业示范区、绿色产业园区等一系列项目相继建成。

崇明生态农业的现状

推广绿色生态农业技术

在农业生产中，崇明大力推广绿色生态农业技术，实现了农业生产的低碳、环保、可持续发展。崇明岛的生态农业技术包括有机农业、生态养殖、绿色种植等。有机农业注重土壤保护和生态平衡，采用天然有机肥料和生物防治方法，不使用化学农药和化肥。生态养殖则注重动物福利和环境保护，采用自然饲养和养殖方式，不使用激素和抗生素。绿色种植则采用科学种植技术，注重生态平衡和土壤保护，不使用化学农药和化肥。这些技术的应用有助于提高农产品的品质和安全性，保护环境，促进可持续发展。此外，崇明生态农业还探索了一系列生态农业模式，如"生态农业+旅游""农村旅游+休闲度假"等，为农业产业转型升级提供了新的思路。

建设生态农业示范区和绿色产业园区

崇明县于2011年10月成功向国家农业部申报创建国家现代农业示范区项目，2012年1月被农业部列为国家级现代农业示范区。崇明生态农业示范区是国家级农业科技示范区和国家农业产业化重点龙头企业示范区，主要由光明集团的崇明农垦部和上海实业集团东滩现代农业园区组成。它以绿色、有机、生态为发展方向，涵盖了蔬菜、水果、畜禽养殖、水产养殖等领域。同时，崇明生态农业示范区还积极探索农业产业化发展之路，推进农业科技创新和现代化经营管理，打造了一批绿色有机产品品牌。

提高农产品品质和知名度

崇明生态农业的农产品品质得到了广泛认可，特色农产品如崇明稻米、崇明老毛蟹、崇明白山羊、蔬菜等深受消费者喜爱。崇明蔬菜以其独特的品种和绿色生态的生产方式，成为上海本地市场的重要供应商之一。此外，崇明柑橘也以其鲜美的口感和高品质的质量，成为了国内外市场的热门产品之一。崇明还积极开展品牌建设和宣传推广，如举办生态农产品展销会、推出"崇明生态农业"品牌等，提高了农产品的知名度和美誉度。

探索农旅融合发展模式

崇明生态农业还推动农旅融合发展，探索"生态农业+旅游""农村旅游+休闲度假"等模式，促进了农业和旅游业的互动发展。例如，崇明生态农园、北部垦区的生态农园基地和崇明岛许多村镇开展了农家乐、采摘游、民宿等活动，吸引了大量游客前来参观、采摘和体验，为农业增加了附加值，同时也推动了旅游业的发展。

结语

综上所述，崇明生态农业在政府的倡导和企业的努力下，取得了显著的成效。崇明生态农业的发展不仅为生态环境保护和农业产业的转型升级提供了新的思路和模式，同时也为人们提供了更加健康、安全的农产品。崇明生态农业的成功经验和做法，对其他地区的生态农业发展也具有一定的借鉴意义。相信在未来，崇明生态农业将继续发扬光大，为中国的农业生产和生态环境保护作出更大的贡献。

译文

Chongming Island, a coastal island in the East China Sea, has become one of the important demonstration zones for China's ecological agriculture development due to its unique ecological environment and rich cultural heritage. This article introduces the development history and current situation of Chongming's ecological agriculture.

Development History of Chongming's Ecological Agriculture

The development of Chongming's ecological agriculture can be traced back to the 1990s when the district began to implement innovative green and ecological agriculture to promote agricultural transformation and upgrading. In the early 2000s, the Chongming government proposed the development strategy of building an "ecological island" with ecological agriculture as an important development task. With the country's emphasis on the ecological environment, in 2010, the Shanghai government designated Chongming as the main base for Shanghai's ecological island construction and incorporated the development of ecological agriculture into the national strategy. Since then, Chongming's ecological agriculture has gradually grown, and a series of projects such as ecological agriculture demonstration zones and green industrial parks have been built.

Current Situation of Chongming's Ecological Agriculture

Promotion of green ecological agriculture technology

Chongming vigorously promotes green ecological agriculture technology to achieve low-carbon, environmentally friendly, and sustainable agricultural production. Chongming's ecological agriculture technology includes organic agriculture, ecological breeding, and green planting. Organic agriculture focuses on soil protection and ecological balance, using natural organic fertilizers and biological control methods without chemical pesticides and fertilizers. Ecological breeding focuses on animal welfare and environmental protection, using natural feeding and breeding methods without hormones and antibiotics. Green planting uses scientific planting techniques, focusing on ecological balance and soil protection, without using chemical pesticides and fertilizers. The application of these technologies helps improve the quality and safety of agricultural products, protect the environment, and promote sustainable development. In addition, Chongming's ecological agriculture has also explored a series of ecological agriculture models, such as "ecological agriculture + tourism" and "rural tourism + leisure vacation", providing new ideas for the transformation and upgrading of the agricultural industry.

Construction of Eco-agriculture Pilot Zones and Green Industrial Parks

In October 2011, Chongming successfully applied to the Ministry of Agriculture to create a national project of modernized agriculture demonstration zone, which was listed as a national demonstration zone by the Ministry of Agriculture in January 2012. The Chongming ecological agriculture demonstration zone is a national agricultural science and technology demonstration zone and a key leading enterprise demonstration zone for national agricultural industrialization, mainly composed of the Chongming Agriculture Reclamation Department of Bright Dairy Group and the Dongtan Modern Agriculture Park of Shanghai Industrial Group. It is oriented towards green, organic, and ecological development, covering multiple areas such as vegetables, fruits, livestock breeding, and aquaculture. At the same time, Chongming's ecological agriculture demonstration zone actively explores the path of agricultural industrialization development, promotes agricultural scientific and technological innovation and modern management, and has created a number of green organic product brands.

Improving the Quality and Reputation of Agricultural Products

Chongming's ecological agriculture products have been widely recognized for their quality, with characteristic agricultural products such as Chongming rice, Chongming hairy crabs, Chongming white goats, and vegetables being popular among consumers. Chongming vegetables have become one of the important suppliers in the Shanghai market due to their unique varieties and green ecological production methods. In addition, Chongming citrus has become a popular product in domestic and foreign markets due to its delicious taste and high-quality. Chongming also actively carries out brand building and promotion, such as holding ecological agricultural product exhibitions and launching the "Chongming Ecological Agriculture" brand, which enhances the visibility and reputation of agricultural products.

Exploring the Model of Integrated Development of Agritainment

Chongming's ecological agriculture also promotes the integrated development of agriculture and tourism by exploring models such as "ecological agriculture + tourism" and "rural tourism + leisure vacation," which promotes the interactive development of agriculture and tourism. For example, Chongming's ecological farms, farm bases in the northern reclamation area, and many villages on Chongming Island have carried out activities such as agritourism, fruit picking tours, and home inns, attracting a large number of tourists to visit and experience, adding value to agriculture while promoting the development of tourism.

Summary

Overall, with the advocacy of the government and the efforts of enterprises, Chongming's ecological agriculture has achieved significant results. The development of Chongming's ecological agriculture not only provides new ideas and models for environmental protection and the transformation and upgrading of the agricultural industry but also provides people with healthier and safer agricultural products. The successful experience and practices of Chongming's ecological agriculture also have certain reference significance for the development of ecological agriculture in other regions. It is believed that in the future, Chongming's ecological agriculture will continue to flourish and make greater contributions to China's agricultural production and environmental protection.

例句赏析

例1:

原文：崇明县于2011年10月成功向国家农业部申报创建国家现代农业示范区项目，2012年1月被农业部列为国家级现代农业示范区。崇明生态农业示范区是国家级农业科技示范区和国家农业产业化重点龙头企业示范区，主要由光明集团的崇明农垦部和上海实业集团东滩现代农业园区组成。

译文：In October 2011, Chongming successfully applied to the Ministry of Agriculture to create a national project of modernized agriculture demonstration zone, which was listed as a national demonstration zone by the Ministry of Agriculture in January 2012. The Chongming ecological agriculture demonstration zone is a national agricultural science and technology demonstration zone and a key leading enterprise demonstration zone for national agricultural industrialization, mainly composed of the Chongming Agriculture Reclamation Department of Bright Dairy Group and the Dongtan Modern Agriculture Park of Shanghai Industrial Group.

赏析：原文介绍了崇明县生态农业示范区的建设过程。原文两个主句都比较长，主要由组织机构的名称构成，两主句均由一个主动句和一个被动句构成。两个句子在被动分句的衔接上处理方式不同，第一句采用 which 定语从句衔接，而第二句则采用过去分词衔接，虽然本质都为定语，但形式却不同。原文难点在于组织机构名称的翻译，有些组织机构本身有英文名并挂在机构官网上，而有些组织机构主要面向国内市场，并无英文名，需要译者重新命名。组织机构名称的大小写也包含了一些信息，小写代表原文的"示范区"不是特指某一个地点，而大写则代表特指某个地点，如"光明集团的崇明农垦部"就指众多示范区中的某个特定区域。

例 2：

原文：例如，崇明生态农园、北部垦区的生态农园基地和崇明岛许多村镇开展了农家乐、采摘游、民宿等活动，吸引了大量游客前来参观、采摘和体验，为农业增加了附加值，同时也推动了旅游业的发展。

译文：For example, Chongming's ecological farms, farm bases in the northern reclamation area, and many villages on Chongming Island have carried out activities such as agritourism, fruit picking tours, and home inns, which attracted a large number of tourists to visit and experience, added value to agriculture and promoted the development of tourism.

赏析：原文介绍了崇明区生态园和村镇的生态旅游活动和效果。原文句子的主语和谓语所占篇幅较长，一般为"一主多谓"结构，谓语动词"开展了""吸引了""增加了""推动了"，均采用"了"的过去时后缀。然而，翻译时，译文将这种并列的谓语分成了主从句结构，谓语动词采用了 which 引导的定语从句或分词结构来衔接，译文使得表达更为精简。在翻译"参观、采摘和体验"时，译文减译了"采摘"，因为"体验"本身就包含了"采摘"。

例 3：

原文：随着国家对生态环境的重视，2010 年，上海市政府明确崇明为上海生态岛建设的主阵地，并将生态农业发展纳入国家战略。此后，崇明生态农业逐步壮大，生态农业示范区、绿色产业园区等一系列项目相继建成。

译文：With the country's emphasis on the ecological environment, in 2010, the Shanghai government designated Chongming as the main base for Shanghai's ecological island construction and incorporated the development of ecological agriculture into the national strategy. Since then, Chongming's ecological agriculture has gradually grown, and a series of projects such as ecological agriculture demonstration zones and green industrial parks have been built.

赏析：原文强调了市政府对崇明发展的重视和措施。对于政策类文本的翻译，战略术语是难点，例如"明确……为""主阵地"，表示某个行动或决策占据某个领域或行业的重要地位，因此可译为"designated... as the main base"。另外，汉语的被动义是隐藏在逻辑含义里的，而非表现在显性的语言形式上，如"一系列项目相继建成"形式上为主动，但逻辑上"项目"与"建成"是被动关系，翻译时需要显性化。

例 4：

原文：崇明生态农业的农产品品质得到了广泛认可，特色农产品如崇明稻米、崇明老毛蟹、崇明白山羊、蔬菜等深受消费者喜爱。崇明蔬菜以其独特的品种和绿色生态的生产方式，成为上海本地市场的重要供应商之一。

译文：Chongming's ecological agriculture products have been widely recognized for their quality, with characteristic agricultural products such as Chongming rice, Chongming hairy crabs, Chongming white goats, and vegetables being popular among consumers. Chongming vegetables have become one of the important suppliers in the Shanghai market due to their unique varieties and green ecological production methods.

赏析：原文为崇明岛特产的罗列和介绍。在全国农业发达的今日，稻米、毛蟹、山羊、蔬菜可能算不上某个地方的特产，但崇明岛作为上海的"菜园"，即主要的粮食供应地，建立了许多食品品牌，在江浙沪一带具有一定知名度。凭借其良好的生态环境和生态农业的经营，崇明一直以来都以"生态和健康"作为推广农产品的特色和口号。由此，农产品的译文需和原文一致，保留"崇明"二字。原文第二句中"以……生产方式"引导的是方式状语，而译文转化为 due to 的原因状语，说明了方式与原因在逻辑关系上的相似性。

☞ **练习**

（一）将下列短语翻译成英文。

1. 生态环境
2. 绿色农业
3. 创新发展
4. 生态岛
5. 发展战略

（二）将下列句子翻译成英文。

1. 崇明岛以其独特的生态环境和丰富的文化底蕴，成为中国生态农业发展的重要示范区之一。

2. 崇明生态农业的发展历程可追溯至20世纪90年代。

3. 在农业生产中，崇明大力推广绿色生态农业技术，实现了农业生产的低碳、环保、可持续发展。

4. 有机农业、生态养殖、绿色种植等是崇明岛的生态农业技术。

5. 崇明大力推广绿色生态农业技术，实现了农业生产的低碳、环保、可持续发展。

(三)将下面段落翻译成英文。

在农业生产中，崇明大力推广绿色生态农业技术，实现了农业生产的低碳、环保、可持续发展。崇明岛的生态农业技术包括有机农业、生态养殖、绿色种植。有机农业专注于土壤保护和生态平衡，使用天然有机肥料和生物控制方法，不使用化学农药和化肥。生态养殖专注于动物福利和环保措施，采用天然饲养和养殖方法，不使用激素和抗生素。绿色种植使用科学种植技术，专注于生态平衡和土壤保护，不使用化学农药和化肥。这些技术的应用有助于提高农产品的品质和安全，保护环境，促进可持续发展。此外，崇明的生态农业还探索了一系列生态农业模式，如"生态农业+旅游"和"乡村旅游+休闲度假"，为农业产业转型升级提供了新思路。

☞ 参考答案

(一)

1. ecological environment

2. green agriculture

3. innovative development

4. ecological island

5. development strategy

(二)

1. Chongming Island has become one of the important demonstration zones for China's ecological agriculture development due to its unique ecological environment and rich cultural heritage.

2. The development of Chongming's ecological agriculture can be traced back to the 1990s.

3. Chongming vigorously promotes green ecological agriculture technology to achieve low-carbon, environmentally friendly, and sustainable agricultural production.

4. Organic agriculture, ecological breeding, and green planting are ecological agriculture technologies on Chongming Island.

5. Chongming vigorously promotes green ecological agriculture technology to achieve low-

carbon, environmentally friendly, and sustainable agricultural production.

（三）

In agricultural production, Chongming vigorously promotes green ecological agriculture technology to achieve low-carbon, environmentally friendly, and sustainable agricultural production. Chongming's ecological agriculture technology includes organic agriculture, ecological breeding, and green planting. Organic agriculture focuses on soil protection and ecological balance, using natural organic fertilizers and biological control methods without chemical pesticides and fertilizers. Ecological breeding focuses on animal welfare and environmental protection, using natural feeding and breeding methods without hormones and antibiotics. Green planting uses scientific planting techniques, focusing on ecological balance and soil protection, without using chemical pesticides and fertilizers. The application of these technologies helps improve the quality and safety of agricultural products, protect the environment, and promote sustainable development. In addition, Chongming's ecological agriculture has also explored a series of ecological agriculture models, such as " ecological agriculture + tourism" and "rural tourism + leisure vacation," providing new ideas for the transformation and upgrading of the agricultural industry.

二、崇明生态农业的特色和优势

翻译简介

本文介绍了崇明生态农业的产品、品牌、经营的优势和特色。译文能准确地表达原文的核心内容，没有出现明显的漏译或误译现象。术语翻译，采用了不同的翻译方法，如音译+解释、音译、忠实企业译法等，以便于读者的理解和查询。在语言风格上，译文符合英语表达习惯，流畅自然。在句型结构方面，译文采用了不同的衔接手法来连接分句，如当原文的并列句转化为主从句结构时，采用动词不定式、分词结构来衔接。该译文不仅提供了一些关于英汉翻译、语言差异的思考和启示，也提供了一些专业术语翻译、句型调整、表达效果等方面的参考。

词汇表

生态农业：ecological agriculture

地理环境：geographical environment

长江口：Yangtze River mouth

气候温和：mild climate

雨量充沛：abundant rainfall

阳光充足：ample sunshine

四季分明：distinct four seasons

土壤质量：soil quality

有机质：organic matter

矿物质：mineral matter

酸碱度：pH

湿地：wetlands

沼泽：swamps

鸟类和动物栖息地：habitats for birds and animals

渔业资源：fishery resources

海域：waters around the island

海洋生物：marine organisms

淡水资源：freshwater resources

科技创新驱动：technology innovation-driven

现代农业科技：modern agricultural technology

农业管理经验：agricultural management experience

数字农业：digital agriculture

精品农业：boutique agriculture

品牌农业：brand agriculture

农业信息化建设：agricultural information construction

农产品质量：agricultural product quality

可追溯性：traceability

原文

崇明生态农业的特色和优势主要体现在以下几个方面：

独特的地理环境

崇明岛地处长江口，气候温和、雨量充沛、阳光充足、四季分明。这种气候条件非常适合农业生产，特别是对于水稻、蔬菜、水果等农作物的种植非常有利。此外，崇明岛的土壤质量非常好，富含有机质和矿物质，土壤酸碱度适中，非常适合农作物的生长。崇明岛还拥有大片的湿地和沼泽，是很多鸟类和动物的栖息地，它们在这里繁殖和生长，也为崇明生态农业提供了非常好的生态条件。崇明岛位于上海市东北部，三面环海，地理位置优越，拥有得天独厚的渔业资源。岛周围的海域水质清澈、水深适中，富含各种海洋生物。此外，崇明岛还有丰富的淡水资源，如长江、黄浦江等，这为崇明岛的渔业发展提供了更多的机遇和优势。

科技创新驱动

崇明生态农业大力发展现代农业科技，引进国内外先进的农业技术和管理经验，提高农业生产效率和质量。崇明与各大高校深度合作，大力推动种源农业、数字农业、精品农业、品牌农业发展。崇明区政府与中国农业大学、中科院分子植物科学卓越创新中心等农科创新机构签约，协同研究水产、花卉、生态、种源等农业发展的问题。此外，崇明生态农业还非常注重农业信息化建设，建立了全岛农业信息系统，实现了农产品质量追溯和生产管理的全过程监控和数据共享。

优质农产品

崇明生态农业注重农产品的内在品质，以安全、绿色、健康为核心，生产出一批具有地域特色的优质农产品，如崇明稻米、崇明老毛蟹、崇明白山羊、崇明蔬菜等。这些产品以其独特的品质和口感，深受消费者的喜爱。为管控农产品的质量，崇明建成了"1个总仓+16个门店"，实现农产品溯源的一网管控。此外，崇明还注重对农产品的品牌建设和营销，成功注册"两无化""山水"商标，通过品牌推广和线上线下的多渠道销售，对接盒马生鲜、叮咚买菜等新零售企业，将崇明农产品打造成了一张响亮的品牌。此外，"崇明白扁豆""崇明金瓜""崇明水仙""崇明香酥芋"和"崇明黄杨"获得了地理标志证明商标，"崇明老毛蟹"和"崇明老白酒"成为了地理标志保护产品。

产业融合

崇明生态农业积极探索农业与旅游、文化等产业的深度融合，发展休闲农业、农业体验等多元化业态，拓宽农业发展空间。例如，崇明生态农业开发了农家乐、特色民宿、农旅融合等多种业态，吸引了越来越多的游客前来参观、体验，既促进了农民增收，又加强了农业与旅游业的互动和融合。另外，崇明生态农业还开发了农业文化旅游、农业科普教育、农业生态旅游等多种形式的农业旅游项目，将农业与文化、教育等产业进行深度融合，推动了农业产业的转型升级。

生态保护与可持续发展

崇明生态农业在生产过程中非常注重生态保护和可持续发展。崇明岛拥有大片的湿地和沼泽，这些地方是很多鸟类和动物的栖息地，为了保护这些生态系统，崇明生态农业采用生态农业种植方式，不使用化肥、农药等化学物质，持续推动化肥农药减量化，避免对环境造成污染。此外，崇明生态农业还积极推进农业循环经济，推广"基地+村"农业废弃物循环利用模式，将农业废弃物和农业生产过程中的废弃物进行资源化利用，达到了资源再利用和减少污染的目的。

崇明生态农业的特色和优势主要体现在其独特的地理环境、科技创新驱动、优质农产品、产业融合和生态保护与可持续发展等方面。通过不断创新和发展，崇明生态农业将继续展现出其独特的魅力和竞争力，为推动中国生态农业的发展作出更大的贡献。同时，崇明生态农业的经验和模式也具有借鉴意义，可以为其他地区的生态农业发展提供有益的参考和借鉴。

译文

The characteristics and advantages of Chongming's ecological agriculture are mainly reflected in the following aspects:

Unique geographical environment

Chongming Island is located at the mouth of the Yangtze River, with a mild climate, abundant rainfall, ample sunshine, and distinct four seasons. This climate condition is very suitable for agricultural production, especially for the cultivation of crops such as rice, vegetables, and fruits. In addition, the soil quality of Chongming Island is very good, rich in organic and mineral matter, and the soil pH is moderate, which is very suitable for crop growth. Chongming Island also has large wetlands and swamps, which are habitats for many birds and animals. They breed and grow here, providing excellent ecological conditions for Chongming's ecological agriculture. Moreover, Chongming Island is located in the northeast of Shanghai, surrounded by the sea on three sides, with a superior geographical location and abundant fishery resources. The waters around the island are clear and deep, rich in various marine organisms. In addition, Chongming Island also has abundant freshwater resources such as the Yangtze River and Huangpu River, which provide more opportunities and advantages for the development of Chongming's fishery.

Technology innovation

Chongming's ecological agriculture vigorously develops modern agricultural technology, introduces advanced agricultural technology and management experience from domestic and foreign sources, and improves agricultural production efficiency and quality. Chongming cooperates deeply with major universities to promote the development of seed source, digital agriculture, boutique agriculture, and brand agriculture. The Chongming District Government has signed agreements with agricultural innovation institutions such as China Agricultural University and the CAS Center for Excellence in Molecular Plant Sciences to collaborate on research issues related to aquatic products, flowers, ecology, seed source, etc. In addition, Chongming's ecological agriculture also attaches great importance to agricultural information construction, establishing a comprehensive island-wide agricultural information system to achieve full-process monitoring and data sharing of agricultural product's quality, traceability and production management.

High-quality agricultural products

Chongming's ecological agriculture focuses on the intrinsic quality of agricultural products, with safety, greenness, and health as its core, producing a batch of high-quality agricultural products with regional characteristics such as Chongming rice, Chongming hairy crabs, Chongming white goats, and Chongming vegetables. These products are deeply loved by consumers for their unique quality and taste. To control the quality of agricultural products, Chongming has built "one warehouse plus 16 stores" to achieve network control of agricultural product traceability. In addition, Chongming also attaches great importance to the branding and marketing of agricultural products. It has successfully registered the "Liǎng Wú Huà (chemical free)" and "Shān Shuǐ (implying high reliability)" trademarks. Through brand promotion and multi-channel sales both online and offline, it has connected with new retail enterprises such as Fresh Hippo and Dingdong Maicai, making Chongming's agricultural products a resounding brand. In addition, "Chongming White Hyacinth Bean" "Chongming Golden Melon" "Chongming Narcissus" "Chongming Crispy Taro" and "Chongming Boxwood" have obtained the certification trademarks of geographical indications, and "Chongming Hairy Crab" and "Chongming Rice Liquor" are also under the protection by geographical indications.

Industry integration

Chongming's ecological agriculture actively explores the deep integration of agriculture with tourism, culture, and other industries, develops diversified formats such as leisure agriculture and agricultural experience to broaden the space for agricultural development. For example, Chongming's ecological agriculture has developed various formats such as farmhouse tourism, characteristic homestays, and agricultural-tourism integration, attracting many tourists to visit and experience. This not only promotes farmers' income but also strengthens the interaction and integration between agriculture and tourism industries. In addition, Chongming's ecological agriculture has also developed various forms of agricultural tourism projects such as agricultural cultural tourism, agricultural science popularization, and agricultural ecological tourism to deeply integrate agriculture with culture, education, and other industries, promoting the transformation and upgrading of the agricultural industry.

Ecological protection and sustainable development

Chongming's ecological agriculture attaches great importance to ecological protection and sustainable development in the production process. Chongming Island has large wetlands and swamps that are habitats for many birds and animals. In order to protect these ecosystems, Chongming's ecological agriculture adopts ecological farming methods without using chemical substances such as fertilizers and pesticides. It continues to promote the reduction of fertilizer and pesticide use to avoid environmental pollution. In addition, Chongming's ecological agriculture actively promotes agricultural circular economy, promotes the "base + village" agricultural waste recycling model, and utilizes agricultural waste and waste generated during the agricultural production process for reusing recycling to achieve resource reuse and pollution reduction.

The characteristics and advantages of Chongming's ecological agriculture are mainly reflected in its unique geographical environment, technology innovation-driven development, high-quality agricultural products, industry integration, ecological protection, and sustainable development. Through continuous innovation and development, Chongming's ecological agriculture will continue to demonstrate its unique charm and competitiveness, making greater contributions to the development of China's ecological agriculture. At the same time, the experience and model of Chongming's ecological agriculture also have reference significance and can provide useful references for the development of ecological agriculture in other regions.

例句赏析

例1：

原文：崇明岛地处长江口，气候温和、雨量充沛、阳光充足、四季分明。这种气候条件非常适合农业生产，特别是对于水稻、蔬菜、水果等农作物的种植非常有利。此外，崇明岛的土壤质量非常好，富含有机质和矿物质，土壤酸碱度适中，非常适合农作物的生长。

译文：Chongming Island is located at the mouth of the Yangtze River, with a mild climate, abundant rainfall, ample sunshine, and distinct four seasons. This climate condition is very suitable for agricultural production, especially for the cultivation of crops such as rice, vegetables, and fruits. In addition, the soil quality of Chongming Island is very good and rich in organic and mineral matter, and the soil pH is moderate, which is very suitable for crop growth.

赏析：译文的准确度非常高，几乎每个词汇都能准确地表达原文的含义，没有出现明显的漏译或误译现象。原文的句型结构较为零散，为崇明岛气候特征的简单罗列，给翻译造成了一些衔接难度，如"崇明岛地处长江口，气候温和、雨量充沛、阳光充足、四季分明"。原文分句为"名词+形容词"结构，翻译时，为了保持一致，采用了以 with 引出气候特征的罗列。第二句的衔接难度较大，需要将各个分句主从化，如"崇明岛的土壤""土壤酸碱度"，译文对两个主句用 and 衔接，后一个分句则处理成 which 引导的定语从句。

例2：

原文：崇明生态农业大力发展现代农业科技，引进国内外先进的农业技术和管理经验，提高农业生产效率和质量。崇明与各大高校深度合作，大力推动种源农业、数字农业、精品农业、品牌农业发展。

译文：Chongming's ecological agriculture vigorously develops modern agricultural technology, introduces advanced agricultural technology and management experience from domestic and foreign sources, and improves agricultural production efficiency and quality. Chongming cooperates deeply with major universities to promote the development of seed source, digital agriculture, boutique agriculture, and brand agriculture.

赏析：这一段主要阐述了崇明生态农业发展的具体举措，在翻译时，为了使译文更加自然流畅，符合英语表达习惯，在句型结构方面，译者采用 and 并列句、动词不定式结构等将各个分句衔接起来。译者还采用了一些生动的程度副词、形容词和动词，如"vigorously develops""introduces advanced""cooperates deeply"等，使得整个句子更加生动有力。首先将谓语动词"大力发展""引进""提高"处理成并列结构，然后将第二句的谓语动词"深度合作""大力推动"处理成主从句结构，因为逻辑上"大力推动"是"深度合作"的目的，而汉语的逻辑关系依赖语境，英文的逻辑关系则需要显性化。这是英汉语一个较为突出的语言风格差异。

例3：

原文：另外，崇明还注重对农产品的品牌建设和营销，成功注册"两无化""山水"商标，通过品牌推广和线上线下的多渠道销售，对接盒马生鲜、叮咚买菜等新零售企业，将崇明农产品打造成了一张响亮的品牌。

译文：In addition, Chongming also attaches great importance to the branding and marketing of agricultural products. It has successfully registered the "Liáng Wú Huà（chemical free）" and "Shān Shuǐ（implying high reliability）" trademarks. Through brand promotion and multi-channel sales both online and offline, it has connected with new retail enterprises such as Fresh Hippo and Dingdong Maicai, making Chongming's agricultural products a resounding brand.

赏析：原文介绍了崇明岛生态农业产品的营销路径。因为涉及较多的术语翻译，译者采用了"音译+解释"的翻译方式，如将"两无化"翻译为"chemical free"，将"山水"翻译为"implying high reliability"，其解释越过了字面而直击深层含义，用词精简。对于"盒马生鲜""叮咚买菜"的翻译，译者按照企业实际的英文来翻译，这样利于外文读者对品牌名称的查询。除了"盒马生鲜"的企业官网有英文名外，"叮咚买菜"只有拼音翻译，但出于指代和查询的准确性，仍然要尊重企业本身的译法。

例4：

原文：另外，崇明生态农业还开发了农业文化旅游、农业科普教育、农业生态旅游等多种形式的农业旅游项目，将农业与文化、教育等产业进行深度融合，推动了农业产业的转型升级。

译文：In addition, Chongming's ecological agriculture has also developed various forms of agricultural tourism projects such as agricultural cultural tourism, agricultural science popularization, and agricultural ecological tourism to deeply integrate agriculture with culture, education, and other industries, promoting the transformation and upgrading of the agricultural industry.

赏析：原文罗列了崇明岛开发的生态旅游项目。译文覆盖了原文所有的信息和细节，翻译准确度较高，在翻译"深度融合""转型升级"时，许多译者容易忽略掉"深度"与"转型"。篇幅上，虽然译文一般要力求精简，但精简性优势会导致歧义和表意不清楚，如"农业文化旅游、农业科普教育、农业生态旅游"中，"农业"为重复出现的词，如果删减重复词，"科普教育""生态旅游"的内容范围就超出了农业。译者对原文的三个谓语动词"开发了""深度融合""推动了"，分别采用动词不定式结构、分词短语作状语的结构来衔接上下文，表示递进关系。

☞ 练习

（一）将以下短语翻译成英文。

1. 生态农业
2. 地理环境
3. 气候温和
4. 雨量充沛
5. 阳光充足
6. 四季分明
7. 水稻
8. 蔬菜
9. 水果
10. 土壤质量

（二）将以下句子翻译成英文。

1. 崇明岛的气候条件非常适合农业生产，特别是对于水稻、蔬菜、水果等农作物的种植非常有利。

2. 崇明岛还拥有大片的湿地和沼泽，这些地方是很多鸟类和动物的栖息地。

3. 崇明生态农业大力发展现代农业科技，引进国内外先进的农业技术和管理经验，提高农业生产效率和质量。

4. 崇明与中国农业大学、中科院分子植物科学卓越中心等农业创新机构签署了协议，共同研究与水产品、花卉、生态、种子来源等相关的问题。

5. 崇明的生态农业还非常重视农业信息化建设，建立了全岛范围内的农业信息系统，实现了农产品质量、追溯和生产管理的全过程监控和数据共享。

（三）将下面段落翻译成英文。

崇明岛地处长江口，气候温和、雨量充沛、阳光充足、四季分明。这种气候条件非常适合农业生产，特别是对于水稻、蔬菜、水果等农作物的种植非常有利。此外，崇明岛的土壤质量非常好，富含有机质和矿物质，土壤酸碱度适中，非常适合农作物的生长。崇明岛还拥有大片的湿地和沼泽，这些地方是很多鸟类和动物的栖息地，它们在这里繁殖和生长，也为崇明生态农业提供了非常好的生态条件。崇明岛位于上海市东北部，三面环海，地理位置优越，拥有得天独厚的渔业资源。岛周围的海域水质清澈、水深适中，富含各种海洋生物。此外，崇明岛还有丰富的淡水资源，如长江、黄浦江等，这为崇明岛的渔业发展提供了更多的机遇和优势。

☞ **参考答案**

(一)

1. ecological agriculture

2. geographical environment

3. mild climate

4. abundant rainfall

5. ample sunshine

6. distinct four seasons

7. rice

8. vegetables

9. fruits

10. soil quality

(二)

1. The climate condition of Chongming Island is very suitable for agricultural production, especially for the cultivation of crops such as rice, vegetables, and fruits.

2. Chongming Island also has large wetlands and swamps, which are habitats for many birds and animals.

3. Chongming's ecological agriculture vigorously develops modern agricultural technology, introduces advanced agricultural technology and management experience from domestic and foreign sources, and improves agricultural production efficiency and quality.

4. Chongming has signed agreements with agricultural innovation institutions such as China Agricultural University and the CAS Center for Excellence in Molecular Plant Sciences to collaborate on research issues related to aquatic products, flowers, ecology, seed source, etc.

5. Chongming's ecological agriculture also attaches great importance to agricultural information construction, establishing a comprehensive island-wide agricultural information system to achieve full-process monitoring and data sharing of agricultural product's quality, traceability and production management.

(三)

Chongming Island is located at the mouth of the Yangtze River, with a mild climate, abundant rainfall, ample sunshine, and distinct four seasons. This climate condition is very suitable for agricultural production, especially for the cultivation of crops such as rice, vegetables, and fruits. In addition, the soil quality of Chongming Island is very good, rich in organic and mineral matter, and the soil pH is moderate, which is very suitable for crop growth. Chongming Island also has large wetlands and swamps, which are habitats for many birds and animals. They breed and grow here, providing excellent ecological conditions for Chongming's ecological agriculture. Moreover, Chongming Island is located in the northeast of Shanghai, surrounded by the sea on three sides, with a superior geographical location and abundant fishery resources. The waters around the island are clear and deep, rich in various marine organisms. In addition, Chongming Island also has abundant freshwater resources such as the Yangtze River and Huangpu River, which provide more opportunities and advantages for the development of Chongming's fishery.

三、崇明生态农业的旅游项目和体验活动

翻译简介

本文介绍了崇明生态农业旅游的项目和活动，包括精致的民宿、花卉基地、农家乐、博物馆和公园等。翻译难点在于原文中状语从句和定语从句的篇幅较长，另外，景区地名的翻译也存在一定难度，一些地名本身没有现有译文，需要创译，要求译者能呈现出地点的功能和定位信息。由于英汉两种语言对地点分类的细化程度不同，因此翻译汉语地名时容易造成歧义。例如许多民宿会用"舍"字，但翻译时可有三种译法，如 homestay, guesthouse, inn，所以译者要按照民宿的规模、服务种类、游客体验、民宿专业度来选择具体译法。

词汇表

自然资源：natural resources
生态环境：ecological environment
地理环境：geographical environment
科技创新驱动：technology innovation
优质农产品：high-quality agricultural products
产业融合：industry integration
综合性农业园区：comprehensive agricultural park

农业生产：agricultural production

生态旅游：ecological tourism

农业体验：agricultural experience

田园风光游：countryside scenery tour

绿色田园：pastoral village

丰收的稻田：rice fields

金黄的麦地：golden wheat fields

绿意盎然的果园：lush orchards

田园生活：rural life

宁静与美好：tranquility and beauty

绿色的田野：green fields

泥土的气息：scent of earth

大自然的力量：power of nature

具体的田园风光景点：specific rural homestays

天鹅苑：Swan Garden

楠舍：Nan She Guesthouse

水云乡：Shuiyun Town

香朵开心农场：Xiangduo Happy Farm

西岸氧吧：West Bank Oxygen Bar

高家庄园：Gaojia Manor

九园草堂：Jiuyuan Caotang

港沿园艺村：Gangyan Horticulture Village

玖居民宿：Jiuju Homestay

水仙花基地：Narcissus Base

农业体验活动：agricultural experience activities

农耕文化的魅力：charm of farming culture

农业的艰辛和收获：hardships and gains of agriculture

手工艺制作：local handicrafts

竹编和传统纺织品：bamboo weaving and traditional textile

户外活动：outdoor activities

农业课堂：agricultural classroom

生态意识：ecological awareness

原文

崇明岛作为上海市的后花园，拥有得天独厚的自然资源和生态环境，以其独特的地理环境、科技创新驱动、优质农产品和产业融合等优势，发展成了集农业生产、生态旅游、农业体验于一体的综合性农业园区。崇明生态农园的旅游项目和体验活动丰富多样，既有自然风光观赏，也有丰富的农业体验。

田园风光游

游客可以漫步于绿色田园，欣赏丰收的稻田、金黄的麦地、绿意盎然的果园等自然风光，感受田园生活的宁静与美好。在这里，游客可以看到一片片绿色的田野，闻到泥土的气息，感受到大自然的力量，让人心旷神怡。崇明岛具体的田园风光景点包括天鹅苑、楠舍、水云乡、香朵开心农场、乡舍、西岸氧吧、林舍、高家庄园、九园草堂、里园、港沿园艺村、耘舍、玖居民宿、水仙花基地、逅院等。

农业体验活动

崇明生态农园提供多样化的农业体验活动，如亲手种植蔬菜、摘取新鲜水果、体验农家乐等，让游客领略农耕文化的魅力，亲身感受收获的喜悦。在这里，游客可以亲手体验农业生产的全过程，了解农业的辛苦和收获，感受到大自然的魅力。游客在崇明景区的农家乐，能够体验到当地竹编、土布等手工制作，户外钓虾、钓鱼、钓螃蟹、果蔬采摘、动物投喂等农业活动。具体景点包括瀛东度假村、天鹅苑、耘舍、水云乡、香朵开心农场、高家庄园、九园草堂、港沿园艺村、水仙花基地等。

农事课堂

崇明生态农园开设了一系列农事课堂，如绿色种植技术、有机肥料制作、农产品加工等，让游客了解农业知识，提高生态意识。在这里，游客可以学习到科学、环保、健康的农业生产知识，了解到崇明生态农业的发展历程和成就。具体景点包括瀛东度假村、西沙明珠湖景区、花博文化园、东平国家森林公园、东滩湿地公园、前哨当代艺术中心、中华鲟保护基地、灶文化博物馆、学宫博物馆等。

生态旅游

崇明生态农园还具备丰富的生态旅游资源，如湿地观光、鸟类观赏、生态徒步、自行车观光等，游客可以放松身心，尽享生态之美。在这里，游客可以欣赏到独特的湿地生态系统，观赏到珍稀的鸟类和动物，感受到大自然的神奇和美丽。具体景点包括西沙明珠湖景区、花博文化园、东平国家森林公园、自行车公园、东滩湿地公园、中华鲟保护基地等。

乡村民宿

游客还可以选择入住崇明生态农园周边的乡村民宿，体验乡村生活，品尝地道的农家菜肴，感受乡村风情。在这里，游客可以感受到真正的乡村生活，品尝到地道的农家菜肴，体验到乡村风情的独特魅力。具体民宿包括天鹅苑、楠舍、乡舍、西岸氧吧、林舍、花雨花畔、里园、金油桥、如砚民宿、云舍居、东禾九谷、瀛杏湾、耘舍、知谷 1984、玖居民宿、地铁小镇、逅院等。

总之，崇明生态农园是一个集农业生产、生态旅游和农业体验于一体的综合性农业园区，是一个宝贵的自然资源和生态环境的绿洲。它不仅让游客感受到了大自然的魅力，也为当地农业经济的发展作出了积极贡献，更为重要的是，它提供了一个了解自然、了解农业、了解环保的机会，让游客更加重视生态环境保护，更加关注可持续发展的重要性。

译文

As a backyard of Shanghai, Chongming Island boasts unique natural resources and ecological environment. With advantages such as its unique geographical environment, technology innovation, high-quality agricultural products, and industry integration, it has developed into a comprehensive agricultural park integrating agricultural production, ecological tourism, and agricultural experience. The tourist projects and experience activities in Chongming Ecological Farm are diverse, featuring both natural scenery and agricultural experience.

Rural Landscape

Tourists can stroll through the pastoral village, enjoy the natural scenery of the rice fields, golden wheat fields, lush orchards, and other landscapes, and experience the tranquility and beauty of rural life. Here, tourists can see green fields, smell the scent of earth, feel the power of nature, and be refreshed. Specific rural homestays in Chongming Island include Swan Garden, Nan She Guesthouse, Shuiyun Town, Xiangduo Happy Farm, Xiang She Guesthouse, West Bank Oxygen Bar, Lin She Guesthouse, Gaojia Manor, Jiuyuan Caotang Guesthouse, Liyuan Guesthouse, Gangyan Horticulture Village, Yun She Guesthouse, Jiuju Homestay, Narcissus Base and Houyuan Homestay.

Agricultural Experience Activities

Chongming Ecological Farm provides a variety of agricultural experience activities such as planting vegetables, picking fresh fruits, and experiencing rural life to let tourists appreciate the charm of farming culture and the joy of harvest. Here, tourists can experience the entire process of agricultural production firsthand, understand the hardships and gains of agriculture, and feel the charm of nature. At Chongming scenic spots' rural homestays, tourists can experience local handicrafts such as bamboo weaving and traditional textile. They can also participate in outdoor activities such as fishing shrimp, fish and crab, picking fruit and vegetable, and feeding animal. Specific agritourism spots include Yingdong Resort Village, Swan Garden, Yun She Guesthouse, Shuiyun Town, Xiangduo Happy Farm, Gaojia Manor, Jiuyuan Caotang Guesthouse, Gangyan Horticulture Village, Narcissus Base.

Agricultural Classroom

Chongming Ecological Farm has set up a series of agricultural classrooms such as green planting technology, organic fertilizer production, and agricultural product processing to let tourists understand agricultural knowledge and improve their ecological awareness. Here, tourists can learn scientific, environmentally friendly, and healthy agricultural production knowledge and understand the development process and achievements of Chongming's ecological agriculture. Specific spots for agricultural education include Yingdong Resort Village, Xisha Mingzhu Lake Scenic Area, Flower Expo Cultural Park, Dongping National Forest Park, Dongtan Wetland Park, Outpost Contemporary Art Center, Chinese Sturgeon Protection Base, Stove Culture Museum, Academy Palace Museum.

Eco-tourism

Chongming Ecological Farm also has rich ecological tourism resources such as wetland sightseeing, bird watching, ecological hiking, and bicycle sightseeing. Tourists can relax and enjoy the beauty of nature. Here they can appreciate the unique wetland ecosystem, rare birds, animals and feel the magic and beauty of nature. Specific scenic spots include Xisha Pearl Lake Scenic Area, Flower Expo Cultural Park, Dongping National Forest Park, Bicycle Park, Dongtan Wetland Park, Chinese Sturgeon Protection Base.

Country Homestay

Tourists can also choose to stay in rural homestays around Chongming Ecological Farm to experience rural life, taste authentic farmhouse cuisine and feel the charm of the countryside. Here tourists can experience the real rural life and taste authentic farmhouse cuisine while experiencing the unique charm of rural life. Specific homestays include Swan Garden, Nan She Guesthouse, Xiang She Guesthouse, West Bank Oxygen Bar, Lin She Guesthouse, Flower Rain Bank, Liyuan Guesthouse, Jin You Qiao Inn, Ruyan Homestay, Yun She Homestay, Donghe Jiugu Homestay Village, Yingxing Bay Homestay Village, Yun She Homestay, Zhi Gu 1984 Homestay, Jiu Ju Homestay, Subway Town, Hou Yuan Homestay.

In summary, Chongming Ecological Farm is a comprehensive agricultural park integrating agricultural production, ecological tourism and agricultural experience. It is a precious oasis of natural resources and ecological environment. It not only allows tourists to feel the charm of nature but also makes a positive contribution to the development of local agricultural economy. More importantly, it provides an opportunity for tourists to understand nature, agriculture and environmental protection so that they can pay more attention to ecological environment protection and sustainable development.

例句赏析

例1:

原文:崇明岛作为上海市的后花园,拥有得天独厚的自然资源和生态环境,以其独特的地理环境、科技创新驱动、优质农产品和产业融合等优势,发展成了集农业生产、生态旅游、农业体验于一体的综合性农业园区。

译文:As a backyard of Shanghai, Chongming Island boasts unique natural resources and ecological environment. With advantages such as its unique geographical environment, technology innovation, high-quality agricultural products, and industry integration, it has developed into a comprehensive agricultural park integrating agricultural production, ecological tourism, and agricultural experience.

赏析:原文介绍了崇明岛的生态农业发展方式。原文为"一主双谓语"结构,状语从句和定语从句较长。在翻译"后花园"时,译文保留了该比喻,但在冠词的选择上,采用了"a",因为上海周边有多处景点也采用了"后花园"绰号,不具有特指性。由于原文篇幅较长,所以翻译时对上下文的衔接就会带来一定的难度,如果和原文一样译成一个整句,篇幅就会拉长，不利于读者阅读。由此，译者采用断句法，从"以……"的方式状语从句开始断开；"集……于一体"的定语从句则采用分词结构来衔接；"以……等优势"为信息的罗列，译者采用 such as 结构来衔接罗列的信息。

例 2：

原文：崇明岛具体的田园风光景点包括天鹅苑、楠舍、水云乡、香朵开心农场、乡舍、西岸氧吧、林舍、高家庄园、九园草堂、里园、港沿园艺村、耘舍、玖居民宿、水仙花基地、逅院等。

译文：Specific rural homestays in Chongming Island include Swan Garden, Nan She Guesthouse Guesthouse, Shuiyun Town, Xiangduo Happy Farm, Xiang She Guesthouse, West Bank Oxygen Bar, Lin She Guesthouse, Gaojia Manor, Jiuyuan Caotang Guesthouse, Liyuan Guesthouse, Gangyan Horticulture Village, Yun She Guesthouse, Jiuju Homestay, Narcissus Base and Houyuan Homestay.

赏析：原文罗列了崇明岛典型的生态田园景点，以民宿、农家乐、花卉种植基地为主。原文的句型结构简单，主要以举例、名词并列为主，但翻译时，对地名的翻译存在一定的难度。因为许多地名没有现有的英文名，需要创造性翻译。另外地名翻译还存在音译和意译两种形式，音译利于交流中对地名的定位，而意译则利于传播地点的特色和意境，能呈现地点的文化特色。翻译时通常的做法是"音译+地点功能"，这样利于地点的定位，例如 Garden，Farm，Bar，Manor，Village，Homestay，Base 等。然而，有些中文地名在功能的分类上和英文有所差异，例如，楠舍、乡舍、林舍、耘舍中的"舍"，虽为同一个字，但其译法却有 homestay，guesthouse，inn。Homestay 通常指的是民宿主人将自己的住所出租给旅客居住，旅客可以和房东一起生活，共用厨房、客厅等公共区域，homestay 也显得更加亲近、温馨，容易让旅客更好地适应和了解当地的文化和生活方式。Guesthouse 则是专门为旅客提供住宿服务的建筑物，通常由专业的经营者经营。旅客可以租用独立的房间或公寓，在公共区域和其他旅客互动和交流。Guesthouse 的特点是独立性强，旅客可以更加自由地安排自己的行程。Inn 指的是提供住宿和餐饮服务的旅馆，通常由专业的经营者经营。

例 3：

原文：游客在崇明景区的农家乐，能够体验到当地竹编、土布等手工制作，户外钓虾、钓鱼、钓螃蟹，果蔬采摘、动物投喂等农业活动。具体景点包括瀛东度假村、天鹅苑、耘舍、水云乡、香朵开心农场、高家庄园、九园草堂、港沿园艺村、水仙花基地等。

译文：At Chongming scenic spots' rural homestays, tourists can experience local handicrafts such as bamboo weaving and traditional textile. They can also participate in outdoor activities such as fishing shrimp, fish, crab, and picking fruit, vegetable, and feeding animal.

Specific agritourism spots include Yingdong Resort Village，Swan Garden，Yun She Guesthouse，Shuiyun Town，Xiangduo Happy Farm，Gaojia Manor，Jiuyuan Caotang Guesthouse，Gangyan Horticulture Village，Narcissus Base.

赏析：原文罗列了崇明岛的农家乐活动和一些典型的民宿。第一句罗列了户内和户外两种活动，翻译时，译者采用断译法，使段落更加条理清晰。原文中的"钓虾"的"虾"很难确定是龙虾还是对虾，翻译时，译者根据崇明的养殖特点和当地饮食偏好，认定该词指的是"对虾"，因此译为 shrimp，而非 crayfish。另外对田园风光民宿和景点的罗列翻译均体现了原文的发音和地点的功能，利于外国游客问路，以及游客需求的匹配。

例 4：

原文：具体景点包括瀛东度假村、西沙明珠湖景区、花博文化园、东平国家森林公园、东滩湿地公园、前哨当代艺术中心、中华鲟保护基地、灶文化博物馆、学宫博物馆等。

译文：Specific spots for agricultural education include Yingdong Resort Village，Xisha Mingzhu Lake Scenic Area，Flower Expo Cultural Park，Dongping National Forest Park，Dongtan Wetland Park，Outpost Contemporary Art Center，Chinese Sturgeon Protection Base，Stove Culture Museum，Academy Palace Museum.

赏析：原文为崇明景区地名的罗列，包括公园、度假村、博物馆。翻译地名时，译文均呈现了地点的功能和属性，但在音译和意译上针对不同的地名采用了不同的技巧。一些地名更强调地名的定位作用，不要求游客理解地名的寓意、来历，例如中国游客在看到瀛东、西沙、东平、东滩时，并不会深究和理解其名字的寓意，更关注的是地点的特色、功能和地理距离。能直接表意和理解的是"西"和"东"，表达了该地点在崇明的相对位置，而"瀛""沙""平""滩"所传达的地点属性不如"湿地""森林""公园"强，更多强调的是对地点标记和定位的作用，因此类似地名的左半部分多采用音译。

☞ **练习**

（一）将下列短语翻译成英文。

1. 生态环境
2. 产业融合
3. 田园风光游
4. 绿色田园
5. 丰收的稻田
6. 绿意盎然的果园
7. 农业体验活动

8. 种植蔬菜

9. 采摘新鲜水果

10. 农产品加工

(二)将下列句子翻译成英文。

1. 崇明岛拥有得天独厚的自然资源和生态环境。

2. 崇明生态农园的旅游项目和体验活动丰富多样。

3. 游客可以漫步于绿色田园，欣赏丰收的稻田、金黄的麦地、绿意盎然的果园等自然风光。

4. 在这里，游客可以看到一片片绿色的田野，闻到泥土的气息，感受到大自然的力量，让人心旷神怡。

5. 崇明生态农园提供多样化的农业体验活动，让游客感受农业文化的魅力和丰收的喜悦。

(三)将下面段落翻译成英文。

崇明岛作为上海市的后花园，拥有得天独厚的自然资源和生态环境，以其独特的地理环境、科技创新驱动、优质农产品和产业融合等优势，发展成了集农业生产、生态旅游、农业体验于一体的综合性农业园区。崇明生态农园的旅游项目和体验活动丰富多样，既有自然风光观赏，也有丰富的农业体验。

☞ **参考答案**

(一)

1. ecological environment

2. industry integration

3. countryside scenery tour

4. pastoral village

5. rice fields of abundant harvest

6. lush orchards

7. agricultural experience activities

8. planting vegetables

9. picking fresh fruits

10. agricultural product processing

(二)

1. Chongming Island boasts unique natural resources and ecological environment.

2. The tourist projects and experience activities in Chongming Ecological Farm are diverse.

3. Tourists can stroll through the pastoral village, enjoy the natural scenery of the rice fields, golden wheat fields, lush orchards, and other landscapes.

4. Here, tourists can see green fields, smell the scent of earth, feel the power of nature, and be refreshed.

5. Chongming Ecological Farm provides a variety of agricultural experience activities to let tourists appreciate the charm of farming culture and the joy of harvest.

(三)

As a backyard of Shanghai, Chongming Island boasts unique natural resources and ecological environment. With advantages such as its unique geographical environment, technology innovation, high-quality agricultural products, and industry integration, it has developed into a comprehensive agricultural park integrating agricultural production, ecological tourism, and agricultural experience. The tourist projects and experience activities in Chongming Ecological Farm are diverse, featuring both natural scenery and agricultural experience.

第四章　崇明生态民宿

一、崇明生态民宿的概念和发展趋势

翻译简介

首先，本文介绍了崇明生态民宿的概念和发展趋势，并附有大量生动的例子。生态民宿强调环保，亲近自然，因而本文出现了大量与自然生态相关的专业术语，这也成了本文翻译的难点之一。其次，本文列举了丰富生动贴切的事例，大量具体翔实的动作、动作的层次、前后逻辑等也是翻译需要注意的重点。译文采用了伴随句式来表达动作之间的层次，如 with 结构、分词短语结构等。而在段落内部分句之间的关系上，译文基本做到了忠实于原文。

词汇表

生态民宿：ecological guesthouses

崇明区：Chongming District

生态环保：ecology and environmental protection

和谐共生：harmonious coexistence

低碳：low-carbon

可持续：sustainable

可再生能源：renewable energy sources

太阳能：solar power

风能：wind power

特色文化：local cultural characteristics

风土人情：local customs

竹屋：bamboo houses

声音隔离效果：sound insulation effects

电力消耗：electricity consumption

节能照明灯具：energy-saving lighting fixtures

当地特色美食：local specialty foods

传统手工艺品：traditional handicrafts

人文氛围：humanistic atmosphere

消耗品：disposable items

原文

崇明生态民宿是指位于上海市崇明区的一种特殊类型的民宿，它以生态环保为主题，强调与自然和谐共生，提供舒适宜人的住宿体验。这种类型的民宿在近年来得到了迅速发展，吸引了越来越多的游客前来体验。

随着生态旅游的兴起，崇明生态民宿正朝着绿色、低碳、可持续的方向发展。例如，一些民宿开始利用太阳能、风能等可再生能源，减少对环境的污染。此外，民宿还注重对当地特色文化的保护和传承，让游客在体验自然之美的同时，更加了解和尊重当地的风土人情。

崇明生态民宿的发展趋势可以从以下几个方面进行分析：

绿色环保

崇明生态民宿注重环保，采用低碳、零排放的建筑材料和设备，致力于减少对自然环境的影响。同时，民宿还通过垃圾分类、回收等方式，促进垃圾减量和资源循环利用。例如，位于崇明岛东海岸的一家生态民宿，采用了天然材料，如竹子、木材、稻草等，建造了一批独具特色的竹屋，这些竹屋不仅具有良好的隔音效果，还能很好地融入当地的自然环境中，让游客感受到自然与人类和谐共生的美好。

利用可再生能源

崇明生态民宿开始利用可再生能源，如太阳能、风能等，减少对环境的污染。这些民宿通过安装太阳能电池板或者风力发电机，将自然能源转化为电能，为自己的用电提供了可靠的保障。例如，位于崇明岛的一家生态民宿，通过在屋顶安装太阳能电池板，为自己的用电提供一定的保障。同时，民宿还在每个房间内安装了节能灯具和空调，进一步减少用电量和对环境的影响。

保护当地文化

崇明生态民宿注重对当地特色文化的保护和传承，让游客在体验自然之美的同时，更加了解和尊重当地的风土人情。这些民宿通过提供当地特色美食、传统手工艺品等活动，让游客感受到浓郁的民俗文化和人文气息。例如，崇明岛的一家生态民宿为游客提供了丰富多彩的当地特色美食，如鲜美的崇明大闸蟹、清香的崇明稻花鱼等，让游客在品尝美食的同时，更好地了解当地的特色文化。此外，民宿还组织了一些传统手工艺品制作活动，如剪纸、编织等，让游客在体验当地文化的同时，还能亲身参与当地文化的传承。

推广可持续发展

崇明生态民宿致力于推广可持续发展，通过自身的努力和示范，引导更多的旅游从业者和游客参与可持续发展。这些民宿通过实施节水、节能、减排等措施，向游客展示了一种可持续的旅游方式，引导游客从消费者到参与者的转变。例如，崇明岛的某家生态民宿，通过推广绿色出行方式，如骑行、徒步等，引导游客减少对环境的影响。同时，民宿还鼓励游客使用环保型的个人物品，如水杯、购物袋等，减少对一次性用品的使用，保护环境。

总之，崇明生态民宿的兴起，推动了崇明岛生态旅游的发展，为游客提供了一种独特的住宿体验。未来，我们相信崇明生态民宿将继续朝着绿色、低碳、可持续的方向发展，为环境保护和可持续发展作出更大的贡献。

译文

Chongming ecological guesthouses refer to a special type of guesthouse located in Chongming District, Shanghai. With ecology and environmental protection as their main theme, they emphasize harmonious coexistence with nature and provide a comfortable and pleasant living experience. This type of guesthouse has rapidly developed in recent years, attracting more and more tourists to experience it.

With the rise of ecotourism, Chongming ecological guesthouses are developing towards a green, low-carbon, and sustainable direction. For example, some guesthouses have started to use renewable energy sources such as solar and wind power to reduce environmental pollution. In addition, guesthouses also pay attention to the protection and inheritance of local cultural characteristics, allowing tourists to better understand and respect local customs while experiencing the beauty of nature.

The development trend of Chongming ecological guesthouses can be analyzed from the following aspects:

Green Environmental Protection

Chongming ecological guesthouses focus on environmental protection, using low-carbon and zero-emission building materials and equipment to reduce their impact on the natural environment. At the same time, guesthouses also promote waste reduction and resource recycling through garbage classification and recycling. For example, an ecological guesthouse located on the east coast of Chongming Island has built a group of unique bamboo houses using natural materials such as bamboo, wood, and straw. These bamboo houses not only have good sound insulation effects but also blend well with the local natural environment, allowing tourists to experience the beauty of harmonious coexistence between nature and humans.

Use of Renewable Energy Sources

Chongming ecological guesthouses have started to use renewable energy sources such as solar and wind power to reduce environmental pollution. By installing solar panels or wind turbines, these guesthouses convert natural energy into electricity, providing reliable guarantees for their own electricity consumption. For example, an ecological guesthouse located on Chongming Island has installed solar panels on the roof to provide a certain guarantee for its electricity consumption. At the same time, the guesthouse has also installed energy-saving lighting fixtures and air conditioning in each room to further reduce electricity consumption and its impact on the environment.

Protecting Local Culture

Chongming ecological guesthouses focus on the protection and inheritance of local cultural characteristics, allowing tourists to better understand and respect local customs while experiencing the beauty of nature. These guesthouses provide local specialty foods, traditional handicrafts, and other activities to let tourists feel the rich folk culture and humanistic atmosphere. For example, an ecological guesthouse located on Chongming Island provides tourists with a variety of local specialty foods such as delicious Chongming hairy crabs and fragrant Chongming rice-field fish, allowing tourists to better understand the local culture while enjoying the food. In addition, the guesthouse also organizes traditional handicraft activities such as paper cutting and weaving, allowing tourists to experience local culture and participate in its inheritance.

Promoting Sustainable Development

Chongming ecological guesthouses are committed to promoting sustainable development and guiding more tourism practitioners and tourists to participate in sustainable development through their own efforts and demonstration. These guesthouses demonstrate a sustainable tourism model by implementing measures such as water conservation, energy conservation, and emission reduction, guiding tourists to transform from consumers to participants. For example, an ecological guesthouse located on Chongming Island promotes green travel methods such as cycling and hiking, guiding tourists to reduce their impact on the environment. At the same time, the guesthouse encourages tourists to use environmentally friendly personal items such as water bottles and shopping bags, reducing the use of disposable items and protecting the environment.

In conclusion, the rise of Chongming ecological guesthouses has promoted the development of ecotourism on Chongming Island and provided tourists with a unique accommodation experience. In the future, we believe that Chongming ecological guesthouses will continue to develop towards a green, low-carbon, and sustainable direction, making greater contributions to environmental protection and sustainable development.

例句赏析

例1：

原文：崇明生态民宿是指位于上海市崇明区的一种特殊类型的民宿，它以生态环保为主题，强调与自然和谐共生，提供舒适宜人的住宿体验。

译文：Chongming ecological guesthouses refer to a special type of guesthouse located in Chongming District, Shanghai. With ecology and environmental protection as their main theme, they emphasize harmonious coexistence with nature and provide a comfortable and pleasant living experience.

赏析：该句中文是对崇明生态民宿的定义，内容丰富，语体正式。虽为一句话，但前后两个小句之间是总—分的关系，第二个小句出现了多个动词并列使用的现象。因此，译文将该句中文译成两个句子，以此体现两个小句之间的逻辑关系。其中，译文将三个动词进行层次划分，"以……为主题"译为"with … as their main theme"作为伴随状语出现，emphasize 和 provide 则通过连词 and 进行连接，使得译文层次分明而又不显得累赘。

例 2：

原文：随着生态旅游的兴起，崇明生态民宿正朝着绿色、低碳、可持续的方向发展。例如，一些民宿开始利用太阳能、风能等可再生能源，减少对环境的污染。此外，民宿还注重对当地特色文化的保护和传承，让游客在体验自然之美的同时，更加了解和尊重当地的风土人情。

译文：With the rise of ecotourism, Chongming ecological guesthouses are developing towards a green, low-carbon, and sustainable direction. For example, some guesthouses have started to use renewable energy sources such as solar and wind power to reduce environmental pollution. In addition, guesthouses also pay attention to the protection and inheritance of local cultural characteristics, allowing tourists to better understand and respect local customs while experiencing the beauty of nature.

赏析：该段第一句中文为与环境保护相关的术语，例如低碳、可持续、太阳能、风能、可再生能源等，其对应的译文术语为"low-carbon, sustainable, solar power, wind power, renewable energy sources"。另外，该段第二句中文出现了一系列动作，分别是"注重""让……体验""了解和尊重"，译文将这几个动作处理为三层，以 pay attention to 为谓语，"让"即"allowing... to"作为伴随状语，"understand and respect... while experiencing"作为复合结构的宾语补足语来修饰"tourists"。

例 3：

原文：例如，崇明岛的一家生态民宿为游客提供了丰富多彩的当地特色美食，如鲜美的崇明大闸蟹、清香的崇明稻花鱼等，让游客在品尝美食的同时，更好地了解当地的特色文化。此外，民宿还组织了一些传统手工艺品制作活动，如剪纸、编织等，让游客在体验当地文化的同时，也能亲身参与当地文化的传承。

译文：For example, an ecological guesthouse located on Chongming Island provides tourists with a variety of local specialty foods such as delicious Chongming hairy crabs and fragrant Chongming rice-field fish, allowing tourists to better understand the local culture while enjoying the food. In addition, the guesthouse also organizes traditional handicraft activities such as paper cutting and weaving, allowing tourists to experience local culture and participate in its inheritance.

赏析：该段的中文列举了一些专业术语，例如"大闸蟹""稻花鱼""剪纸"等，其对应的译文翻译为 hairy crabs, rice-field fish, paper cutting。原文中的两个例子句式比较相似，译文也保留了原文的这个特征，选用了相同的句式，与原文段落的层次感和逻辑性保持一致。

☞ 练习

(一)将下列短语翻译成英文。

1. 自然资源

2. 生态环境

3. 独特的生态之旅

4. 高品质的体验

5. 私密性和安静度

(二)将下列句子翻译成英文。

1. 崇明生态民宿致力于提供高品质的服务和设施，为游客提供舒适的住宿环境，注重客房的私密性和安静度。

2. 住宿环境是旅游体验的重要组成部分之一，崇明生态民宿注重客房的私密性和安静度，确保游客在忙碌的旅程中得到充分休息。

3. 例如，"竹林小屋"生态民宿，其客房均为独立木质结构，每个房间都拥有私人庭院，让游客在享受自然环境的同时，也能够得到充分的私密性和安静度。

(三)将下面段落翻译成英文。

1. 崇明生态民宿

崇明岛是上海市的一个县级市，位于长江口上游，是中国第三大岛，也是长江口地区最大的自然岛屿。崇明岛地势平坦、河流众多，拥有丰富的自然资源和生态环境。随着旅游业的发展，越来越多的游客来到崇明岛，寻求一次独特的生态之旅。崇明生态民宿应运而生，成为许多游客的首选。

2. 高品质的体验与充分的私密性和安静度

崇明生态民宿致力于提供高品质的服务和设施，为游客提供舒适的住宿环境，注重客房的私密性和安静度，让游客在忙碌的旅程中得到充分休息。

3. 独特的住宿选择

"竹林小屋"生态民宿就是崇明岛上独特的住宿选择之一。每个客房都采用独立的木质结构，并配有私人庭院，让游客在享受自然环境的同时，也能够得到充分的私密性和安静度。除了舒适的住宿环境外，崇明生态民宿还提供各种休闲活动，如瑜伽、农耕体验、烹饪课程等，让游客在享受住宿体验的同时，也能够充分融入当地的生活。

☞ 参考答案

(一)

1. natural resources

2. ecological environment

3. unique ecological journey

4. high-quality experience

5. privacy and quietness

（二）

1. Chongming ecological guesthouses are committed to providing high-quality services and facilities, offering comfortable accommodation with emphasis on privacy and quietness of the guest rooms.

2. The accommodation environment is an important part of the travel experience, and Chongming ecological guesthouses focus on privacy and quietness of the guest rooms to ensure tourists can fully rest during their busy journey.

3. For example, the "Bamboo House" ecological guesthouse features independent wooden structures for each guest room, and each room has a private courtyard, allowing tourists to enjoy the natural environment while also ensuring privacy and quietness.

（三）

1. Chongming Ecological Guesthouses

Chongming Island is a county-level city in Shanghai and the third largest island in China, with abundant natural resources and a rich ecological environment. With the development of tourism, more and more tourists are coming to Chongming Island for a unique ecological journey, and Chongming ecological guesthouses have emerged as their preferred accommodation option.

2. High-quality Experience with Sufficient Privacy and Quietness

Chongming ecological guesthouses are committed to providing high-quality experiences in both services and facilities. First and foremost, they offer comfortable accommodation with privacy and quietness of the guest rooms, allowing tourists to fully rest during their busy journey.

3. Unique Accommodation Options

The "Bamboo House" ecological guesthouse is an example of the unique accommodation options available on Chongming Island. Each guest room features an independent wooden structure and a private courtyard, allowing tourists to enjoy the natural environment while also ensuring privacy and quietness. In addition to comfortable accommodation, Chongming ecological guesthouses also offer a variety of leisure activities, such as yoga, farming experiences, cooking courses, etc. , allowing tourists to fully immerse themselves in local life while enjoying their stay.

二、崇明生态民宿的类型和特点

翻译简介

本文主要在于说明崇明生态民宿的类型和特点，其中民宿名称的翻译是难点和重点。"悠然见南山"因为有其文化渊源，在翻译时需要进行仔细比较，同时又因用作店名，所以在篇幅和用词上需要符合其语境。篇幅不能过长，用词需精简，最能体现悠然的意境。"水岸芦苇荡""竹林小屋"的翻译，亦是如此。

词汇表

周浦崇明生态旅游区：Zhoupu Chongming ecological tourism area

和谐共处：harmonious coexistence

舒适愉悦的居住体验：comfortable and pleasant living experience

农家乐客栈：farmhouse guesthouses

水岸客栈：waterfront guesthouses

森林小屋：forest cabins

农村风光客栈：rural scenery guesthouses

农业文化：farming culture

农产品：agricultural products

环保材料：environmentally friendly materials

绿色出行方式：green travel methods

湿地景观客栈：wetland landscape guesthouses

湿地公园：wetland parks

观察鸟类栖息地：observe world-class bird habitats

室内装饰：interior decoration

竹林小屋：bamboo forest cabins

木质结构：wooden structure

资源保护和再利用：resource conservation and reuse

环保意识增强：enhance environmental awareness

人文文化：human culture

原文

生态民宿是崇明岛上的一种特殊类型的住宿，以生态环保为主题，强调与自然和谐共生，提供舒适宜人的住宿体验。崇明生态民宿具有多种类型，包括田园风光民宿、湿地景观民宿、森林小屋等。这些民宿各具特色，但都强调环保理念和自然氛围。

田园风光民宿

田园风光民宿位于崇明岛的农村地区，它们通常建立在农田或果园旁边，环境优美、空气清新，游客可以感受到浓郁的乡村气息和自然之美。这些民宿以农业为主题，让游客亲身体验农耕文化，品尝当地新鲜的农产品。同时，这些民宿还注重环保理念，采用环保材料进行装修，提供绿色出行方式，如自行车，鼓励游客环保出行。例如，位于崇明岛的"悠然见南山"民宿，就是一家典型的田园风光民宿。它位于农田之中，周围环绕着稻田、果园，游客可以亲身体验农耕文化，品尝当地新鲜的农产品。此外，民宿还提供绿色出行方式，如自行车，鼓励游客环保出行。

湿地景观民宿

湿地景观民宿位于崇明岛的湿地地区，它们通常建立在湿地公园附近，让游客能够在身临其境的环境中体验湿地生态之美，观赏世界级的鸟类栖息地。这些民宿内部装修采用环保材料，与周围的湿地景观相得益彰，让游客在舒适的环境中感受到自然之美。例如，位于崇明岛东滩国家级湿地公园内的"水岸芦苇荡"民宿，是一家典型的湿地景观民宿。民宿紧邻崇明东滩国家级湿地公园，让游客能够身临其境，体验湿地生态之美，观赏世界级的鸟类栖息地。民宿内部装修采用环保材料，与周围的湿地景观相得益彰。

森林小屋

森林小屋位于崇明岛的森林地区，它们通常建立在森林深处，让游客能够在原始森林中感受自然之美，享受大自然的恩赐。这些民宿通常采用木质结构，让游客在舒适的环境中感受到自然的气息。例如，位于崇明岛的"竹林小屋"民宿，是一家典型的森林小屋。民宿建立在竹林深处，让游客能够在原始森林中感受自然之美，享受大自然的恩赐。民宿采用木质结构，让游客在舒适的环境中感受到自然的气息。此外，民宿还提供绿色出行方式，如徒步旅行，让游客更好地融入自然环境中。

崇明生态民宿的共同特点是注重环保理念和自然氛围。这些民宿在建设和运营中，采用环保材料、提供绿色出行方式、注重资源的节约和再利用，让游客在享受住宿的同时，也能够学习生态保护知识，增强环保意识。

崇明生态民宿融合了自然和人文。它们让游客置身于自然之中，感受自然之美，了解当地的生态文化，同时也让游客更好地了解生态保护的重要性。在这里，游客可以享受一次难忘的生态之旅，感受到大自然的神奇和魅力。

译文

Chongming ecological guesthouses are a special type of accommodation on Chongming Island, with ecology and environmental protection as their main theme. They emphasize harmonious coexistence with nature and provide a comfortable and pleasant living experience. Chongming ecological guesthouses come in various types, including farmhouse guesthouses, waterfront guesthouses, forest cabins, and more. Each of these guesthouses has its unique features but all emphasize the concept of environmental protection and a natural atmosphere.

Rural Scenery Guesthouses

Rural scenery guesthouses are located in rural areas of Chongming Island, usually built next to farmland or orchards, with beautiful surroundings and fresh air. Tourists can feel the strong rural atmosphere and natural beauty. These guesthouses focus on agriculture, allowing tourists to experience farming culture and taste local fresh agricultural products. At the same time, these guesthouses also emphasize environmental protection, using environmentally friendly materials for decoration, providing green travel methods such as bicycles, and encouraging tourists to travel in an environmentally friendly way. For example, the guesthouse "Gaze Afar Towards the Southern Mountains" located on Chongming Island is a typical rural scenery guesthouse. It is located in the middle of farmland, surrounded by rice fields and orchards. Tourists can experience farming culture and taste local fresh agricultural products. In addition, the guesthouse provides green travel methods such as bicycles, encouraging tourists to travel in an environmentally friendly way.

Wetland Landscape Guesthouses

Wetland landscape guesthouses are located in the wetland areas of Chongming Island, usually built near wetland parks, allowing tourists to experience the beauty of wetland ecology in an immersive environment and observe world-class bird habitats. The interior decoration of these guesthouses uses environmentally friendly materials, complementing the surrounding wetland landscape, allowing tourists to feel the beauty of nature in a comfortable environment. For example, the guesthouse "Waterfront Reed" located in Dongtan National Wetland Park on Chongming Island is a typical wetland landscape guesthouse. It is adjacent to Dongtan National Wetland Park, allowing tourists to be immersed in the beauty of wetland ecology and observe world-class bird habitats. The interior decoration of the guesthouse uses environmentally friendly materials, complementing the surrounding wetland landscape.

Forest Cabins

Forest cabins are located in the forested areas of Chongming Island, usually built deep in the forest, allowing tourists to feel the beauty of nature in the original forest and enjoy the gifts of nature. These guesthouses usually use wooden structures, allowing tourists to feel the natural atmosphere in a comfortable environment. For example, "Bamboo Chalets" guesthouse located on Chongming Island is a typical forest cabin. The guesthouse is built deep in the bamboo forest, allowing tourists to feel the beauty of nature in the original forest and enjoy the gifts of nature. The guesthouse uses wooden structures, allowing tourists to feel the natural atmosphere in a comfortable environment. In addition, the guesthouse provides green travel methods such as hiking, allowing tourists to better integrate into the natural environment.

The common feature of Chongming ecological guesthouses is their emphasis on environmental protection and natural atmosphere. These guesthouses use environmentally friendly materials during construction and operation, provide green travel methods, emphasize resource conservation and reuse, allowing tourists to learn about ecological protection knowledge and enhance environmental awareness while enjoying their stay.

Chongming ecological guesthouses provide a unique accommodation experience that combines nature and human culture. They allow tourists to immerse themselves in nature, feel the beauty of nature, understand local ecological culture, and also increase awareness of ecological protection. Here, tourists can enjoy an unforgettable ecological journey and feel the magic and charm of nature.

例句赏析

例 1:

原文：生态民宿是崇明岛上的一种特殊类型的住宿，以生态环保为主题，强调与自然和谐共生，提供舒适宜人的住宿体验。崇明生态民宿具有多种类型，包括田园风光民宿、湿地景观民宿、森林小屋等。

译文：Chongming ecological guesthouses are a special type of accommodation on Chongming Island, with ecology and environmental protection as their main theme. They emphasize harmonious coexistence with nature and provide a comfortable and pleasant living experience. Chongming ecological guesthouses come in various types, including farmhouse guesthouses, waterfront guesthouses, forest cabins, and more.

赏析：这段中文分为两层，一是介绍生态民宿的概念，二是列举生态民宿的种类。译文将其分为三句进行翻译，将第一句中的生态民宿的属性与特征分开，层次更加分明，句型也更为紧凑。原文中"具有多种类型"，译文采用动词"come"，体现出多种民宿出现的动态性，英文中 there be 结构也可表达"有"这一概念，但由于 be 动词表存在、状态，是一个静态动词，而不同种类的生态民宿应该是先后出现，动态存在的，因而 come 这一词的运用更为合适。

例 2：

原文：位于崇明岛的"悠然见南山"民宿，就是一家典型的田园风光民宿。它位于农田之中，周围环绕着稻田、果园，游客可以亲身体验农耕文化，品尝当地新鲜的农产品。

译文：… the guesthouse "Gaze Afar Towards the Southern Mountains" located on Chongming Island is a typical rural scenery guesthouse. It is located in the middle of farmland, surrounded by rice fields and orchards. Tourists can experience farming culture and taste local fresh agricultural products.

赏析：该句的翻译难点为民宿的名称"悠然见南山"。该店名出自东晋诗人陶渊明《饮酒·其五》："结庐在人境，而无车马喧。问君何能尔？心远地自偏。采菊东篱下，悠然见南山。山气日夕佳，飞鸟相与还。此中有真意，欲辨已忘言。"全诗宗旨是归复自然，诗人在自己的庭园中随意地采摘菊花，偶然间抬起头来，目光恰与南山（诗人居所南面的庐山）相会。"悠然见南山"描述的是一种人闲逸自在的状态。古今中外很多翻译家都翻译过此诗。其中"采菊东篱下，悠然见南山"，杨宪益和戴乃迭[1]将其翻译为：While picking asters 'neath the eastern fence, My gaze upon the southern mountains rests. 汪榕培[2]的版本为：I pluck hedge-side chrysanthemums with pleasure, And see the tranquil Southern Mount in leisure. 许渊冲[3]则译为：I pick fence-side chrysanthemums at will, And leisurely I see the

---

① 杨宪益，戴乃迭. Poetry and Prose of the Tang and Song. Beijing: Chinese Literature Press, 1984.

② 汪榕培. 陶渊明诗歌英译比较研究[M]. 北京：外语教学与研究出版社，2000.

③ 许渊冲. 中国古诗选三百首[M]. 北京：北京大学出版社，1996.

southern hill. William Acker① 的版本为：I pluck chrysanthemums under the eastern hedge, And gaze afar towards the southern mountains. 几家翻译各有所长，但作为民宿的名称，首先篇幅不能太长，其次要最大限度地表现出闲适悠然的状态。于是，William Acker 的版本最为符合。

例3：

原文：位于崇明岛东滩国家级湿地公园内的"水岸芦苇荡"民宿，是一家典型的湿地景观民宿。民宿紧邻崇明东滩国家级湿地公园，让游客能够身临其境，体验湿地生态之美，观赏世界级的鸟类栖息地。民宿内部装修采用环保材料，与周围的湿地景观相得益彰。

译文：…the guesthouse "Waterfront Reed" located in Dongtan National Wetland Park on Chongming Island is a typical wetland landscape guesthouse. It is adjacent to Dongtan National Wetland Park, allowing tourists to be immersed in the beauty of wetland ecology and observe world-class bird habitats. The interior decoration of the guesthouse uses environmentally friendly materials, complementing the surrounding wetland landscape.

赏析：该段主要以"水岸芦苇荡"为例，描述了湿地景观民宿的特点。翻译的难点在于"水岸芦苇荡"这一民宿名称。"芦苇荡"在中文语境中较有文学性，"蒹葭苍苍，白露为霜。所谓伊人，在水一方"。其中"蒹葭"指的就是芦苇。而该民宿开在东滩湿地，故名称译为"Waterfront Reed"。另一翻译难点在于成语"身临其境"和"相得益彰"的翻译，译文将其翻译为"be immersed in"和"complement"，简洁而准确。

☞ **练习**

（一）将下列短语翻译成英文。

1. 生态环保

2. 与自然和谐共生

3. 住宿体验

4. 湿地景观民宿

5. 农耕文化

（二）将下列句子翻译成英文。

1. 崇明生态民宿是一种特殊类型的住宿，以生态环保为主题，强调与自然和谐共生，提供舒适宜人的住宿体验。

2. 田园风光民宿位于崇明岛的农村地区，它们通常建立在农田或果园旁边，环境优

---

① William Acker. T'ao the Hermit：Sixty Poems by T'ao Ch'ien（365-427）［M］. London：Thames and Hudson，1952.

美、空气清新。

3. 湿地景观民宿是一种特殊类型的住宿，位于崇明岛的湿地景观区域，提供舒适宜人的住宿体验。

4. 田园风光民宿让游客亲身体验农耕文化，品尝当地新鲜的农产品。

5. 湿地景观民宿注重环保理念，采用环保材料进行装修，提供绿色出行方式。

(三)将下面段落翻译成英文。

1. 崇明生态民宿是一种特殊类型的住宿，以生态环保为主题，强调与自然和谐共生，提供舒适宜人的住宿体验。崇明生态民宿具有多种类型，包括田园风光民宿、湿地景观民宿、森林小屋等。这些民宿各具特色，但都强调环保理念和自然氛围。

2. 田园风光民宿位于崇明岛的农村地区，它们通常建立在农田或果园旁边，环境优美、空气清新，游客可以感受到浓郁的乡村气息和自然之美。这些民宿以农业为主题，让游客亲身体验农耕文化，品尝当地新鲜的农产品。同时，这些民宿还注重环保理念，采用环保材料进行装修，提供绿色出行方式，如自行车，鼓励游客环保出行。

3. 湿地景观民宿是一种特殊类型的住宿，位于崇明岛的湿地景观区域，提供舒适宜人的住宿体验。这些民宿注重环保理念，采用环保材料进行装修，提供绿色出行方式。同时，游客可以在这里欣赏到湿地独特的自然风光和生态系统。例如，"月光草原"湿地景观民宿就是一家非常受欢迎的民宿，在这里游客可以欣赏到美丽的月光草原景色。

☞ **参考答案**

(一)

1. ecological conservation

2. harmonious coexistence with nature

3. accommodation experience

4. wetland landscape guesthouse

5. agricultural culture

(二)

1. Chongming Ecological guesthouses are a special type of accommodation that focuses on ecological conservation and emphasizes harmonious coexistence with nature, providing a comfortable and pleasant accommodation experience.

2. Rural guesthouses are located in the countryside of Chongming Island, usually built next to farmland or orchards, with beautiful surroundings and fresh air.

3. Wetland landscape guesthouses are a special type of accommodation located in the wetland landscape area of Chongming Island, providing a comfortable and pleasant

accommodation experience.

4. Rural guesthouses allow tourists to experience agricultural culture firsthand and taste fresh local produce.

5. Wetland landscape guesthouses emphasize environmental protection, using environmentally friendly materials for decoration and providing green travel options.

（三）

1. Chongming Ecological guesthouses are a special type of accommodation that focuses on ecological conservation and emphasizes harmonious coexistence with nature, providing a comfortable and pleasant accommodation experience. Chongming Ecological guesthouses come in various types, including rural guesthouses, wetland landscape guesthouses, forest cabins, etc. These guesthouses all have their own unique features, but they all emphasize environmental protection and a natural atmosphere.

2. Rural guesthouses are located in the countryside of Chongming Island, usually built next to farmland or orchards, with beautiful surroundings and fresh air. Tourists can experience the rich rural atmosphere and natural beauty here. These guesthouses have agriculture as their theme, allowing tourists to experience agricultural culture firsthand and taste fresh local produce. At the same time, these guesthouses also emphasize environmental protection, using environmentally friendly materials for decoration and providing green travel options such as bicycles, encouraging tourists to travel in an environmental-friendly way.

3. Wetland landscape guesthouses are a special type of accommodation located in the wetland landscape area of Chongming Island, providing a comfortable and pleasant accommodation experience. These guesthouses emphasize environmental protection, using environmentally friendly materials for decoration and providing green travel options. At the same time, tourists can appreciate the unique natural scenery and ecosystem of wetlands here. For example, "Moonlight Grassland" Wetland Landscape Guesthouse is a very popular guesthouse where tourists can enjoy the beautiful scenery of the moonlit grassland.

三、崇明生态民宿的服务和设施

翻译简介

本文描写了崇明生态民宿的服务和设施。崇明因为其得天独厚的地理条件，成为许多生态民宿的不二选择。东滩湿地、森林公园均有非常独特的民宿。为了吸引游客，这些民宿充分利用优美的自然生态，同时又十分重视生态保护，不断地向游客们分享环保理念。因此与生态地理、清洁能源相关的术语就成为翻译的难点和重点，例如长江口、太阳能热水器、地源热泵等，相应地译为 Yangtze River estuary, solar water heaters, ground-source heat pumps。

词汇表

长江口：Yangtze River estuary

长江三角洲地区：Yangtze River Delta region

平坦地形：flat terrain

独立木制结构：independent wooden structures

私人庭院：private courtyard

可重复使用拖鞋和浴袍：reusable slippers and bathrobes

环保知识共享活动：environmental knowledge sharing activities

参与环保活动：participation in environmental protection activities

环保讲座和垃圾分类知识共享：environmental lectures and waste sorting knowledge sharing

养成良好的环保习惯：develop good environmental habits

植树造林和河流清理：afforestation and river cleaning

清洁能源技术：clean energy technologies

太阳能热水器和地源热泵：solar water heaters and ground-source heat pumps

有机蔬菜：organic vegetables

理解如何减少浪费和实现绿色生活：understand how to reduce waste and achieve a green lifestyle

原文

崇明岛是上海市的一个县级市，位于长江口上游，是中国第三大岛，也是长江口地区最大的自然岛屿。崇明岛地势平坦、河流众多，拥有丰富的自然资源和生态环境。随着旅游业的发展，越来越多的游客来到崇明岛，寻求一次独特的生态之旅。崇明生态民宿应运而生，成为许多游客的首选。

首先，众所周知，住宿环境是旅游体验的重要组成部分之一。崇明生态民宿在提供住宿环境时，注重客房的私密性和安静度，让游客在忙碌的旅程中得到充分休息。例如，"竹林小屋"生态民宿，其客房均为独立木质结构，每个房间都拥有私人庭院，让游客在享受自然环境的同时，也能够得到充分的私密性和安静度。

其次，民宿还会提供丰富的休闲活动，如瑜伽、农耕体验、烹饪课程等，让游客在享受自然风光的同时，充分融入当地的生活。以"林中小居"为例，这家位于崇明森林公园的民宿，提供户外烧烤、徒步等活动，让游客在感受森林的氛围中，度过愉快的时光。

在享受自然风光的同时，崇明生态民宿也提供了多种有趣的休闲活动，让游客能够充分融入当地的生活。例如，"悠然见南山"生态民宿，会定期举行摄影比赛、农耕体验等活动，让游客感受当地的农耕文化和自然之美。此外，许多生态民宿还提供瑜伽、烹饪课程等活动，让游客在放松身心的同时，也能够学习新技能，丰富旅行体验。

最后，崇明生态民宿还注重环保理念的推广。许多民宿会在客房内提供环保用品，如可重复使用的拖鞋、浴袍等，减少一次性用品的使用。同时，民宿还会开展环保知识普及活动，提高游客的环保意识和参与度。例如，"绿野仙踪"生态民宿，在入住期间会组织环保讲座和垃圾分类知识分享，引导游客养成良好的环保习惯。此外，该民宿还与周边的环保组织合作，组织游客参加志愿者活动，如植树造林、清理河道等，实践绿色出行的理念。

在环保理念的推广方面，崇明生态民宿做得非常到位。例如，"田园牧歌"生态民宿，采用太阳能热水器和地源热泵等清洁能源技术，减少对环境的影响。此外，该民宿还在自己的农田里种植有机蔬菜，为游客提供健康美味的餐食。同时，民宿还积极推广垃圾分类和资源回收利用，让游客了解如何减少垃圾的产生，实现绿色生活。

总之，崇明生态民宿以其独特的自然风光、丰富的休闲活动和环保理念，吸引了越来越多的游客。这些民宿不仅为游客提供了高品质的住宿环境和旅游体验，还让游客了解和尊重当地文化、自然环境，为地球的可持续发展作出了贡献。如果你想体验一次独特的生态之旅，崇明岛的生态民宿是你不容错过的选择。

译文

Chongming Island is a county-level city in Shanghai, located upstream of the Yangtze River estuary. It is the third largest island in China and the largest natural island in the Yangtze River Delta region. With its flat terrain, numerous rivers, and rich natural resources and ecological environment, Chongming Island has become a popular destination for tourists seeking a unique ecological journey. Chongming ecological guesthouses have emerged as a popular choice for many tourists, offering high-quality services and facilities.

Firstly, these guesthouses provide comfortable accommodation with privacy and quietness, allowing tourists to rest fully during their busy journey. For example, "Bamboo Chalets" Ecological Guesthouse has independent wooden structures for each guest room, and each room has a private courtyard, allowing guests to enjoy the natural environment while also having privacy and quietness.

Secondly, these guesthouses offer a variety of leisure activities such as yoga, farming experiences, and cooking classes, allowing tourists to fully immerse themselves in local life while enjoying the natural scenery. For example, "Forest Cottage" Guesthouse located in Chongming Forest Park offers outdoor activities such as barbecue and hiking, allowing guests to spend a pleasant time in the forest atmosphere.

Thirdly, these guesthouses promote environmental protection concepts. Many guesthouses provide environmentally friendly products in guest rooms, such as reusable slippers and bathrobes, to reduce the use of disposable items. They also organize environmental knowledge sharing activities to raise awareness among tourists and encourage their participation in environmental protection activities. For example, "The Wizard of Oz" Guesthouse organizes environmental lectures and waste sorting knowledge sharing during guests' stay, guiding them to develop good environmental habits. In addition, the guesthouse cooperates with local environmental organizations to organize volunteer activities such as afforestation and river cleaning, practicing the concept of green travel.

Chongming Ecological guesthouses have done a very good job in promoting the concept of environmental protection. For example, "Idyllic Pastoral" adopts clean energy technologies such as solar water heaters and ground-source heat pumps to reduce their impact on the environment. They also plant organic vegetables in their own fields to provide healthy and delicious meals for guests. These guesthouses actively promote waste sorting and resource recycling to help guests understand how to reduce waste and achieve a green lifestyle.

In summary, Chongming ecological guesthouses have attracted more and more tourists with their unique natural scenery, rich leisure activities, and environmental protection concepts. These guesthouses not only provide high-quality accommodation and travel experiences for tourists but also help them understand and respect local culture and natural environment, contributing to the sustainable development of the earth. If you want to experience a unique ecological journey, Chongming Island's ecological guesthouses are a choice not to be missed.

例句赏析

例1：

原文： 崇明岛是上海市的一个县级市，位于长江口上游，是中国第三大岛，也是长江口地区最大的自然岛屿。崇明岛地势平坦、河流众多，拥有丰富的自然资源和生态环境。随着旅游业的发展，越来越多的游客来到崇明岛，寻求一次独特的生态之旅。崇明生态民宿应运而生，成为许多游客的首选。

译文： Chongming Island is a county-level city in Shanghai, located upstream of the Yangtze River estuary. It is the third largest island in China and the largest natural island in the Yangtze River Delta region. With its flat terrain, numerous rivers, and rich natural resources and ecological environment, Chongming Island has become a popular destination for tourists seeking a unique ecological journey. Chongming ecological guesthouses have emerged as a popular choice for many tourists, offering high-quality services and facilities.

赏析： 该段原文介绍了崇明岛的自然资源，相关术语是翻译的难点，例如长江口上游、地势平坦等，相应的翻译是 the upstream of the Yangtze River estuary, flat terrain。另外，原文中"县级市"是中国特有的行政划分，翻译为"county-level city"。中文中"……级"，在英文中可以译为"...-level""...-class""...wide"，例如 county-level, world-class, nationwide。

例2：

原文： 首先，众所周知，住宿环境是旅游体验的重要组成部分之一。"竹林小屋"生态民宿，其客房均为独立木质结构，每个房间都拥有私人庭院，让游客在享受自然环境的同时，也能够得到充分的私密性和安静度。

译文： Firstly, these guesthouses provide comfortable accommodation with privacy and quietness, allowing tourists to rest fully during their busy journey. For example, "Bamboo Chalets" Ecological Guesthouse has independent wooden structures for each guest room, and each room has a private courtyard, allowing guests to enjoy the natural environment while also having privacy and quietness.

赏析： 该段文字主要强调生态民宿注重私密性和安静度，中文中常出现具有概括性的一些名词，比如该段中的"私密性"和"安静度"，在英译的过程中"性"和"度"通常是不用译出的。译文将其翻译为"privacy"和"quietness"。本段另一处难点为民宿店名"竹林小屋"的翻译，译文将其译为"Bamboo Chalets"，"Chalets"为林中或海边度假小屋，与店名非常匹配。

例3:

原文:在环保理念的推广方面,崇明生态民宿做得非常到位。例如,"田园牧歌"生态民宿,采用太阳能热水器和地源热泵等清洁能源技术,减少对环境的影响。此外,该民宿还在自己的农田里种植有机蔬菜,为游客提供健康美味的餐食。同时,民宿还积极推广垃圾分类和资源回收利用,让游客了解如何减少垃圾的产生,实现绿色生活。

译文: Chongming Ecological guesthouses have done a very good job in promoting the concept of environmental protection. For example, "Idyllic Pastoral" adopts clean energy technologies such as solar water heaters and ground-source heat pumps to reduce their impact on the environment. They also plant organic vegetables in their own fields to provide healthy and delicious meals for guests. The guesthouse actively promotes waste sorting and resource recycling to help guests understand how to reduce waste and achieve a green lifestyle.

赏析:该段的一个翻译难点为"田园牧歌",要既表现出生态民宿的田园特色又表达出一种放松有限的气质。Idyllic 与 pastoral 均有田园悠闲之意,故而较为契合。该段的第二个翻译难点为能源技术相关的术语,例如太阳能热水器、地源热泵,可译为 solar water heater 和 ground-source heat pump。另外,"垃圾分类""资源回收利用"也是近些年来环保的热门词汇,分别译为 waste sorting 和 resource recycling。

☞ **练习**

(一)将下列短语翻译成英文。

1. 崇明岛

2. 自然岛屿

3. 生态民宿

4. 服务和设施

5. 住宿环境

6. 私密性和安静度

7. 休闲活动

(二)将下列句子翻译成英文。

1. 崇明岛是上海市的一个县级市,位于长江口上游,是中国第三大岛,也是长江口地区最大的自然岛屿。

2. 崇明生态民宿在服务和设施方面都致力于提供高品质的体验。

3. 众所周知，住宿环境是旅游体验的重要组成部分之一。

4. "竹林小屋"生态民宿，其客房均为独立木质结构，每个房间都拥有私人庭院，让游客在享受自然环境的同时，也能够得到充分的私密性和安静度。

5. 其次，民宿还会提供丰富的休闲活动，如瑜伽、农耕体验、烹饪课程等，让游客在享受自然环境的同时，也能够参与各种有趣的活动。

(三)将下面段落翻译成英文。

崇明生态民宿应运而生，成为许多游客的首选。崇明生态民宿在服务和设施方面都致力于提供高品质的体验。首先，民宿会提供舒适的住宿环境，注重客房的私密性和安静度，让游客在忙碌的旅程中能够得到充分休息。其次，民宿还会提供丰富的休闲活动，如瑜伽、农耕体验、烹饪课程等，让游客在享受自然环境的同时，也能够参与各种有趣的活动。这些都为游客提供了一次难忘的生态之旅。

☞ 参考答案

(一)

1. Chongming Island

2. natural island

3. ecological guesthouse

4. service and facilities

5. accommodation environment

6. privacy and quietness

7. leisure activities

(二)

1. Chongming Island is a county-level city in Shanghai, located upstream of the Yangtze River estuary. It is the third largest island in China and the largest natural island in the Yangtze River estuary region.

2. Chongming ecological guesthouses are committed to providing high-quality experiences in terms of service and facilities.

3. It is well-known that the accommodation environment is one of the important components of the travel experience.

4. "Bamboo Chalets" Ecological Guesthouse has independent wooden structures for each guest room, and each room has a private courtyard, allowing guests to enjoy the natural

environment while also having sufficient privacy and quietness.

5. Secondly, guesthouses also provide a variety of leisure activities, such as yoga, farming experiences, cooking courses, etc. , allowing guests to enjoy various interesting activities while enjoying the natural environment.

（三）

Chongming ecological guesthouses have emerged as many tourists' preferred choice, as they are committed to providing high-quality experiences in terms of service and facilities. Firstly, guesthouses provide comfortable accommodation environments, emphasizing privacy and quietness of the guest rooms, allowing guests to have sufficient rest during their busy journeys. Secondly, guesthouses also provide a variety of leisure activities, such as yoga, farming experiences, cooking courses, etc. , allowing guests to enjoy various interesting activities while enjoying the natural environment. All of these provide tourists with an unforgettable ecological trip experience.

第五章　崇明生态民俗

一、崇明传统文化的历史和演变

翻译简介

　　本文侧重描写崇明传统文化的历史和演变，回顾了崇明的悠久历史，也涉及与历史、文化、宗教相关的诸多术语。首先，本段涉及诸多历史相关术语，例如考古遗址、新石器时代晚期、宋元时期、明清时期等，对应的英文是 archaeological sites, the late Neolithic period, the Song and Yuan dynasties, the Ming and Qing dynasties。其次，中文民间谚语集民间智慧于一身，语言简练、道理深刻，通常还会押韵，英译时应该尽量贴近原文，在表达清楚的基础上，注意语言的韵律。另外，对于文化、宗教相关的术语翻译，应首先清楚明白其语义，然后再采取相应归化或者异化的手法进行翻译。

词汇表

　　东海：the East China Sea

　　文化遗产：cultural heritages

　　考古遗址：archaeological sites

　　新石器时代晚期：the late Neolithic period

　　宋元时期：the Song and Yuan dynasties

　　农业谚语：agricultural proverbs

　　民间故事：folk stories

　　明清时期：the Ming and Qing dynasties

　　贸易港口：trading port

　　民间文化：folk cultures

农历：the lunar calendar

佛教节日：Buddhist festival

祭祖：worship ancestors

民间艺术节目：folk art programs

龙舟赛：dragon-boat races

秧歌舞蹈：Yangko dances

渔民文化：fishermen's culture

渔歌：fish songs

拖渔网：lifting fishing nets

肥沃的土地：fertile land

稻苗：rice seedlings

水乡文化：water town culture

竹筏：bamboo rafts

荡秋千船：swing boats

宗教信仰：religious beliefs

佛教文化：Buddhist culture

庙会：temple fair

芦笋：asparagus

花菜：cauliflower

原文

　　崇明岛位于长江口上游，是中国东海海域最大的岛屿之一。这个岛屿拥有悠久的历史，自古以来就是人类活动的重要地区。在这片土地上，形成了独特的崇明传统文化，这些文化遗产至今仍然被人们保留和传承。

　　自古以来，崇明地区就有人类活动的痕迹。考古学家所发现的遗址证明，早在新石器时代晚期，崇明地区就有人类居住。在宋元时期，崇明地区逐渐形成了属于自己的特色。主要的生产方式是渔猎和农耕，这促进了崇明文化的发展。崇明人民在长期的生产生活中，创造出了许多有关农业和渔猎的谚语和民间故事，这些故事流传至今，成了崇明传统文化的一部分。例如，"秋天种麦，春天种稻，一年种两季，农民不会老"。

　　明清时期，崇明成了一个重要的贸易港口。在这个时期，各种民俗文化在这里交融，使得崇明传统文化更加丰富多彩。例如，每年的农历二月初二，崇明岛上都会举行"二月二龙抬头"文化旅游节。人们会在这个节日里祭祀先辈和神灵，同时也会表演一些传统的民间艺术节目，如龙舟赛、舞蹈、山歌等。

此外，崇明传统文化中还有许多具有代表性的文化遗产。渔家文化是其中之一。由于岛上地处长江口，渔业一直是岛民的主要经济来源。渔民们在长期的生产生活中创造了许多有关渔业的传统文化，如渔歌、捞起鱼网等。而农耕文化也是崇明岛上的一大特色。岛上的土地肥沃，适宜种植水稻、蔬菜等农作物，崇明的农民们在长期的农耕生产中也创造了许多有关农业的传统文化，如耕牛、插秧、晒粮等。

水乡文化是崇明传统文化中的另一大特色。岛上的河流、湖泊、水塘等水域资源非常丰富，这也造就了崇明的水乡文化。在这里，人们可以欣赏到许多美丽的水乡风光，同时也有许多传统的水上活动和水上运输方式，如竹筏、渡船、秋千船等。

在崇明传统文化中，还有一些与宗教信仰相关的传统文化遗产。例如，崇明岛上的佛教文化非常发达，盂兰节是岛上最重要的佛教节日之一。每年的农历正月初一，崇明岛上还会举行一场盛大的庙会，这场庙会是为了祭祀岛上的土地神和城隍爷，同时也是人们欢度新年的重要活动之一。

除了以上的传统文化遗产，崇明传统文化中还有许多其他特色。例如，岛上的土特产非常丰富，如崇明芦笋、崇明大米、崇明花菜等，这些土特产也成了崇明传统文化的一部分。此外，岛上的民间艺术也非常发达，如崇明民间音乐、崇明民间舞蹈等，这些艺术形式也体现了崇明传统文化的独特魅力。

总的来说，崇明传统文化是一个非常庞大、丰富、多元化的文化体系，它蕴含着岛上人民的智慧和传统，是中国传统文化的一个重要组成部分。随着时代的变迁，崇明传统文化也在不断地发展和演变，但是我们应该尽力去保护和传承这些文化遗产，让它们在未来的岁月里继续传承下去。

译文

Chongming Island, located in the upper reaches of the Yangtze River estuary, is one of the largest islands in the East China Sea. This island has a long history and has been an important area for human activity since ancient times. On this land, a unique Chongming traditional culture has been formed, and these cultural heritages are still preserved and inherited by people today.

Since ancient times, there have been traces of human activity in the Chongming area. According to archaeological sites discovered by archaeologists, humans have lived in the Chongming area as early as the late Neolithic period. During the Song and Yuan dynasties, the Chongming area gradually formed its own characteristics. The main production methods were fishing and farming, which promoted the development of Chongming culture. In the long-term production and life, Chongming people have created many agricultural and fishing proverbs and folk stories. These stories have been passed down to this day and have become part of Chongming's traditional culture. For example, "Plant wheat in autumn, plant rice in spring, plant two seasons a year, and farmers will not grow old."

During the Ming and Qing dynasties, Chongming became an important trading port. During this period, various folk cultures blended here, making Chongming's traditional culture more colorful. For example, every year on the second day of the second lunar month, Chongming Island holds the Dragon Head Tourism Festival. People will worship ancestors and gods during this festival and also perform some traditional folk art programs such as dragon-boat races and folk dance and song.

In addition, there are many representative cultural heritages in Chongming's traditional culture. Fishermen's culture is one of them. As the island is located at the mouth of the Yangtze River, fishing has always been the main source of income for islanders. Fishermen have created many traditional cultures related to fishing in their long-term production and life, such as fish songs and lifting fishing nets. Farming culture is also a major feature of Chongming Island. The island's fertile land is suitable for planting rice, vegetables and other crops. Chongming's farmers have also created many traditional cultures related to agriculture in their long-term farming production, such as plowing with oxen, transplanting rice seedlings and drying grains.

Water town culture is another major feature of Chongming's traditional culture. The island's water resources such as rivers, lakes, and ponds are very rich, which also create Chongming's water town culture. Here, people can enjoy many beautiful water town scenery and also participate in many traditional water activities and transportation methods such as bamboo rafts, ferries, and swing boats.

In Chongming's traditional culture, there are also some traditional cultural heritages related to religious beliefs. For example, Buddhist culture on Chongming Island is very developed. The Ghost Festival is one of the most important Buddhist festivals on the island. Every year on the first day of the lunar calendar, Chongming Island also holds a grand temple fair to worship the local earth god and city god. It is also an important activity for people to celebrate the new year.

In addition to the above-mentioned traditional cultural heritages, there are many other features in Chongming's traditional culture. For example, the island's local specialties are very rich, such as Chongming asparagus, Chongming rice, Chongming cauliflower, etc., which have also become part of Chongming's traditional culture. In addition, folk art on the island is also very developed, such as Chongming folk music and Chongming folk dance. These art forms also reflect the unique charm of Chongming's traditional culture.

Overall, Chongming's traditional culture is a very large, rich and diverse cultural system that embodies the wisdom and traditions of the island's people. It is an important part of Chinese traditional culture. With the changes of time, Chongming's traditional culture is also constantly developing and evolving. However, we should try our best to protect and inherit these cultural heritages so that they can continue to be passed down in the future years.

例句赏析

例1：

原文：自古以来，崇明地区就有人类活动的痕迹。考古学家所发现的遗址证明，早在新石器时代晚期，崇明地区就有人类居住。在宋元时期，崇明地区逐渐形成了属于自己的特色。主要的生产方式是渔猎和农耕，这促进了崇明文化的发展。崇明人民在长期的生产生活中，创造出了许多有关农业和渔猎的谚语和民间故事，这些故事流传至今，成了崇明传统文化的一部分。例如，"秋天种麦，春天种稻，一年种两季，农民不会老"。

译文：Since ancient times, there have been traces of human activity in the Chongming area. According to archaeological sites discovered by archaeologists, humans have lived in the Chongming area as early as the late Neolithic period. During the Song and Yuan dynasties, the Chongming area gradually formed its own characteristics. The main production methods were fishing and farming, which promoted the development of Chongming culture. In the long-term production and life, Chongming people have created many agricultural and fishing proverbs and folk stories. These stories have been passed down to this day and have become part of Chongming's traditional culture. For example, "Plant wheat in autumn, plant rice in spring, plant two seasons a year, and farmers will not grow old."

赏析：该段中文涉及诸多历史相关的术语，例如遗址、新石器时代晚期、宋元时期，分别译为 archaeological sites, the late Neolithic period, the Song and Yuan dynasties。本段另一个翻译要点是时态，很多行为活动是从古代延续至今的，因而使用的多为现在完成时态。另外，本段还引用了一句民间谚语。谚语的翻译也是难点之一。中文谚语语言简练，道理深刻。译文采用直译的方式将自古以来农民的智慧一语道出。

例2：

原文：明清时期，崇明成了一个重要的贸易港口。在这个时期，各种民俗文化在这里交融，使得崇明传统文化更加丰富多彩。例如，每年的农历二月初二，崇明岛上都会举行"二月二龙抬头"文化旅游节。人们会在这个节日里祭祀先辈和神灵，同时也会表演一些传统民间艺术节目，如龙舟赛、舞蹈、山歌等。

译文：During the Ming and Qing dynasties, Chongming became an important trading port. During this period, various folk cultures blended here, making Chongming's traditional culture more colorful. For example, every year on the second day of the second lunar month, Chongming Island holds the Dragon Head Tourism Festival. People will worship ancestors and gods during this festival and also perform some traditional folk art programs such as dragon-boat races and folk dance and song.

赏析：该段中文描写的是崇明的各种民俗和节日。因为是贸易港口，所以各种民俗文化都在这里交融，译文采用"blend"来描述这种情况，表现了多种文化相互融合的现象。本段的另一个翻译难点与传统节假日相关。首先，农历的英文是 the lunar calendar，译文中用非限制性定语从句来修饰盂兰节，使该句的表达节奏更为合理恰当。其次，盂兰节不能直接使用音译法，归化的翻译方式会使得目标读者一头雾水。盂兰节即中元节，也被称为鬼节，因而采用 the Ghost Festival 更为贴切。而像龙舟赛、秧歌等传统的民间艺术节目的翻译，需要平时的不断积累。

例3：

原文：在崇明传统文化中，还有一些与宗教信仰相关的传统文化遗产。例如，崇明岛上的佛教文化非常发达，盂兰节是岛上最重要的佛教节日之一。每年的农历正月初一，崇明岛上还会举行一场盛大的庙会，这场庙会是为了祭祀岛上的土地神和城隍爷，同时也是人们欢度新年的重要活动之一。

译文：In Chongming's traditional culture, there are also some traditional cultural heritages related to religious beliefs. For example, Buddhist culture on Chongming Island is very developed. The Ghost Festival is one of the most important Buddhist festivals on the island. Every year on the first day of the lunar calendar, Chongming Island also holds a grand temple fair to worship the local earth god and city god. It is also an important activity for people to celebrate the new year.

赏析：该段的翻译难点为与宗教祭祀相关的术语翻译。首先，"庙会"的英文翻译是"temple fair"，fair 通常指"集市"，而中文中的庙会也是为人们提供买卖和游乐的场所，因而非常贴切。其次是"土地神"和"城隍爷"的翻译，作为地道的中文本土词汇，这两个词饱含着丰富的中国文化内涵。译文采用意译的方法，将"土地神"译作 the local earth god，而将"城隍爷"译作 city god，目标读者便能轻而易举理解原文的意思了。

☞ 练习

（一）将下列短语翻译成英文。

1. 文化遗产

2. 考古遗址

3. 新石器时代晚期

4. 宋元时期

5. 农业谚语

（二）将下列句子翻译成英文。

1. 在这片土地上，形成了独特的崇明传统文化，这些文化遗产至今仍然被人们保留和传承。

2. 崇明人民在长期的生产生活中，创造出了许多有关农业和渔猎的谚语和民间故事，这些故事流传至今，成了崇明传统文化的一部分。

3. 岛上的土地肥沃，适宜种植水稻、蔬菜等农作物，崇明的农民们在长期的农耕生产中也创造了许多有关农业的传统文化，如耕牛、插秧、晒粮等。

4. 在这里，人们可以欣赏到许多美丽的水乡风光，同时也有许多传统的水上活动和水上运输方式，如竹筏、渡船、秋千船等。

5. 随着时代的变迁，崇明传统文化也在不断地发展和演变，但是我们应该尽力去保护和传承这些文化遗产，让它们在未来的岁月里继续传承下去。

（三）将下面段落翻译成英文。

明清时期，崇明成了一个重要的贸易港口。在这个时期，各种民俗文化在这里交融，使得崇明传统文化更加丰富多彩。例如，每年的农历八月十五日，崇明岛上都会举行盂兰节，这是一个传统的佛教节日，人们会在这个节日里祭祀先辈和神灵，同时也会表演一些传统民间艺术节目，如龙舟赛、秧歌等。

☞ 参考答案

（一）

1. cultural heritages

2. archaeological sites

3. the late Neolithic period

4. the Song and Yuan dynasties

5. agricultural proverbs

（二）

1. On this land, a unique Chongming traditional culture has been formed, and these cultural heritages are still preserved and inherited by people today.

2. In the long-term production and life, Chongming people have created many agricultural and fishing proverbs and folk stories. These stories have been passed down to this day and have become part of Chongming's traditional culture.

3. The island's fertile land is suitable for planting rice, vegetables and other crops. Chongming's farmers have also created many traditional cultures related to agriculture in their long-term farming production, such as plowing with oxen, transplanting rice seedlings and drying grains.

4. Here, people can enjoy many beautiful water town scenery and also participate in many traditional water activities and transportation methods such as bamboo rafts, ferries, and swing boats.

5. With the changes of time, Chongming's traditional culture is also constantly developing and evolving. However, we should try our best to protect and inherit these cultural heritages so that they can continue to be passed down in the future years.

（三）

During the Ming and Qing dynasties, Chongming became an important trading port. During this period, various folk cultures blended here, making Chongming's traditional culture more colorful. For example, every year on the 15th day of the lunar calendar, Chongming Island holds the Ghost Festival, which is a traditional Buddhist festival. People will worship ancestors and gods during this festival and also perform some traditional folk art programs such as dragon boat races and Yangko dances.

二、崇明传统文化的代表性元素和特点

翻译简介

本文介绍了崇明的传统习俗和工艺，这些习俗和工艺都是崇明文化的代表性元素和特点。本文重点介绍了赶海节和顶针线这两种习俗。赶海是住在海边的居民才有的习俗，人们前往海滩，仔细搜寻海产品，因而在翻译时不仅要注意音译还要注意意译。顶针线是一种崇明特有的刺绣工艺，而不是一种针线，所以在翻译时需要特别标明。本文中文段落在描述传统习俗特征时运用了并列句式，英语翻译时为了避免单调，常常选用不同的动词，搭配由 with 短语或者动词现在分词形式来表示伴随状况。另外本文相关术语的翻译也是一个难点。

词汇表

生态宝藏：ecological treasure

文化库存：cultural repository

代表性元素：representative elements

收获季节：time of harvest

祭海：offering sacrifices to the sea

祈祷：praying for blessings

龙舟赛：dragon-boat races

海神：sea god

祈求平安顺利：pray for peace and smoothness

感受到对自然的敬畏：reflect people's awe of nature

顶针绣：thimble embroidery

刺绣工艺：embroidery craftsmanship

花卉布置：flower arrangement

麻编：hemp weaving

挂毯：tapestry

刺绣针：embroidery needles

细线：fine threads

刺绣布料：embroidered fabrics

精美：exquisiteness

艺术吸引力：artistic appeal

厨艺文化：culinary culture

特色食品：local specialty food

八宝鸭：eight-treasure duck

鲈鱼：sea bass

毛蟹饼干：crab cakes

中药材料：Chinese medicinal materials

新鲜口感和丰富营养：fresh taste and rich nutrition

海洋文化特色：marine cultural characteristic

渔民为主体：fishermen as the main body

水景观：waterscape views

渔业文化氛围：fishing culture atmosphere

吹糖人：sugar blowing

花灯笼：flower lanterns

唢呐：suona horn

岛屿风情：unique island style

加深对这个地方的了解和认识，更好地保护和传承这些珍贵的文化遗产：deepen their understanding and recognition of this place，help better protect and inherit these precious cultural heritages

原文

崇明岛是一个生态宝地，也是一个文化宝库。在这个美丽的岛屿上，有着丰富多彩的传统文化。崇明传统文化是一个非常庞大、丰富、多元化的文化体系，其中有许多具有代表性的元素和特点，下面我们将介绍其中的一些典型例子。

赶海节是崇明地区一年一度的传统节日。每年农历四月初，当地渔民将迎来丰收的时刻。届时，渔民们会举行隆重的庆祝活动，包括祭海、祈福、赛龙舟等。这些活动既是对海神的感恩，也是表达对来年风调雨顺、海船顺利出海的祈求。赶海节不仅展示了当地渔民的传统文化，也体现了人们对自然的敬畏之心。

顶针线是崇明地区的一种传统手工艺，以其精美的刺绣工艺闻名于世。传统的顶针线包括插花、披麻、织毯等多种技艺。顶针线的起源可以追溯到宋代，经过几百年的发展，如今已成为崇明传统文化的一部分。顶针线作品在国内外市场上备受欢迎，成为崇明地区的一张独特名片。顶针线的制作过程需要用到多种工具和材料，如刺绣针、细线、绣布等，制作过程十分烦琐，需要工匠们耐心细致地完成。顶针线作品以其细腻、精美、富有艺术感染力等特点，深受人们的喜爱。

崇明菜是一种具有地方特色的美食。崇明菜以当地丰富的农产品为基础，以其独特的烹饪手法和口感受到了人们广泛的喜爱。如崇明八宝鸭、崇明鲈鱼、崇明蟹肉糕等，都是崇明地区的美食代表。崇明八宝鸭是崇明地区的传统名菜之一，以选用当地特产鸭子和多种中药材料为原料，经过独特的工艺烹饪而成。崇明鲈鱼则是以岛上盛产的鲈鱼为主料，配以当地特产蔬菜和调味料，口感鲜美、营养丰富。崇明蟹肉糕则是以当地特产大闸蟹为原料，加入精选的米粉和调味料制成的一款美食。这些美食不仅味道鲜美，还体现了当地人民对美食的热爱和追求。

除了以上的代表性元素，崇明传统文化中还有许多其他特色。如渔家文化，源远流长，它以渔民为主体，具有浓郁的海洋文化特色。在这里，人们可以欣赏到许多美丽的水乡风光，感受到浓厚的渔家文化氛围。此外，崇明还有传统的民间艺术，如吹糖人、打花灯、唢呐等，这些艺术形式既富有地方特色，又具有浓厚的历史文化底蕴，是崇明传统文化的重要组成部分。

崇明岛是一个富有生态、人文、历史、文化资源的地方。在这个美丽的岛屿上，人们可以感受到浓郁的传统文化氛围，领略到独特的岛屿风情。通过了解和传承崇明传统文化，不仅可以加深人们对这个地方的了解和认识，还可以帮助人们更好地保护和传承这些宝贵的文化遗产。

译文

Chongming Island is an ecological treasure and a cultural repository. On this beautiful island, there is a rich and colorful traditional culture. Chongming's traditional culture is a very large, rich, and diverse cultural system, with many representative elements and characteristics. Below, we will introduce some typical examples.

The Beachcombing Festival is an annual traditional festival in the Chongming area. Every year in early April of the lunar calendar, local fishermen will usher in a time of harvest. At that time, the fishermen will hold grand celebrations, including offering sacrifices to the sea, praying for blessings, and dragon boat races. These activities are not only an expression of gratitude to the sea god but also a prayer for a smooth sailing in the coming year. The Beachcombing Festival not only showcases the traditional culture of local fishermen but also reflects people's awe of nature.

Thimble embroidery is a traditional handicraft in the Chongming area, famous for its exquisite embroidery craftsmanship. Traditional thimble embroidery includes various techniques such as flower arrangement, hemp weaving, and tapestry. The origin of thimble embroidery can be traced back to the Song Dynasty and has become a part of Chongming's traditional culture after hundreds of years of development. Thimble embroidery works are popular in both domestic and foreign markets and have become a unique business card of the Chongming area. The production process of thimble embroidery requires the use of various tools and materials such as embroidery needles, fine threads, and embroidered fabrics. The production process is very cumbersome and requires craftsmen to be patient and meticulous. Thimble embroidery works are loved for their delicacy, exquisiteness, and artistic appeal.

Chongming cuisine is a local specialty food with unique cooking methods and flavors based on the abundant local agricultural products. Examples include Chongming eight-treasure duck, Chongming sea bass, and Chongming crab cake, all representing the culinary culture of the Chongming area. Chongming eight-treasure duck is one of the traditional famous dishes in the Chongming area, made from locally produced ducks and various Chinese medicinal materials through unique cooking techniques. Chongming sea bass is made from locally produced sea bass, combined with local vegetables and seasonings, with a fresh taste and rich nutrition. Chongming crab cake is made from locally produced hairy crabs, selected rice flour, and seasonings, creating a delicious delicacy. These foods not only have a delicious taste but also reflect the local people's love and pursuit of food.

In addition to the representative elements mentioned above, there are many other characteristics of traditional culture in Chongming. For example, fishing culture has a long history and features a strong marine cultural characteristic with fishermen as the main body. Here, people can enjoy many beautiful waterscape views and experience a strong fishing culture atmosphere. In addition, Chongming also has traditional folk arts such as sugar blowing, flower lanterns, and suona horn, which are not only rich in local characteristics but also have a strong historical and cultural heritage and are an important part of Chongming's traditional culture.

Chongming Island is a place with rich ecological, cultural, historical, and cultural resources. On this beautiful island, people can feel the strong traditional cultural atmosphere and appreciate the unique island style. By understanding and inheriting Chongming's traditional culture, people can not only deepen their understanding and recognition of this place but also help better protect and inherit these precious cultural heritages.

例句赏析

例1：

原文：赶海节是崇明地区一年一度的传统节日。每年农历四月初，当地渔民将迎来丰收的时刻。届时，渔民们会举行隆重的庆祝活动，包括祭海、祈福、赛龙舟等。这些活动既是对海神的感恩，也是表达对来年风调雨顺、海船顺利出海的祈求。

译文：The Beachcombing Festival is an annual traditional festival in the Chongming area.

Every year in early April of the lunar calendar, local fishermen will usher in a time of harvest. At that time, the fishermen will hold grand celebrations, including offering sacrifices to the sea, praying for blessings, and dragon boat races. These activities are not only an expression of gratitude to the sea god but also a prayer for a smooth sailing in the coming year.

赏析：本段文字重点描写渔民的传统节日，"赶海节"是独有的崇明文化。"赶海"是海岛人民特有的生活习惯，也是英译的难点。"Beachcomb"是一个复合词，由"beach"（沙滩）和"comb"（仔细搜寻）构成，而"赶海"则指在海边沙滩仔细搜寻海产品，所以用"beachcomb"翻译"赶海"非常合适。另外，本段还出现了一些特殊的习俗，如祭海、祈福，译文将其译为"offer sacrifices to the sea""pray for blessings"。

例2：

原文：传统的顶针线包括插花、披麻、织毯等多种技艺。顶针线的起源可以追溯到宋代，经过几百年的发展，如今已成为崇明传统文化的一部分。顶针线作品在国内外市场上备受欢迎，成为崇明地区的一张独特名片。顶针线的制作过程需要用到多种工具和材料，如刺绣针、细线、绣布等，制作过程十分烦琐，需要工匠们耐心细致地完成。顶针线作品以其细腻、精美、富有艺术感染力等特点，深受人们的喜爱。

译文：Traditional thimble embroidery includes various techniques such as flower arrangement, hemp weaving, and tapestry. The origin of thimble embroidery can be traced back to the Song Dynasty and has become a part of Chongming's traditional culture after hundreds of years of development. Thimble embroidery works are popular in both domestic and foreign markets and have become a unique business card of the Chongming area. The production process of thimble embroidery requires the use of various tools and materials such as embroidery needles, fine threads, and embroidered fabrics. The production process is very cumbersome and requires craftsmen to be patient and meticulous. Thimble embroidery works are loved for their delicacy, exquisiteness, and artistic appeal.

赏析：本段文字涉及顶针线这项传统工艺的介绍，相关的术语较多，翻译时难度较大。首先，顶针线并非指一种线，而是指一种用顶针做工具的特殊刺绣。所以在翻译时应当译为 thimble embroidery 而不是 top needlework。其次，与顶针线相关的工艺，如插花、披麻、织毯，也是翻译的难点。顶针线所需要的原材料，如刺绣针、细线、秀布，也涉及相关的专业术语，翻译难度也较大。

例3：

原文：除了以上的代表性元素，崇明传统文化中还有许多其他特色。如渔家文化，源远流长，它以渔民为主体，具有浓郁的海洋文化特色。在这里，人们可以欣赏到许多美丽的水乡风光，感受到浓厚的渔家文化氛围。此外，崇明还有传统的民间艺术，如吹糖人、打花灯、唢呐等，这些艺术形式既富有地方特色，又具有浓厚的历史文化底蕴，是崇明传统文化的重要组成部分。

译文：In addition to the representative elements mentioned above, there are many other characteristics of traditional culture in Chongming. For example, fishing culture has a long history and features a strong marine cultural characteristic with fishermen as the main body. Here, people can enjoy many beautiful waterscape views and experience a strong fishing culture atmosphere. In addition, Chongming also has traditional folk arts such as sugar blowing, flower lanterns, and suona horn, which are not only rich in local characteristics but also have a strong historical and cultural heritage and are an important part of Chongming's traditional culture.

赏析：本段中文讲述了渔家文化的三大特点：历史悠久、以渔民为主、带有浓郁的海洋特色。在翻译时，译者没有采用并列结构，而是采用了不同的表达形式。"具有……特色"译文译成"feature"，"以……为主体"则选用 with 结构作为伴随状语译出。本段当中出现的三种民俗文化，即吹糖人、打花灯、唢呐，也是翻译的难点，需要在理解这些工艺后才能进行恰当的翻译，切记不能进行单纯的音译。

☞ **练习**

(一)将下列短语翻译成英文。

1. 崇明传统文化

2. 赶海节

3. 顶针线

4. 崇明菜

5. 渔家文化

(二)将下列句子翻译成英文。

1. 崇明岛是一个生态宝地，也是一个文化宝库。

2. 赶海节是崇明地区一年一度的传统节日。

3. 顶针线是崇明地区的一种传统手工艺，以其精美的刺绣工艺闻名于世。

4. 崇明菜是一种具有地方特色的美食。

5. 崇明传统文化中还有许多其他特色。

(三)将下面段落翻译成英文。

　　崇明岛是一个富有生态、人文、历史、文化资源的地方。在这个美丽的岛屿上，人们可以感受到浓郁的传统文化氛围，领略到独特的岛屿风情。通过了解和传承崇明传统文化，不仅可以加深人们对这个地方的了解和认识，还可以帮助人们更好地保护和传承这些宝贵的文化遗产。

☞ **参考答案**

　　（一）

1. Chongming traditional culture

2. Beachcombing Festival

3. thimble embroidery

4. Chongming cuisine

5. fishing culture

　　（二）

1. Chongming Island is an ecological treasure trove and a cultural treasury.

2. The Beachcombing Festival is an annual traditional festival in Chongming area.

3. Thimble embroidery is a traditional handicraft in Chongming area, famous for its exquisite embroidery.

4. Chongming cuisine is a local specialty cuisine based on the rich agricultural products in the area.

5. There are many other characteristics in Chongming traditional culture.

　　（三）

Chongming Island is a place rich in ecological, cultural, historical, and cultural resources. On this beautiful island, people can feel the rich traditional cultural atmosphere and appreciate the unique island style. Understanding and inheriting Chongming traditional culture can not only deepen people's understanding and recognition of this place, but also help people better protect and inherit these precious cultural heritages.

三、崇明传统文化的保护和传承

翻译简介

　　本文重点讲解崇明传统文化的保护和传承。崇明政府在崇明岛上设立了多个文化产业基地，以便培育和扶持本土传统文化产业，通过举办各种特色文化活动吸引各地游客，同时对青少年进行传统文化教育，使其得到传承。原文长句较多，举例较多，因此在翻译过程中尤其需要理解句子内部的逻辑结构，丰富句式表达，除了采用并列句式外，还可使用非谓语动词、with 短语等来表达句子内部的并列含义。另外，在碰到超长定语时，应当采用多种策略将其后置，平衡句子结构，增加句子尾重。

词汇表

行政单位：administrative unit

河海交汇岛：river-sea confluence island

赶海节：the Beachcombing Festival

顶针文化：thimble embroidery culture

保护和传承：protection and inheritance

文化产业基地：cultural industry bases

展示和销售渠道：display and sales channels

顶针线博物馆：Thimble Embroidery Museum

传统手工艺人的培训和创新：training and innovation of traditional craftsmen

传统文化主题活动：activities with traditional culture as the theme

民间艺术展览：folk art exhibition

传承和推广：inheriting and promoting

渔民的传统文化：traditional culture of local fishermen

自然的敬畏：awe of nature

祭海、龙舟比赛和舞狮表演等传统活动：traditional activities such as fishermen offering sacrifices to the sea, dragon boat races, and lion dances

学校课程和社区活动的形式：various forms such as school curriculum and community activities

认同感和传承意识：sense of identity and inheritance awareness

文化艺术家、工匠和其他传承人：cultural artists, craftsmen, and other inheritors

旅游开发：tourism development

特色旅游景点：tourist attractions with local characteristics

合理规划和利用：reasonable planning and utilization

独特自然景观和丰富的生态资源：unique natural scenery and rich ecological resources

生态旅游项目如观鸟、探险和垂钓等：eco-tourism projects such as bird watching, adventure，and fishing

原文

　　崇明岛是上海市辖区内的一个县级行政单位，位于长江口外东海中部，是中国第三大岛，也是全国最大的江海交汇洲。这里有着丰富多彩的传统文化，如赶海节、顶针线等，这些文化元素丰富多彩，成了崇明地区的独特名片。近年来，崇明地区对传统文化的保护和传承给予了越来越高的重视，政府部门积极采取措施，推动传统文化的传承与发展。

　　崇明政府设立了多个文化产业基地，以便培育和扶持本土传统文化产业。这些基地不仅为当地的传统手工艺人提供了展示和销售渠道，同时也吸引了众多游客前来参观体验，从而提高了崇明传统文化的影响力。例如，崇明顶针线博物馆就是一个非常好的例子。这个博物馆收藏了大量的顶针线作品和资料，展示了顶针线的历史和制作技艺，吸引了许多游客前来参观。另外，政府还积极支持传统手工艺人的培训和创新，让传统手工艺得到更好的发展。

　　为了让更多人了解和认识崇明传统文化，崇明地区每年都会举办各种以传统文化为主题的活动。例如，崇明赶海节、崇明民间艺术展、崇明美食节等。通过这些活动，让游客和市民们亲身参与到传统文化的体验中，更好地传承和弘扬崇明地区的传统文化。例如，崇明赶海节是崇明地区的一张独特名片，它不仅展示了当地渔民的传统文化，也体现了人们对自然的敬畏之心。在赶海节期间，人们可以看到渔民祭海、赛龙舟、舞狮子等传统活动，感受崇明传统文化的魅力。

　　崇明地区重视对青少年的传统文化教育，通过学校课程、社区活动等多种形式，让青少年了解本土的传统文化，从而培养他们对传统文化的认同感和传承意识。例如，崇明中学开设了传统文化课程，让学生们了解崇明的传统文化和历史。另外，还鼓励文化艺术家、手工艺人和其他传承人到学校、社区等地开展讲座、示范等活动，将传统文化知识传授给下一代。

　　在保护崇明生态环境的同时，政府还积极开展了以传统文化为特色的旅游业发展。通过合理规划和利用，打造了一批具有地方特色的旅游景点。例如，崇明东滩湿地公园是一个生态公园，以其独特的自然风光和丰富的生态资源而闻名；崇明顶针线博物馆则是一个展示顶针线文化的博物馆，吸引了众多游客前来参观。这些景点在保护传统文化资源的基础上，为游客提供了丰富的旅游体验，从而推动了崇明传统文化的传播与发展。例如，游客可以在崇明东滩湿地公园体验各种生态旅游项目，如赏鸟、探险、垂钓等，感受这片生态环境的独特魅力。

总之，崇明地区丰富的生态资源和独特的民俗文化使其成为一个具有魅力的旅游目的地。通过不断地保护、传承和发展传统文化，崇明将继续为世人展示其独特的文化魅力。崇明地区的传统文化，不仅是一种文化遗产，更是一种文化资源。只有通过不断地保护、传承和发展，才能让这些文化元素得以传承下去，为我们的文化多样性和人类文明的发展作出贡献。

译文

Chongming Island is a county-level administrative unit within Shanghai, located in the middle of the East China Sea outside the mouth of the Yangtze River. It is the third largest island in China and the largest river-sea confluence island in the country. Here, there is a rich and colorful traditional culture, such as the Beachcombing Festival and thimble embroidery, which have become unique business cards of the Chongming area. In recent years, Chongming has attached increasing importance to the protection and inheritance of traditional culture. Government departments have taken active measures to promote the inheritance and development of traditional culture.

The Chongming government has established multiple cultural industry bases to cultivate and support local traditional cultural industries. These bases not only provide display and sales channels for local traditional craftsmen, but also attract many tourists to visit and experience, thereby enhancing the influence of Chongming's traditional culture. For example, the Chongming Thimble Embroidery Museum is a very good example. The museum collects a large number of thimble embroidery works and materials, displaying the history and production techniques of thimble embroidery, attracting many visitors. In addition, the government actively supports the training and innovation of traditional craftsmen, allowing traditional handicrafts to develop better.

In order to let more people understand and recognize Chongming's traditional culture, Chongming holds various activities with traditional culture as the theme every year. For example, the Chongming clamming festival, Chongming folk art exhibition, Chongming food festival, etc. Through these activities, tourists and citizens can participate in the experience of traditional culture, better inheriting and promoting Chongming's traditional culture. For example, the Chongming clamming festival is a unique business card of Chongming area, which not only showcases the traditional culture of local fishermen but also reflects people's awe of nature. During the clamming festival, people can see traditional activities such as fishermen offering sacrifices to the sea, dragon boat races, and lion dances, feeling the charm of Chongming's traditional culture.

Chongming attaches importance to traditional cultural education for young people. Through various forms such as school curriculum and community activities, young people can learn about local traditional culture, thereby cultivating their sense of identity and inheritance awareness of traditional culture. For example, Chongming Middle School offers traditional cultural courses to let students understand Chongming's traditional culture and history. In addition, cultural artists, craftsmen, and other inheritors are encouraged to give lectures and demonstrations in schools and communities to pass on traditional cultural knowledge to the next generation.

While protecting the ecological environment of Chongming, the government also actively develops tourism with traditional culture as its feature. Through reasonable planning and utilization, a group of tourist attractions with local characteristics have been created. For example, Chongming Dongtan Wetland Park is an ecological park famous for its unique natural scenery and rich ecological resources; the Chongming Thimble Embroidery Museum is a museum displaying thimble embroidery culture that attracts many visitors. These attractions provide rich tourism experiences for tourists on the basis of protecting traditional cultural resources, thereby promoting the spread and development of Chongming's traditional culture. For example, tourists can experience various eco-tourism projects such as bird watching, adventure, and fishing in Chongming Dongtan Wetland Park, feeling the unique charm of this ecological environment.

In conclusion, Chongming's rich ecological resources and unique folk culture make it a charming tourist destination. By continuously protecting, inheriting, and developing traditional culture, Chongming will continue to showcase its unique cultural charm to the world. The traditional culture of Chongming is not only a cultural heritage but also a cultural resource. Only by continuously protecting, inheriting, and developing it can these cultural elements be inherited and contribute to our cultural diversity and the development of human civilization.

例句赏析

例 1：

原文：崇明政府设立了多个文化产业基地，以便培育和扶持本土传统文化产业。这些基地不仅为当地的传统手工艺人提供了展示和销售渠道，同时也吸引了众多游客前来参观体验，从而提高了崇明传统文化的影响力。例如，崇明顶针线博物馆就是一个非常好的例子。这个博物馆收藏了大量的顶针线作品和资料，展示了顶针线的历史和制作技艺，吸引了许多游客前来参观。

译文： The Chongming government has established multiple cultural industry bases to cultivate and support local traditional cultural industries. These bases not only provide display and sales channels for local traditional craftsmen, but also attract many tourists to visit and experience, thereby enhancing the influence of Chongming's traditional culture. For example, the Chongming Thimble Embroidery Museum is a very good example. The museum collects a large number of thimble embroidery works and materials, displaying the history and production techniques of thimble embroidery, attracting many visitors.

赏析： 该段中文介绍了崇明政府设立产业基地、扶持文化产业、振兴传统手工艺的举措。翻译该段需要注意句子内部的逻辑结构。该段中文第二句，使用"不仅""同时""从而"来表达语义之间的逻辑联系，译文中相应地使用 not only... but also...来表达并列的逻辑关系，用 thereby 来表示目的。该段中文运用"收藏""展示""吸引"三个动词来说明顶针线博物馆的功能，而译文则使用 collect 为主动词，display 和 attract 的现在分词作为伴随状语来说明，使用动词现在分词来作伴随状语，表示与主句动作同时发生的动作。

例 2：

原文： 在保护崇明生态环境的同时，政府还积极开展了以传统文化为特色的旅游业发展。通过合理规划和利用，打造了一批具有地方特色的旅游景点。例如，崇明东滩湿地公园是一个生态公园，以其独特的自然风光和丰富的生态资源而闻名；崇明顶针线博物馆则是一个展示顶针线文化的博物馆，吸引了众多游客前来参观。

译文： While protecting the ecological environment of Chongming, the government also actively develops tourism with traditional culture as its feature. Through reasonable planning and utilization, a group of tourist attractions with local characteristics have been created. While protecting the ecological environment of Chongming, the government also actively develops tourism with traditional culture as its feature. For example, Chongming Dongtan Wetland Park is an ecological park famous for its unique natural scenery and rich ecological resources; the Chongming Thimble Embroidery Museum is a museum displaying thimble embroidery culture that attracts many visitors.

赏析： 本段中文主要介绍政府开发的地方特色旅游景点。第一句中文出现了较长的定语"以传统文化为特色的"，按照英文的表达习惯，通常较长的定语可以通过从句、非谓语动词、介词短语等后置来增加句子的尾重，从而实现句子内部的稳定和平衡。所以本句译文就采用了 with 的结构后置来修饰 tourism，避免了头重脚轻，实现了句子的均衡。在翻译第三句"以……而闻名"时则采用的是形容词短语"（be）famous for"来限定"park"来实现平衡。另外，译文将原文的第二句翻译成被动结构，避免了句型的单一重复。

例 3：

原文： 总之，崇明地区丰富的生态资源和独特的民俗文化使其成为一个具有魅力的旅游目的地。通过不断地保护、传承和发展传统文化，崇明将继续为世人展示其独特的文化魅力。崇明地区的传统文化，不仅是一种文化遗产，更是一种文化资源。只有通过不断地保护、传承和发展，才能让这些文化元素得以传承下去，为我们的文化多样性和人类文明的发展作出贡献。

译文： In conclusion, Chongming's rich ecological resources and unique folk culture make it a charming tourist destination. By continuously protecting, inheriting, and developing traditional culture, Chongming will continue to showcase its unique cultural charm to the world. The traditional culture of Chongming is not only a cultural heritage but also a cultural resource. Only by continuously protecting, inheriting, and developing it can these cultural elements be inherited and contribute to our cultural diversity and the development of human civilization.

赏析： 该段中文总结了崇明独特的民俗文化所带来的得天独厚的优势。在翻译该段中文时，译者除了运用普通的陈述句外，还使用了并列句和倒装句。第一句使用"主+谓+宾+宾补"的结构，简洁精练；第二句中采用"showcase"翻译"展示"，暗含崇明的生态和民俗文化就像博物馆一样向世人尽情地展示。

☞ **练习**

（一）将下列短语翻译成英文。

1. 赶海节

2. 保护和传承

3. 文化产业基地

4. 传统手工艺人的培训和创新

5. 特色旅游景点

（二）将下列句子翻译成英文。

1. 崇明地区对传统文化的保护和传承给予了越来越高的重视。

2. 崇明政府设立了多个文化产业基地，以便培育和扶持本土传统文化产业。

3. 崇明顶针线博物馆就是一个非常好的例子。

4. 政府还积极支持传统手工艺人的培训和创新，让传统手工艺得到更好的发展。

5. 崇明地区每年都会举办各种以传统文化为主题的活动。

(三)将下面段落翻译成英文。

在保护崇明生态环境的同时，政府还积极开展了以传统文化为特色的旅游业。通过合理规划和利用，打造了一批具有地方特色的旅游景点。例如，崇明东滩湿地公园是一个生态公园，以其独特的自然风光和丰富的生态资源而闻名；崇明顶针线博物馆则是一个展示顶针线文化的博物馆，吸引了众多游客前来参观。这些景点在保护传统文化资源的基础上，为游客提供了丰富的旅游体验，从而推动了崇明传统文化的传播与发展。例如，游客可以在崇明东滩湿地公园体验各种生态旅游项目，如赏鸟、探险、垂钓等，感受到这片生态环境的独特魅力。

☞ **参考答案**

(一)

1. the Beachcombing festival

2. protection and inheritance

3. cultural industry base

4. training and innovation of traditional craftsmen

5. tourist attractions with local characteristics

(二)

1. Chongming attaches increasing importance to the protection and inheritance of traditional culture.

2. The Chongming government has established multiple cultural industry bases to cultivate and support local traditional cultural industries.

3. The Chongming Thimble Embroidery Museum is a very good example.

4. The government also actively supports the training and innovation of traditional artisans, allowing traditional handicrafts to have better development.

5. Chongming holds various activities with traditional culture as the theme every year.

(三)

While protecting the ecological environment of Chongming, the government also actively develops tourism with traditional culture as its feature. Through reasonable planning and utilization, a group of tourist attractions with local characteristics have been created. For example, Chongming Dongtan Wetland Park is an ecological park famous for its unique natural scenery and rich ecological resources; the Chongming Thimble Embroidery Museum is a museum displaying thimble embroidery culture that attracts many visitors. These attractions provide rich tourism experiences for tourists on the basis of protecting traditional cultural resources, thereby promoting the spread and development of Chongming's traditional culture. For example, tourists can experience various eco-tourism projects such as bird watching, adventure, and fishing in Chongming Dongtan Wetland Park, feeling the unique charm of this ecological environment.

第六章　崇明生态美食

一、崇明本土美食的历史和特色

翻译简介

　　本文重点介绍了崇明的本土美食，如大闸蟹、黄鳝等，详细地描述了挑选食材的过程和烹饪方法。中餐选材讲究，制作过程严格，因而在翻译时需要特别准确。本文涉及的诸多地道的中餐美食，给翻译带来了不小的难度。首先，关于食材的翻译，要真正了解食材的来源，切记望文生义，诸如大闸蟹、黄鳝的翻译。大闸蟹的学名叫作"中华绒螯蟹"，因为蟹爪上有毛，所以被翻译为"hairy crab"，也常被译作"Chinese mitten crab"。而黄鳝因为常在稻田、水沟处被发现，因而译作"rice field eel"。其次，对于调料、烹饪手法和过程的翻译，应注重相关术语的积累，注意遵循烹饪顺序。

词汇表

　　本土美食：local cuisine

　　文化内涵：cultural connotations

　　选材讲究：careful selection of ingredients

　　口味清淡：light taste

　　宋、元、明、清：Song, Yuan, Ming, and Qing dynasties

　　海鲜资源：seafood resources

　　重要渔场：important fishing grounds

　　农业基地：agricultural base

　　特产：specialties

　　大闸蟹：hairy crabs

鲜美的口感：delicious taste

营养价值丰富：rich nutritional value

黄鳝：rice field eel

美味的肉质：delicious meat

无腥味：no fishy smell

调味料：seasonings

保留原味：retain the original flavor

亚热带海洋性气候带：subtropical marine climate zone

轻爽可口：light, delicious, and refreshing

原文

崇明岛是中国大陆最大的岛屿之一，位于上海市区东北部，是一个以生态旅游为主题的旅游胜地。除了生态景观，崇明还以其丰富的本土美食而闻名，这些美食不仅口感鲜美，而且具有浓郁的地方特色和文化内涵。本文将从崇明本土美食的历史、选材讲究、独特的烹饪技艺、口味清淡等几个方面介绍崇明本土美食的特色和魅力。

崇明本土美食的历史可以追溯到宋、元、明、清等各个朝代。在古时候，崇明岛周边水域丰富、海鲜资源丰富，成为当时的重要渔场之一。同时，崇明也是一个重要的农业基地，以种植稻谷、蔬菜等农作物为主。这些自然资源为崇明本土美食的发展提供了坚实的基础。

随着时间的推移，崇明本土美食逐渐形成了独特的特色和风味。崇明美食注重选用当地优质、新鲜的食材，以保证菜品的品质和口感。例如，崇明大闸蟹是当地的特产之一，以其鲜美的口感和丰富的营养价值而闻名。大闸蟹的产地主要在崇明岛周边的水域，这里的水质清澈、富含营养，是大闸蟹生长的理想环境。在选用大闸蟹时，崇明美食注重挑选个头适中、身体壳体完整、膏黄饱满的大闸蟹，以保证菜品的品质和口感。除了大闸蟹，崇明黄鳝也是当地的一道经典美食。崇明黄鳝是在崇明的池塘、水沟中自然生长的鳝鱼，以其鲜美的口感和独特的风味而广受欢迎。在选用黄鳝时，崇明美食同样注重选用体型适中、肉质鲜美、无腥味的黄鳝，以保证菜品的品质和口感。

崇明美食的制作方法丰富多样，有独特的烹饪技巧，如炖、煮、蒸、烧等。例如，崇明大闸蟹最为经典的做法是清蒸。清蒸大闸蟹的方法是将蒸锅加水烧开后，将大闸蟹放入蒸锅中，然后撒上一些葱、姜、蒜、料酒等调料，蒸制 10 至 15 分钟即可。这种做法可以保留大闸蟹的原汁原味，使其口感更加鲜美。另外，崇明黄鳝也有独特的烹饪方法。崇明黄鳝最为经典的做法是烤制。在烤制黄鳝时，先将黄鳝去皮、切段，然后用酱油、料酒、白糖等调味料腌制一段时间，最后放到烤箱中烤制。这种做法可以使黄鳝的肉质更加鲜嫩、口感更加醇厚。崇明美食的烹饪方法注重保留食材的原汁原味，并且富有创意和变化，让人们在品尝美食的同时也能感受到独特的文化和历史。

崇明本土美食的口味以清淡为主，注重突出食材的本质味道。这种口味的特点与崇明的气候环境有关：崇明岛属于亚热带海洋性气候，夏季炎热潮湿，人们不喜欢吃太油腻、太重口味的食物，而更喜欢清淡爽口的口感。因此，崇明美食讲究清淡、鲜美、爽口，并且富有营养价值，深受人们的喜爱。

崇明本土美食以其独特的历史、选材讲究、独特的烹饪技艺和清淡的口味，成为当地文化和旅游的重要组成部分。在崇明旅游时，品尝崇明本土美食，不仅可以满足味蕾的享受，还能感受到当地的历史和文化，是一次难得的生态之旅。

译文

Chongming Island is one of the largest islands in China's mainland, located in the northeast of Shanghai, and is a tourist destination with an eco-tourism theme. In addition to its ecological landscape, Chongming is also famous for its rich local cuisine, which not only tastes delicious but also has strong local characteristics and cultural connotations. This article will introduce the characteristics and charm of Chongming's local cuisine from several aspects such as the history of local cuisine, careful selection of ingredients, unique cooking techniques, and light taste.

The history of Chongming's local cuisine can be traced back to various dynasties such as the Song, Yuan, Ming, and Qing. In ancient times, the waters around Chongming Island were abundant, and the seafood resources were rich, making it one of the important fishing grounds at that time. At the same time, Chongming is also an important agricultural base, mainly planting rice, vegetables and other crops. These natural resources provide a solid foundation for the development of Chongming's local cuisine.

With the passage of time, Chongming's local cuisine has gradually formed unique characteristics and flavors. Chongming cuisine emphasizes the use of local high-quality and fresh ingredients to ensure the quality and taste of the dishes. For example, Chongming hairy crabs are one of the local specialties, famous for their delicious taste and rich nutritional value. The main habitat of hairy crabs is in the waters around Chongming Island, where the water is clear and nutrient-rich, making it an ideal environment for hairy crab growth. When selecting hairy crabs, Chongming cuisine pays attention to choosing crabs with moderate size, intact body shells, and full crab roe to ensure the quality and taste of the dishes. In addition to hairy crabs,

Chongming rice field eel is also a classic local delicacy. Chongming rice field eel is a naturally grown eel in Chongming's ponds and waterways, widely popular for its delicious taste and unique flavor. When selecting rice field eels, Chongming cuisine also pays attention to choosing eels with moderate size, delicious meat, and no fishy smell to ensure the quality and taste of the dishes.

Chongming cuisine has a rich variety of cooking methods and unique cooking techniques, such as stewing, boiling, steaming, and roasting. For example, the most classic way to cook hairy crabs in Chongming is steaming. The method of steaming hairy crabs is to boil water in a steamer, put the crabs into the steamer, then sprinkle some scallions, ginger, garlic, cooking wine and other seasonings on them, and steam them for 10-15 minutes. This method can retain the original flavor of hairy crabs and make them more delicious. In addition, Chongming rice field eel also has a unique cooking method. The most classic way to cook Chongming rice field eel is roasting. When roasting rice field eels, first remove their skin and cut them into sections, then marinate them with soy sauce, cooking wine, sugar, and other seasonings for a period of time before putting them into the oven for roasting. This method can make the meat of rice field eels more tender and delicious with a fragrant taste. The cooking methods of Chongming cuisine emphasize retaining the original flavor of ingredients while being creative and changeable, allowing people to feel the unique culture and history while tasting delicious food.

The taste of Chongming's local cuisine is mainly light, emphasizing highlighting the essence taste of ingredients. This taste characteristic is related to Chongming's climate environment. Chongming Island belongs to a subtropical marine climate zone. In summer it is hot and humid, people do not like to eat too greasy or heavy-tasting food but prefer light and refreshing tastes. Therefore, Chongming cuisine emphasizes lightness, deliciousness, refreshing taste, and rich nutritional value, which are deeply loved by people.

Chongming's local cuisine has unique characteristics and charm with its distinctive history, careful selection of ingredients, unique cooking techniques, and light taste.

例句赏析

例1：

原文： 崇明大闸蟹是当地的特产之一，以其鲜美的口感和丰富的营养价值而闻名。大闸蟹的产地主要在崇明岛周边的水域，这里的水质清澈、富含营养，是大闸蟹生长的理想环境。在选用大闸蟹时，崇明美食注重挑选个头适中、身体壳体完整、膏黄饱满的大闸蟹，以保证菜品的品质和口感。

译文：For example, Chongming hairy crabs are one of the local specialties, famous for their delicious taste and rich nutritional value. The main habitat of hairy crabs is in the waters around Chongming Island, where the water is clear and nutrient-rich, making it an ideal environment for hairy crab growth. When selecting hairy crabs, Chongming cuisine pays attention to choosing crabs with moderate size, intact body shells, and full crab roe to ensure the quality and taste of the dishes.

赏析：该段中文重点描述了崇明大闸蟹的特征。大闸蟹的学名叫作"中华绒螯蟹"，因为蟹爪上有毛，所以被翻译为"hairy crab"，也常被译作"Chinese mitten crab"。该段第二句中的"产地"指的是大闸蟹的栖息地，因而翻译时译为"habitat"更为准确。第二句译文使用定语从句来描述限定大闸蟹的生长水域，其中"富含营养"译作"nutrient-rich"，类似的表达还有"protein-rich" "calcium-rich"。当讲到挑选大闸蟹需要注意的事项时，原文将"个头、壳体、膏黄"三个条件进行并列来修饰大闸蟹，而译文则用 with 短语结构后置作定语修饰"crabs"，使得整个句子结构显得平衡而稳定。

例 2：

原文：除了大闸蟹，崇明黄鳝也是当地的一道经典美食。崇明黄鳝是在崇明的池塘、水沟中自然生长的鳝鱼，以其鲜美的口感和独特的风味而广受欢迎。在选用黄鳝时，崇明美食同样注重选用体型适中、肉质鲜美、无腥味的黄鳝，以保证菜品的品质和口感。

译文：In addition to hairy crabs, Chongming rice field eel is also a classic local delicacy. Chongming rice field eel is a naturally grown eel in Chongming's ponds and waterways, widely popular for its delicious taste and unique flavor. When selecting rice field eels, Chongming cuisine also pays attention to choosing eels with moderate size, delicious meat, and no fishy smell to ensure the quality and taste of the dishes.

赏析：该段主要介绍黄鳝的生长环境和选用标准。首先，黄鳝，别名鳝鱼、田鳝、田鳗，英文中 eel 常来表示鳗鱼，而黄鳝多生长在稻田、池塘中，因而英译为 rice field eel。其次，英文中有很多词汇是用来描述食物的，特色美食用 specialty，美味佳肴用 delicacy，而菜系用 cuisine。最后，在选用黄鳝时，译文采用 with 短语结构来体现黄鳝的体型、肉质和味道。

例 3：

原文：另外，崇明黄鳝也有独特的烹饪方法。崇明黄鳝最为经典的做法是烤制。在烤制黄鳝时，先将黄鳝去皮、切段，然后用酱油、料酒、白糖等调味料腌制一段时间，最后放到烤箱中烤制。这种做法可以使黄鳝的肉质更加鲜嫩、口感更加醇厚。

译文：In addition, Chongming rice field eel also has a unique cooking method. The most classic way to cook Chongming rice field eel is roasting. When roasting rice field eels, first remove their skin and cut them into sections, then marinate them with soy sauce, cooking wine, sugar, and other seasonings for a period of time before putting them into the oven for roasting. This method can make the meat of rice field eels more tender and delicious with a fragrant taste.

赏析：本段文字着重描写黄鳝的烹饪手法。中餐烹饪讲究细节，有一定的步骤秩序，因而翻译时也应尤其重视次序，如用"first... then... before"就可将几道工序的顺序简洁明了地表达出来。在翻译黄鳝具体的烹饪步骤时，译文采用了祈使句，更加突出了具体的动作。本段另外一个翻译难点是烹饪方式和调料的翻译，如烤制、腌制、酱油、料酒等，分别译为 roast, marinate, soy sauce, cooking wine。

☞ 练习

(一)将下列短语翻译成英文。

1. 本土美食

2. 地方特色

3. 原料精选

4. 独特的烹饪技巧

5. 清淡的口味

(二)将下列句子翻译成英文。

1. 崇明岛是中国大陆最大的岛屿之一，位于上海东北部，是一个以生态旅游为主题的旅游胜地。

2. 崇明的地方美食不仅味道美味，而且具有浓郁的地方特色和文化内涵。

3. 崇明菜肴强调使用本地优质新鲜原料，以确保菜肴的质量和口感。

4. 崇明菜肴有丰富多样的烹饪方法和独特的烹饪技巧，如炖、煮、蒸和烤等。

5. 崇明菜肴的口味以清淡为主，强调突出原料的本味。

(三)将下面段落翻译成英文。

崇明岛的地方美食历史可以追溯到宋、元、明、清等各个朝代。古时候，崇明岛周围的水域丰富，海产品资源丰富，使其成为当时重要的渔场之一。同时，崇明也是一个重要的农业基地，主要种植水稻、蔬菜等作物。这些自然资源为崇明地方美食的发展奠定了坚实基础。

☞ 参考答案

(一)

1. local cuisine

2. local characteristics

3. careful selection of ingredients

4. unique cooking techniques

5. light taste

（二）

1. Chongming Island is one of the largest islands in China's mainland, located in the northeast of Shanghai, and is a tourist destination with an eco-tourism theme.

2. Chongming's local cuisine not only tastes delicious but also has strong local characteristics and cultural connotations.

3. Chongming cuisine emphasizes the use of local high-quality and fresh ingredients to ensure the quality and taste of the dishes.

4. Chongming cuisine has a rich variety of cooking methods and unique cooking techniques, such as stewing, boiling, steaming, and roasting.

5. The taste of Chongming's local cuisine is mainly light, emphasizing highlighting the essence taste of ingredients.

（三）

The history of Chongming's local cuisine can be traced back to various dynasties such as the Song, Yuan, Ming, and Qing. In ancient times, the waters around Chongming Island were abundant, and the seafood resources were rich, making it one of the important fishing grounds at that time. At the same time, Chongming is also an important agricultural base, mainly planting rice, vegetables and other crops. These natural resources provide a solid foundation for the development of Chongming's local cuisine.

二、崇明本土美食的代表性菜品和餐厅

翻译简介

本文介绍了诸多崇明本土美食的代表性菜品和餐厅，如崇明大闸蟹、高桥鲍汁鳝鱼、白鹅炖蛋等，"鱼巷餐厅""龙门客栈"则是本文推荐的环境清幽的美食餐厅。对于中式菜肴的翻译，方法策略较多，最为常用的是"食材+烹饪方式"，译文也采取这一方法，将以上三道菜肴翻译为 Chongming hairy crab, Gaoqiao braised eel in abalone sauce, white goose stewed egg。而对于餐厅名称的翻译，首要的法则是简洁且吸引人。"龙门客栈"因为同名电影而名声大噪，所以在翻译的时候没有采用音译而是沿用了电影英文名称，以期得到更多顾客的垂青。

词汇表

本地美食：local cuisine

代表性菜肴：representative dishes

味道正宗的当地美食：authentic local delicacies

味道鲜美的蟹肉：tender meat of the crab

美味佳肴：delicious dish

推荐餐厅：recommended restaurant

鲍汁焖鳝鱼：braised eel in abalone sauce

留有余味：lingering aftertaste

保健美食：health-preserving delicacy

白鹅肉：white goose meat

炖蛋：stewed egg

本地食材：local ingredients

独特烹饪技巧：unique cooking techniques

螃蟹粉汤：crab powder soup

炒花生米：fried peanuts

渔巷餐厅：Fish Alley Restaurant

竹叶青景区：Zhuyeqing Scenic Area

古镇东滩：Dongtan Ancient Town

龙门客栈：Dragon Inn

原文

崇明岛是上海市区东北部的一个大岛，以生态旅游和本土美食而闻名。本文将介绍崇明本土美食的代表性菜品和餐厅，让你在前往崇明旅游时，不仅可以欣赏美景，也能品尝到地道的美食佳肴。

崇明大闸蟹是崇明的代表性美食之一。每年的蟹肥时节，游客们络绎不绝地来品尝这一美味佳肴。这道菜品选用当地的大闸蟹，肉质鲜美、膏黄丰满，是崇明的特色之一。崇明大闸蟹的最佳食用时间是每年的 8 月到 11 月，此时正是大闸蟹肥美的时节。推荐餐厅：

崇明大闸蟹馆。这家餐厅是崇明大闸蟹的专业餐厅，提供各种美味的大闸蟹料理，是品尝崇明大闸蟹的不二之选。

高桥鲍汁黄鳝是另一道崇明的特色美食。这道菜品选用崇明特产的黄鳝，搭配鲍汁烹制而成。鲍汁的鲜美和黄鳝的滑嫩相得益彰，让人回味无穷。推荐餐厅：高桥鲍汁黄鳝坊。这家餐厅是崇明黄鳝的专业餐厅，提供各种美味的黄鳝料理，是品尝崇明黄鳝的不二之选。

白鹅炖蛋是崇明的一道养生佳肴。这道菜品选用崇明特产的白鹅肉，搭配鸡蛋炖制而成。白鹅肉滑嫩，鸡蛋蛋黄鲜美，是一道养生佳肴。推荐餐厅：白鹅炖蛋馆。这家餐厅是崇明白鹅炖蛋的专业餐厅，提供各种美味的白鹅炖蛋料理，是品尝崇明白鹅炖蛋的不二之选。

除了以上几道代表性菜品，崇明还有其他美食值得品尝。如崇明蟹粉汤、崇明烤鸭、崇明油炸花生等。这些美食都选用了当地的食材，运用独特的烹饪技艺，口感十分鲜美。

除了品尝美食，崇明的餐厅环境也十分优美。如位于崇明岛南部的"竹叶青风景区"内的"鱼巷餐厅"，这家餐厅环境清幽，建筑风格古朴，是品尝崇明美食的不错选择。还有位于崇明东部的"东滩古镇"内的"龙门客栈"，这家餐厅建筑风格古色古香，环境舒适宜人，让你在品尝美食的同时，也能享受到清幽的古镇风情。

崇明岛是一个集生态旅游和本土美食于一体的旅游胜地。在崇明旅游时，一定要品尝当地的美食佳肴，让你的旅行更加完美。除了以上代表性菜品，还有许多其他美食值得品尝。同时，崇明的餐厅环境也十分优美，让你在品尝美食的同时，也能享受到不同的风景和建筑风格。

译文

Chongming Island is a large island located in the northeast of Shanghai, famous for its ecotourism and local cuisine. This text will introduce the representative dishes and restaurants of Chongming's local cuisine, allowing you to not only enjoy the beautiful scenery but also taste authentic local delicacies during your trip to Chongming.

Chongming hairy crab is one of the representative local delicacies. During the crab fattening season every year, tourists come in droves to taste this delicious dish. This dish uses local hairy crabs, which have tender meat and full crab roe, making it one of Chongming's specialties. The best time to eat Chongming hairy crab is from August to November every year, which is the season when the crabs are at their fattest. Recommended restaurant: Chongming Hairy Crab Restaurant, which is a professional restaurant specializing in

Chongming hairy crab, providing various delicious hairy crab dishes and is the best choice for tasting Chongming hairy crab.

Gaoqiao braised eel in abalone sauce is another featured local cuisine of Chongming. This dish uses Chongming's special rice field eel, cooked with abalone sauce. The deliciousness of the abalone sauce and the tenderness of the rice field eel complement each other, leaving a lingering aftertaste. Recommended restaurant: Gaoqiao Braised Eel Restaurant, which is a professional restaurant specializing in Chongming rice field eel, providing various delicious rice field eel dishes and is the best choice for tasting Chongming rice field eel.

White goose stewed egg with white goose meat is a health-preserving delicacy in Chongming. This dish uses Chongming's special white goose meat, cooked with chicken eggs. The white goose meat is tender and the egg yolk is delicious, making it a health-preserving delicacy. Recommended restaurant: White Goose Stewed Egg Restaurant, which is a professional restaurant specializing in Chongming white goose stewed egg, providing various delicious white goose stewed egg dishes and is the best choice for tasting Chongming white goose stewed egg.

In addition to the above representative dishes, there are other delicacies in Chongming worth trying, such as Chongming crab powder soup, Chongming roast duck, and Chongming fried peanuts. These delicacies all use local ingredients and unique cooking techniques, with a very delicious taste.

In addition to tasting delicious food, the restaurants in Chongming also have beautiful environments. For example, the "Fish Alley Restaurant" located in the "Zhuyeqing Scenic Area" in the south of Chongming Island has a quiet environment and a quaint architectural style, making it a good choice for tasting Chongming cuisine. There is also the "Dragon Inn" located in the "Dongtan Ancient Town" in the east of Chongming Island. This restaurant has an ancient architectural style and a comfortable environment, allowing you to enjoy both delicious food and the quiet charm of an ancient town.

Chongming Island is a tourist destination that combines ecotourism and local cuisine. When traveling to Chongming, you must taste the local delicacies, making your trip more perfect. In addition to the representative dishes introduced above, there are many other delicacies worth trying. At the same time, the restaurants in Chongming also have beautiful environments, allowing you to enjoy different scenery and architectural styles while tasting delicious food.

例句赏析

例1：

原文： 崇明大闸蟹是崇明的代表性美食之一。每年的蟹肥时节，游客们络绎不绝地来品尝这一美味佳肴。这道菜品选用当地的大闸蟹，肉质鲜美、膏黄丰满，是崇明的特色之一。崇明大闸蟹的最佳食用时间是每年的 8 月到 11 月，此时正是大闸蟹肥美的时节。推荐餐厅：崇明大闸蟹馆。这家餐厅是崇明大闸蟹的专业餐厅，提供各种美味的大闸蟹料理，是品尝崇明大闸蟹的不二之选。

译文： Chongming hairy crab is one of the representative local delicacies. During the crab fattening season every year, tourists come in droves to taste this delicious dish. This dish uses local hairy crabs, which have tender meat and full crab roe, making it one of Chongming's specialties. The best time to eat Chongming hairy crab is from August to November every year, which is the season when the crabs are at their fattest. Recommended restaurant: Chongming Hairy Crab Restaurant, which is a professional restaurant specializing in Chongming hairy crab, providing various delicious hairy crab dishes and is the best choice for tasting Chongming hairy crab.

赏析： 本段介绍了崇明大闸蟹的最佳食用时间和餐厅。中文选段措辞简练精致，第二句中的"络绎不绝"用于形容游客数量众多且源源不断，译文译作"come in droves"，既表达了人数众多，又呈现出动作的持续性。第三句中的"肉质鲜美""膏黄丰满"则选择使用非限制性定语从句进行翻译。而在最后，文段推荐了一家专营餐厅，译文用 specialize in 这一词组来表达"专门经营"这一含义。

例2：

原文： 高桥鲍汁黄鳝是另一道崇明的特色美食。这道菜品选用崇明特产的黄鳝，搭配鲍汁烹制而成。鲍汁的鲜美和黄鳝的滑嫩相得益彰，让人回味无穷。推荐餐厅：高桥鲍汁黄鳝坊。这家餐厅是崇明黄鳝的专业餐厅，提供各种美味的黄鳝料理，是品尝崇明黄鳝的不二之选。

译文： Gaoqiao braised eel in abalone sauce is another featured local cuisine of Chongming. This dish uses Chongming's special rice field eel, cooked with abalone sauce. The deliciousness of the abalone sauce and the tenderness of the rice field eel complement each other, leaving a lingering aftertaste. Recommended restaurant: Gaoqiao Braised Eel Restaurant, which is a professional restaurant specializing in Chongming rice field eel, providing various delicious rice field eel dishes and is the best choice for tasting Chongming rice field eel.

赏析：本段主要介绍高桥鲍汁黄鳝，从选材、品尝到推荐餐厅，一应俱全。首先，该道菜名的翻译就颇有难度。该道菜品的主角是黄鳝，烹饪方式是用鲍汁炖煮，而高桥则是上海一地名。因此在翻译菜名的时候，这些元素均得译出，不得直译，所以译文译作"Gaoqiao braised eel in abalone sauce"。原文第三句用了两个成语，即相得益彰和回味无穷，简练而精准地描述了这道菜的品味非凡。译文以"complement"为主动词，表现了这两味原材料互为补充、相互衬托的属性，同时以 leaving a lingering aftertaste 为伴随状语，描述一种不断回味、不断萦绕的美味记忆。

例3：

原文：除了品尝美食，崇明的餐厅环境也十分优美。如位于崇明岛南部的"竹叶青风景区"内的"鱼巷餐厅"，这家餐厅环境清幽，建筑风格古朴，是品尝崇明美食的不错选择。还有位于崇明东部的"东滩古镇"内的"龙门客栈"，这家餐厅建筑风格古色古香，环境舒适宜人，让你在品尝美食的同时，也能享受到清幽的古镇风情。

译文：In addition to tasting delicious food, the restaurants in Chongming also have beautiful environments. For example, the "Fish Alley Restaurant" located in the "Zhuyeqing Scenic Area" in the south of Chongming Island has a quiet environment and a quaint architectural style, making it a good choice for tasting Chongming cuisine. There is also the "Dragon Inn" located in the "Dongtan Ancient Town" in the east of Chongming Island. This restaurant has an ancient architectural style and a comfortable environment, allowing you to enjoy both delicious food and the quiet charm of an ancient town.

赏析：本段主要推荐崇明岛上环境优美的美食餐厅。首先，餐厅名称的翻译是一个难点。"鱼巷餐厅"采用直译的方式译为"Fish Alley Restaurant"，而"龙门客栈"则采用意译的手法，"龙门客栈"背后有一个典故，那就是电影《龙门客栈》，许多中国人是通过该部电影才知道"龙门客栈"的。因此该店名是引用了这一典故，所以在店名的翻译上应体现这一特点，按照电影的英文名，将"龙门客栈"译为"Dragon Inn"。因为这些餐厅环境优美，因此原文中有许多关于环境的描写，例如"环境清幽""风格古朴"，而译文则选用"quiet""quaint"来表现清幽和古朴，十分贴切。

☞ **练习**

（一）将下列短语翻译成英文。

1. 鲍汁焖鳝鱼

2. 大闸蟹

3. 黄鳝

4. 本土美食

5. 独特的烹饪技巧

(二)将下列句子翻译成英文。

1. 每年的八月到十一月是吃崇明大闸蟹的最佳时间,因为这时螃蟹最肥美。

2. 这些美食都采用当地的原料和独特的烹饪技巧,味道非常美味。

3. 除了品尝美食,崇明的餐厅还有优美的环境。

(三)将下面段落翻译成英文。

崇明岛以生态旅游和本土美食闻名。岛上有许多值得品尝的美食,如崇明大闸蟹、高桥鲍汁黄鳝和白鹅炖蛋。崇明大闸蟹是当地的代表性美食之一。每年的螃蟹肥满季节,游客们都会前来品尝这道美味佳肴。此菜肴使用当地的大闸蟹,肉质鲜嫩、蟹黄丰满,是崇明的特色之一。吃崇明大闸蟹的最佳时间是每年的八月到十一月,这是螃蟹最肥美的季节。推荐餐厅:崇明大闸蟹餐厅,这是一家专业从事崇明大闸蟹的餐厅,提供各种美味的大闸蟹菜肴,是品尝崇明大闸蟹的最佳选择。

☞ **参考答案**

(一)

1. braised eel in abalone sauce

2. hairy crab

3. rice field eel

4. local delicacies

5. unique cooking techniques

(二)

1. The best time to eat Chongming hairy crab is from August to November every year, which is the season when the crabs are at their fattest.

2. These delicacies all use local ingredients and unique cooking techniques, with a very delicious taste.

3. In addition to tasting delicious food, the restaurants in Chongming also have beautiful environments.

(三)

Chongming Island is renowned for its ecotourism and local cuisine. The island boasts of several delicacies that are worth trying, such as Chongming hairy crab, Gaoqiao braised eel in abalone sauce, and white goose stewed egg with white goose meat. Chongming hairy crab is one of the representative local delicacies. During the crab fattening season every year, tourists come in droves to taste this delicious dish. This dish uses local hairy crabs, which have tender meat and full crab roe, making it one of Chongming's specialties. The best time to eat Chongming hairy crab is from August to November every year, which is the season when the crabs are at their fattest. Recommended restaurant: Chongming Hairy Crab Restaurant, which is a professional restaurant specializing in Chongming hairy crab, providing various delicious hairy crab dishes and is the best choice for tasting Chongming hairy crab.

三、崇明本土美食的制作方法和食用技巧

翻译简介

本文介绍了崇明本土美食的制作方法和使用技巧，非常翔实。在翻译的过程中，译文需要特别注意菜肴名称、食品制作过程的翻译。本文还对每种美食做了详细的口感描述，译文通过不同的形容词来区分口感的细微差别，同时采用并列结构、with 短语结构、分词短语作伴随状语等结构来描绘不同的口感和质地。译文还采用了不同的动词来描述制作过程中的具体动作，如用 sprinkle 来翻译"沾上……"，具体而自然。

词汇表

高桥鲍汁黄鳝坊：Gaoqiao Braised Eel in Abalone Sauce

蟹粉汤：crab powder soup

油炸花生：fried peanuts

崇明糕：Chongming Cake

糯米粉：glutinous rice flour

红糖：brown sugar

芝麻：sesame seeds

椰子丝：coconut shreds

崇明芦笋：Chongming asparagus

渔家乐：Fish Fun

豆腐花：tofu pudding

　　烤肠：grilled sausage

原文

　　崇明岛是上海市东北部的一个大岛，以其优美的生态环境和多样的本土美食而著名。在这个岛上，游客可以欣赏到美丽的自然风光，同时也可以品尝到地道的美食佳肴。本文将介绍崇明本土美食的代表性菜品和餐厅，让您在前往崇明旅游时，不仅能够感受到大自然的魅力，还能够满足您的味蕾。

崇明大闸蟹

　　崇明大闸蟹是崇明最著名的美食之一。每年的螃蟹肥美季节，岛上的餐厅都会供应这种蟹。崇明大闸蟹的肉质鲜美、膏黄丰满，是崇明特产的代表之一。这种蟹的最佳食用时间是每年的 8 月到 11 月。当地人通常会将大闸蟹煮熟后直接食用，不加任何调料。而在餐厅里，大闸蟹则会被处理成各种精美的料理。如果您想尝一尝正宗的崇明大闸蟹，推荐您去崇明大闸蟹馆，那里是崇明螃蟹的专业餐厅。

崇明黄鳝

　　崇明黄鳝是崇明的另一道特色美食。这种黄鳝生活在崇明岛的水道中，肉质鲜嫩、汁液丰富，被誉为"江南第一黄鳝"。这种食材的最佳食用时间是每年的 5 月到 7 月。崇明的餐厅通常会将黄鳝烹调成许多精美的菜肴，如高桥鲍汁黄鳝、黄鳝炒饭等。如果您想品尝正宗的崇明黄鳝，推荐您去高桥鲍汁黄鳝坊，那里是崇明黄鳝的专业餐厅。

崇明烤鸭

　　崇明烤鸭是一道特色的崇明菜肴。这种烤鸭是由崇明特有的天鹅鸭制成的，肉质鲜嫩、皮脆肉嫩。崇明的餐厅通常会将烤鸭切成薄片，搭配葱花和酱料一起食用。如果您想品尝正宗的崇明烤鸭，推荐您去崇明烤鸭王，那里是崇明烤鸭的专业餐厅。

崇明蟹粉汤

　　崇明蟹粉汤是一道以崇明大闸蟹为主要材料的汤。这种汤的制作方法比较烦琐，需要选用蟹黄鲜美、肉质鲜嫩的崇明大闸蟹，再加入鸡汤和其他食材一起炖煮。这种汤的味道鲜美，非常适合在秋季食用。如果您想品尝正宗的崇明蟹粉汤，推荐您去崇明蟹粉汤馆，那里是崇明蟹粉汤的专业餐厅。

崇明油炸花生

崇明油炸花生是崇明的一道小吃，也是当地人喜欢的零食之一。这种花生选用的是当地产的花生，经过油炸后，口感酥脆、香气四溢。崇明的餐厅通常会将油炸花生作为开胃菜或零食供应。如果您想品尝正宗的崇明油炸花生，可以去崇明岛上的各个小吃摊点或餐厅尝试。

崇明糕

崇明糕是崇明岛上的一道传统美食，以其口感绵软、味道香甜而受到当地人和游客的喜爱。这种糕点主要由糯米粉和红糖制成，是一种健康美味的小吃。以下是崇明糕的制作方法和食用建议。

制作方法：

准备好糯米粉和红糖，按照 2 : 1 的比例混合在一起。

慢慢加入适量的水，搅拌成糊状。

将混合好的糊倒入蒸锅中，用中火蒸 30 分钟。

将蒸好的糕切成小块，放入碟子里备用。

在锅中加入适量的清水和红糖，煮至糖溶解。

将糖水倒入碟子中的糕上，让糕吸收糖水。

最后，放入冰箱冷藏，等到凉爽后即可食用。

食用建议：

崇明糕可以直接食用，也可以与其他小吃搭配食用，如崇明油炸花生、崇明豆腐等。崇明糕口感绵软，不粘牙，味道香甜，非常适合作为下午茶或零食。如果您想更加丰富口感，可以将糕切成小块，沾上芝麻或椰丝等佐料食用。崇明糕还可以作为节日礼品或纪念品送给朋友和家人，展示当地的风土人情和美食文化。

在崇明岛上，您可以在当地的小吃摊点、餐厅和超市等地方购买到崇明糕。其中，以位于崇明岛南部的"崇明糕王"最为著名，这家店的崇明糕口感细腻、味道浓郁，是品尝崇明糕的不错选择。此外，还有位于岛东部的"东滩古镇"内的"崇明糕屋"，这家店的崇明糕口感软糯、甜度适中，也是不容错过的美食店铺。

总之，崇明岛的美食文化非常丰富多彩，每一道菜肴都有其独特的风味和制作工艺。在崇明旅游时，您一定不能错过品尝当地的美食佳肴，让您的旅行更加完美。

译文

Chongming Island is a large island located in the northeast of Shanghai, famous for its beautiful ecological environment and diverse local cuisine. On this island, tourists can enjoy the beautiful natural scenery and also taste authentic local delicacies. This chapter will introduce the representative dishes and restaurants of Chongming's local cuisine, allowing you to not only enjoy the beauty of nature but also satisfy your taste buds.

Chongming Hairy Crab

Chongming Hairy Crab is one of the most famous local delicacies. Every year during the crab fattening season, restaurants on the island serve this crab. Chongming Hairy Crab has tender meat and full crab roe, making it one of the specialties of Chongming. The best time to eat Chongming Hairy Crab is from August to November every year. Locals usually eat the crab boiled without any seasoning. In restaurants, the crab is processed into various exquisite dishes. If you want to taste authentic Chongming Hairy Crab, it is recommended that you go to Chongming Hairy Crab Restaurant, which is a professional restaurant specializing in Chongming Hairy Crab.

Chongming Rice Field Eel

Chongming rice field eel is another featured local cuisine of Chongming. This eel lives in the waterways of Chongming Island, with tender meat and rich juice, known as "the first rice field eel in Jiangnan". The best time to eat this ingredient is from May to July every year. Restaurants in Chongming usually cook rice field eel into many exquisite dishes, such as Gaoqiao Braised Eel in Abalone Sauce and Rice Field Eel Fried Rice. If you want to taste authentic Chongming rice field eel, it is recommended that you go to Gaoqiao Braised Eel Restaurant, which is a professional restaurant specializing in Chongming rice field eel.

Chongming Roast Duck

Chongming Roast Duck is a featured Chongming dish. This roast duck is made from the unique swan goose of Chongming Island, with tender meat and crispy skin. Restaurants in Chongming usually cut the roast duck into thin slices, served with scallions and sauce. If you want to taste authentic Chongming Roast Duck, it is recommended that you go to Chongming

Roast Duck King, which is a professional restaurant specializing in Chongming Roast Duck.

Chongming Crab Powder Soup

Chongming Crab Powder Soup is a soup made mainly from Chongming Hairy Crab. The production method of this soup is relatively complicated, requiring the use of fresh and tender Chongming Hairy Crab roe and meat, along with chicken soup and other ingredients stewed together. This soup has a delicious taste and is very suitable for consumption in autumn. If you want to taste authentic Chongming Crab Powder Soup, it is recommended that you go to Chongming Crab Powder Soup Restaurant, which is a professional restaurant specializing in Chongming Crab Powder Soup.

Chongming Fried Peanuts

Chongming Fried Peanuts is a snack in Chongming and also one of the favorite snacks of locals. This peanut uses locally produced peanuts, which are fried until crispy and fragrant. Restaurants in Chongming usually serve fried peanuts as an appetizer or snack. If you want to taste authentic Chongming Fried Peanuts, you can try them at various snack stalls or restaurants on Chongming Island.

Chongming Cake

Chongming Cake is a traditional delicacy on Chongming Island, loved by locals and tourists for its soft texture and sweet taste. This cake is mainly made of glutinous rice flour and brown sugar, making it a healthy and delicious snack. Below are the production methods and consumption recommendations for Chongming Cake.

Production Method:

Prepare glutinous rice flour and brown sugar, mix them together in a ratio of 2 : 1.

Slowly add a suitable amount of water and stir into a paste.

— Pour the mixed paste into a steamer and steam over medium heat for 30 minutes.

— Cut the steamed cake into small pieces and put them in a dish for later use.

— Add a suitable amount of water and brown sugar to the pot, and cook until the sugar is dissolved.

— Pour the sugar water onto the cake in the dish, allowing the cake to absorb the sugar water.

— Finally, put it in the refrigerator to cool before eating.

Serving Suggestions：

Chongming cake can be eaten directly or paired with other snacks such as Chongming fried peanuts and Chongming tofu. The cake has a soft texture, is not sticky to the teeth, and has a sweet aroma, making it ideal as an afternoon tea or snack. If you want to enhance the flavor, you can cut the cake into small pieces and sprinkle sesame seeds or coconut shreds on top. Chongming cake can also be given as a festival gift or souvenir to friends and family, showcasing local customs and cuisine.

On Chongming Island, you can buy Chongming cake at local snack stalls, restaurants, and supermarkets. Among them, "Chongming Cake King" located in the south of Chongming Island is the most famous. The cakes there have a delicate texture and rich flavor, making it a great choice for tasting Chongming cake. In addition, there is "Chongming Cake House" in "Dongtan Ancient Town" in the east of the island. The cakes there have a soft and chewy texture with moderate sweetness, also a must-try food spot.

In summary, Chongming Island's culinary culture is very rich and colorful, with each dish having its unique flavor and production process. When traveling to Chongming Island, you must not miss tasting local delicacies to make your trip more perfect.

例句赏析

例1：

原文：崇明油炸花生是崇明的一道小吃，也是当地人喜欢的零食之一。这种花生选用的是当地产的花生，经过油炸后，口感酥脆、香气四溢。崇明的餐厅通常会将油炸花生作为开胃菜或零食供应。如果您想品尝正宗的崇明油炸花生，可以去崇明岛上的各个小吃摊点或餐厅尝试。

译文：Chongming Fried Peanuts is a snack in Chongming and also one of the favorite snacks of locals. This peanut uses locally produced peanuts, which are fried until crispy and fragrant. Restaurants in Chongming usually serve fried peanuts as an appetizer or snack. If you want to taste authentic Chongming Fried Peanuts, you can try them at various snack stalls or restaurants on Chongming Island.

赏析：该段中文主要介绍了崇明油炸花生的制作。中文第二句，详细地说明了油炸花生的制作过程。译文用 crispy 和 fragrant 来翻译"口感酥脆""香气四溢"，着重描述油炸的程度，并以这部分作为定语从句修饰"peanuts"，使得整个句子的节奏变得更为舒缓均衡。原文第三句提到"将……作为……供应"，翻译时将其译为"serve...as..."，该短语在饮食翻译中十分常见，"serve"本身亦有服务之义，因而十分贴切。

例2:

原文:崇明糕可以直接食用,也可以与其他小吃搭配食用,如崇明油炸花生、崇明豆腐等。崇明糕口感绵软,不粘牙,味道香甜,非常适合作为下午茶或零食。如果您想更加丰富口感,可以将糕切成小块,沾上芝麻或椰丝等佐料食用。崇明糕还可以作为节日礼品或纪念品送给朋友和家人,展示当地的风土人情和美食文化。

译文:Chongming cake can be eaten directly or paired with other snacks such as Chongming fried peanuts and Chongming tofu. The cake has a soft texture, is not sticky to the teeth, and has a sweet aroma, making it ideal as an afternoon tea or snack. If you want to enhance the flavor, you can cut the cake into small pieces and sprinkle sesame seeds or coconut shreds on top. Chongming cake can also be given as a festival gift or souvenir to friends and family, showcasing local customs and cuisine.

赏析:该段中文着重描写崇明糕的口感和食用方式。中文第一句提及"搭配食用",译文译成 be paired with,"pair"有成双成对的意思,在这里用作动词,表示"一起食用"的意思。后一句讲到崇明糕的口感,颇为细致,翻译时尤需注意。译文将口感绵软、不粘牙、味道香甜作为谓语进行并列,最后以 make 的复合结构作为伴随状语,描述油炸花生在餐食中的地位。原文第三句运用了非常具体的动词,如"切成小块、沾上",译文则将其翻译为 cut...into pieces, sprinkle,颇为传神。

例3:

原文:在崇明岛上,您可以在当地的小吃摊点、餐厅和超市等地方购买到崇明糕。其中,以位于崇明岛南部的"崇明糕王"最为著名,这家店的崇明糕口感细腻、味道浓郁,是品尝崇明糕的不错选择。此外,还有位于岛东部的"东滩古镇"内的"崇明糕屋",这家店的崇明糕口感软糯、甜度适中,也是不容错过的美食店铺。

译文:On Chongming Island, you can buy Chongming cake at local snack stalls, restaurants, and supermarkets. Among them, "Chongming Cake King" located in the south of Chongming Island is the most famous. The cakes there have a delicate texture and rich flavor, making it a great choice for tasting Chongming cake. In addition, there is "Chongming Cake House" in "Dongtan Ancient Town" in the east of the island. The cakes there have a soft and chewy texture with moderate sweetness, also a must-try food spot.

赏析:该段中文介绍了售卖崇明糕的店铺。其中"崇明糕王""崇明糕屋"最为知名,分别译作 Chongming Cake King 和 Chongming Cake House。译文对两家店铺的评价也用了不同的措辞,一为 a great choice,一为 a must-try food spot,丰富了词汇,符合英文表达习惯。该段中文对于口感的描述甚为细致,"口感细腻、味道浓郁",译文使用的是并列结构,即 a delicate texture and rich flavor;"口感软糯、甜度适中",译文则使用 with 短语结构进行复合，即 a soft and chewy texture with moderate sweetness。可见译文在选词及表达结构上，进行了不同程度的选择，这也是英文常见的表达习惯。

☞ 练习

(一)将下列短语翻译成英文。

1. 油炸花生

2. 崇明糕

3. 红糖

4. 高桥鲍汁黄鳝坊

5. 糯米粉

(二)将下列句子翻译成英文。

1. 崇明岛的自然风景非常优美，吸引了很多游客前来观光。

2. 崇明大闸蟹是崇明岛的特产之一，非常美味。

3. 在高桥鲍汁黄鳝坊，你可以品尝到正宗的崇明黄鳝。

4. 崇明糕是一种传统的小吃，口感甜美，深受当地人喜爱。

5. 竹叶青风景区是崇明岛上最著名的旅游景点之一。

(三)将下面段落翻译成英文。

崇明岛是上海市辖区内唯一的县级市，位于长江口南岸，与上海市区隔江相望。岛上生态环境优美，拥有丰富的自然资源和特色美食。崇明大闸蟹、高桥鲍汁黄鳝坊、糯米粉、崇明豆腐等都是岛上著名的美食。此外，岛上还有竹叶青风景区、东滩古镇等旅游景点，吸引了众多游客前来观光游玩。

☞ 参考答案

(一)

1. fried peanuts

2. Chongming Cake

3. brown sugar

4. Gaoqiao Braised Eel in Abalone Sauce

5. glutinous rice flour

(二)

1. The natural scenery of Chongming Island is very beautiful, attracting many tourists to visit.

2. Chongming Hairy Crab is one of the specialties of Chongming Island and is very

delicious.

3. At Gaoqiao Braised Eel in Abalone Sauce, you can taste authentic Chongming rice field eel.

4. Chongming Cake is a traditional snack with a sweet taste and is deeply loved by locals.

5. Zhuyeqing Scenic Area is one of the most famous tourist attractions on Chongming Island.

(三)

Chongming Island is the only county-level city within the jurisdiction of Shanghai, located on the south bank of the Yangtze River, facing Shanghai across the river. The island has a beautiful ecological environment and abundant natural resources and local delicacies, such as Chongming Hairy Crab, Gaoqiao Braised Eel in Abalone Sauce, glutinous rice flour, and Chongming tofu. In addition, there are tourist attractions such as Zhuyeqing Scenic Area and Dongtan Ancient Town on the island, which attract many tourists to visit and enjoy.

第七章　崇明生态交通

一、崇明交通基础设施的现状和发展趋势

翻译简介

本文主要介绍了崇明交通基础设施的现状和发展趋势。本文译文整体质量较高，翻译准确、表达清晰。在用词方面，翻译选用的词语准确，符合语境，没有出现明显的语义偏差。在句子结构方面，翻译采用了和原文相似的结构，使得翻译后的文章语法正确、通顺。在语言风格方面，翻译采用了简洁明了的语言风格，使得翻译后的文章易于理解。译者考虑到中英文化的差异，对一些文化难点进行了合理的处理，使得翻译后的文章符合西方读者的阅读习惯和文化背景。在翻译技巧与策略方面，译者运用适当的翻译技巧和策略，如音译、意译、加注等，使得翻译后的文章更加准确、通顺、易于理解。在修辞方面，译者考虑到原文的修辞手法，在翻译时进行了恰当的转化和处理。

词汇表

长江口：mouth of the Yangtze River

经济：economy

交通基础设施：transportation infrastructure

公路：highway

水上交通：water transportation

公共交通：public transportation

崇明大桥：Chongming Bridge

乡村道路：rural roads

狭窄的道路和公路：narrow roads and highways

绿化覆盖率：greening coverage

交通拥堵：traffic congestion

道路宽敞整洁：spacious and clean roads

交通管理有序：orderly traffic management

水环境保护：water environment protection

湿地生态系统：wetland ecosystem

水生态环境：water ecological environment

地铁：subway

隧道：tunnel

生态交通：ecological transportation

空气污染：air pollution

噪音污染：noise pollution

旅游资源：tourism resources

可持续发展：sustainable development

原文

崇明区是上海市东北部的一个重要区域，位于长江口的崇明岛上。近年来，随着经济的快速发展，崇明交通基础设施建设也取得了显著发展。本文将介绍崇明交通基础设施的现状和发展趋势，包括公路、水上交通、公共交通等形式。

公路交通

崇明区的公路交通发展迅速，目前已经形成了以 S2 崇启高速公路为骨架的公路网络。例如，崇明大桥作为长江口地区的重要桥梁，极大地提高了崇明与上海市区之间的交通便利性。此外，崇明还加强了乡村道路的建设，提高了乡村交通条件。例如，几年前，崇明只有一些狭窄的道路和公路，绿化程度不高，交通拥堵严重。但现在，崇明区的道路宽敞整洁，交通管理有序，绿化覆盖率也在不断提高，为居民和游客提供了更加便利、舒适的交通环境。

水上交通

崇明岛作为长江口的一个重要岛屿，具有丰富的水上交通资源。近年来，崇明加强了与长江沿岸城市的联系，开辟了一批新的水上航线。例如，崇明至南通、崇明至启东等航线的开通，为崇明的旅游业发展带来了新的机遇。另外，崇明还积极开展水域环境保护，保护和修复了长江口湿地生态系统，提高了水域生态环境质量。这些措施对保护长江口地区的生态环境和水上交通安全具有重要意义。

公共交通

在公共交通方面，崇明区政府高度重视公共交通系统的建设，不断完善公共交通设施。目前，崇明区已经形成了以公交为主体，出租车、自行车等多种出行方式相辅相成的公共交通体系。例如，崇明区政府推出的"1.5 小时通勤圈"计划，为居民提供了更加便捷的通勤方式。此外，崇明区还推广低碳出行，推出了公共自行车、电动汽车等多项环保措施，提高了居民和游客的出行体验。

地铁和地下隧道

未来，崇明交通基础设施的建设将进一步完善，一些重要的交通项目也正在规划和建设中。例如，上海市政府正在推进通往崇明岛的地铁建设，计划建设 3 号线和 22 号线，预计于 2024 年开通运营。另外，崇明区政府还计划建设南门隧道，连接崇明岛南门和上海市嘉定区，进一步提高崇明与上海市区的交通便利性。这些交通项目的建设将进一步完善崇明的交通网络，为崇明的旅游业和经济发展带来新的机遇。

崇明生态交通的意义和挑战

随着人们对生态环境的重视程度的不断提高，崇明生态交通的建设也成了崇明区政府的一项重要任务。崇明生态交通的建设既有意义，也面临挑战。

意义

崇明生态交通的建设对于保护崇明岛生态环境具有重要意义。通过加强公共交通的建设，鼓励低碳出行，减少机动车辆的使用，可以有效降低空气污染和噪音污染，保护崇明岛的生态环境。此外，加强水上交通的建设，可以促进长江口地区的旅游业发展，带动区域经济的快速发展。

挑战

崇明生态交通的建设面临着一些挑战。首先，崇明岛与上海市区相距较远，交通运输成本较高。其次，崇明岛的地理条件比较特殊，岛上的道路和桥梁建设存在一定的难度。再次，崇明岛的旅游资源丰富，但交通基础设施建设相对滞后，旅游交通不畅也成为崇明生态交通建设的一大挑战。

崇明生态交通的未来展望

未来，随着崇明生态旅游的快速发展，崇明生态交通的建设也将迎来新的机遇。崇明区政府将进一步完善公路、水上交通和公共交通等多种交通方式，加快地铁和地下隧道等重要交通项目的建设，为崇明生态旅游的发展提供更加便捷、舒适、安全的交通保障。同时，崇明区政府还将加强交通管理，加强对生态环境的保护，促进崇明生态旅游的可持续发展。

译文

Chongming District is an important area in the northeast of Shanghai, located on Chongming Island at the mouth of the Yangtze River. In recent years, with the rapid development of the economy, significant achievements have been made in the construction of transportation infrastructure in Chongming. This text will introduce the current situation and development trend of transportation infrastructure in Chongming, including various forms such as highways, water transportation, and public transportation.

Highway Transportation

The development of highway transportation in Chongming District has been rapid, and a highway network has been formed with S2 Chongming-Qidong Expressway as the backbone. For example, Chongming Bridge, as an important bridge in the Yangtze River Delta region, has greatly improved the transportation convenience between Chongming and Shanghai. In addition, Chongming has strengthened the construction of rural roads and improved rural transportation conditions. For example, a few years ago, Chongming only had narrow roads and highways with low greening coverage and serious traffic congestion. But now, the roads in Chongming District are spacious and clean, traffic management is orderly, and greening coverage is constantly improving, providing residents and tourists with a more convenient and comfortable transportation environment.

Water Transportation

As an important island at the mouth of the Yangtze River, Chongming Island has abundant water transportation resources. In recent years, Chongming has strengthened its connection with cities along the Yangtze River and opened up a batch of new water routes. For example, the opening of routes such as Chongming to Nantong and Chongming to Qidong has brought new opportunities for the development of tourism in Chongming. In addition, Chongming actively carries out water environment protection, protects and restores the wetland ecosystem of the Yangtze River estuary, and improves the quality of the water ecological environment. These measures are of great significance for protecting the ecological environment and water transportation safety in the Yangtze River Delta region.

Public Transportation

Regarding public transportation, the Chongming District government attaches great importance to the construction of the public transportation system and continuously improves public transportation facilities. Currently, Chongming District has formed a public transportation system with buses as the main mode of transportation, complemented by taxis, bicycles, and other modes of transportation. For example, the Chongming District government has launched the "1. 5-hour commuting circle" plan, which provides residents with a more convenient way to commute. In addition, Chongming also promotes low-carbon travel and has introduced a number of environmental protection measures such as public bicycles and electric cars, improving the travel experience for residents and tourists.

Subway and Underground Tunnels

In the future, the construction of Chongming's transportation infrastructure will be further improved, and some important transportation projects are also being planned and constructed. For example, the Shanghai municipal government is promoting the construction of a subway to Chongming Island, planning to build Line 3 and Line 22, which is expected to open in 2024. In addition, the Chongming District government plans to build the Nanmen Tunnel, connecting the south gate of Chongming Island and Jiading District in Shanghai, further improving the transportation convenience between Chongming and Shanghai. The construction of these transportation projects will further improve Chongming's transportation network, bringing new opportunities for Chongming's tourism industry and economic development.

The Significance and Challenges of Chongming's Ecological Transportation

As people's attention to the ecological environment continues to increase, the construction of Chongming's ecological transportation has become an important task for the Chongming District government. The construction of Chongming's ecological transportation has both significance and challenges.

Significance

The construction of ecological transportation in Chongming Island is of great significance for protecting the ecological environment of Chongming Island. By strengthening the construction of public transportation, encouraging low-carbon travel, and reducing the use of motor vehicles, it can effectively reduce air and noise pollution and protect the ecological environment of Chongming Island. In addition, strengthening the construction of water transportation can promote the development of tourism in the Yangtze River estuary region and drive the rapid development of the regional economy.

Challenges

The construction of ecological transportation in Chongming Island faces some challenges. Firstly, Chongming Island is far away from the urban area of Shanghai, and transportation costs are relatively high. Secondly, the geographical conditions of Chongming Island are relatively special, and there are certain difficulties in the construction of roads and bridges on the island. Thirdly, Chongming Island has rich tourism resources, but the construction of transportation infrastructure is relatively lagging behind, and the inconvenience of tourism transportation has also become a major challenge for the construction of ecological transportation in Chongming.

Future Prospects for Ecological Transportation in Chongming

In the future, with the rapid development of ecological tourism in Chongming, the construction of ecological transportation in Chongming will also usher in new opportunities. The Chongming District Government will further improve various transportation methods such as highways, water transportation, and public transportation, accelerate the construction of important transportation projects such as subways and underground tunnels, and provide more convenient, comfortable, and safe transportation guarantees for the development of ecological tourism in Chongming. At the same time, the Chongming District Government will also strengthen traffic management, protect the ecological environment, and promote the sustainable development of ecological tourism in Chongming.

例句赏析

例 1：

原文： 但现在，崇明区的道路宽敞整洁，交通管理有序，绿化覆盖率也在不断提高，为居民和游客提供了更加便利、舒适的交通环境。

译文： But now, the roads in Chongming District are spacious and clean, traffic management is orderly, and greening coverage is constantly improving, providing residents and tourists with a more convenient and comfortable transportation environment.

赏析： 从这个句子来看，该句子的翻译质量较高，符合翻译的基本原则和技巧。首先，译者在语言风格上采用了与原文相似的语言风格，使得翻译后的句子与原文保持一致。其次，在翻译过程中，译者在用词方面准确地传达了原文的意思，并且使用了适当的形容词来描述崇明区的道路、交通管理和绿化覆盖率等方面的情况。此外，在翻译句子结构方面，译者采用了与原文类似的语序，使得翻译后的句子更加自然流畅。最后，该句子的翻译效果良好，能够准确地传达原文的意思，同时也符合英语读者的阅读习惯和表达习惯。总之，译文体现了翻译的基本原则和技巧，同时也体现了译者对语言和文化的敏感度和理解能力。

例 2：

原文： 另外，崇明还积极开展水域环境保护，保护和修复了长江口湿地生态系统，提高了水域生态环境质量。

译文： In addition, Chongming actively carries out water environment protection, protects and restores the wetland ecosystem of the Yangtze River estuary, and improves the quality of the water ecological environment.

赏析： 这段译文是一句简单的陈述句，主要讲述了崇明在开展水域环境保护方面所做的工作。整个句子结构清晰，表达简洁明了，符合英语表达的习惯。译者使用了"actively carries out"表达崇明在保护水域环境方面的积极性，同时使用"protects and restores"表达崇明在保护长江口湿地生态系统方面所做的工作，另外，使用了"improves the quality of the water ecological environment"表达崇明在提高水域生态环境质量方面的成果。整个翻译过程中，译者注重表达原文的信息，并且在语言风格、修辞等方面也做了一些适当的调整，使得译文更符合英语的表达习惯，同时也更加准确地传达了原文的信息。整体来说，这句话的翻译质量较高，符合翻译的基本原则和技巧。

例 3：

原文： 崇明区政府将进一步完善公路、水上交通和公共交通等多种交通方式，加快地铁和地下隧道等重要交通项目的建设，为崇明生态旅游的发展提供更加便捷、舒适、安全的交通保障。

译文： The Chongming District Government will further improve various transportation methods such as highways, water transportation, and public transportation, accelerate the construction of important transportation projects such as subways and underground tunnels, and provide more convenient, comfortable, and safe transportation guarantees for the development of ecological tourism in Chongming.

赏析： 该段中文篇幅较长，包含了崇明区政府将进一步完善公路、水上交通和公共交通等多种交通方式，加快地铁和地下隧道等重要交通项目的建设，为崇明生态旅游的发展提供更加便捷、舒适、安全的交通保障等多个信息。本段译文则较好地表达了原文的意思，同时也遵循了翻译的基本原则，如忠实原文。在用词方面，译文使用了较为简单明了的词汇，如 improve，transportation，subways，comfortable 等，符合英文表达的语言风格。句子结构方面，译文采用并列句的结构，通过逗号来分隔不同的信息，使句子结构清晰明了，易于理解。在翻译技巧与策略方面，译文采用了类比和概括的翻译方法，将原文的"公路、水上交通和公共交通等多种交通方式"译为"various transportation methods such as highways，water transportation，and public transportation"，将"提供更加便捷、舒适、安全的交通保障"译为"provide more convenient，comfortable，and safe transportation guarantees"，使翻译更加贴近英文表达习惯。

☞ **练习**

（一）将下列短语翻译成英文。

1. 长江口地区

2. 农村道路

3. 交通拥堵

4. 公共交通系统

5. 低碳出行

6. 生态旅游

7. 水运资源

8. 水环境保护

9. 交通管理

10. 可持续发展

（二）将下列句子翻译成英文。

1. 随着经济的快速发展，崇明交通基础设施建设取得了显著成就。

2. 崇明岛地理条件比较特殊，在岛上修路、建桥存在一定难度。

3. 崇明区政府重视公共交通系统的建设，并不断完善公共交通设施。

4. 崇明区政府计划修建南门隧道，进一步提高崇明与上海之间的交通便利性。

5. 崇明生态交通的建设面临着一些挑战。

(三)将下面段落翻译成英文。

　　未来，随着崇明生态旅游的快速发展，崇明生态交通建设也将迎来新的机遇。崇明区政府将进一步完善各种交通方式，如公路、水运和公共交通，加快地铁和地下隧道等重要交通项目的建设，为崇明生态旅游发展提供更为便捷、舒适、安全的交通保障。同时，崇明区政府还将加强交通管理，保护生态环境，推动崇明生态旅游的可持续发展。

☞ **参考答案**

(一)

1. Yangtze River Delta region

2. rural roads

3. traffic congestion

4. public transportation system

5. low-carbon travel

6. ecological tourism

7. water transportation resources

8. water environment protection

9. traffic management

10. sustainable development

(二)

1. With the rapid development of the economy, significant achievements have been made in the construction of transportation infrastructure in Chongming.

2. The geographical conditions of Chongming Island are relatively special, and there are certain difficulties in the construction of roads and bridges on the island.

3. The Chongming District government attaches great importance to the construction of the public transportation system and continuously improves public transportation facilities.

4. The Chongming District Government plans to build the Nanmen Tunnel, connecting the south gate of Chongming Island and Jiading District in Shanghai, further improving the transportation convenience between Chongming and Shanghai.

5. The construction of ecological transportation in Chongming Island faces some challenges.

（三）

In the future, with the rapid development of ecological tourism in Chongming, the construction of ecological transportation in Chongming will also usher in new opportunities. The Chongming District Government will further improve various transportation methods such as highways, water transportation, and public transportation, accelerate the construction of important transportation projects such as subways and underground tunnels, and provide more convenient, comfortable, and safe transportation guarantees for the development of ecological tourism in Chongming. At the same time, the Chongming District Government will also strengthen traffic management, protect the ecological environment, and promote the sustainable development of ecological tourism in Chongming.

二、崇明交通出行安全问题及解决方案

翻译简介

本文是一篇关于崇明区交通安全的文章，主要介绍了崇明区政府为了保障居民的出行安全，采取了一系列的措施，包括加强交通安全教育和宣传、改善交通设施、加强交通执法、推广智能交通技术等。本文的用词、句子结构和语言风格简洁明了，符合新闻报道的风格。翻译时，译者在尽可能保留原文意思的基础上，采用了简洁明了的表达方式，使得译文易于理解。同时，译者采用了一些翻译技巧和策略，如在翻译"宣传活动"时，采用了"publicity activities"的表达方式，更加准确地表达了原文的意思。另外，译文中也体现了翻译原则，如在翻译"道路交通安全"时，采用了"road traffic safety"的表达方式，更加符合英语表达习惯。总体来说，本文的翻译质量较高，能够准确地传达原文的意思，并且符合英语表达习惯，使得英语读者易于理解。

词汇表

安全问题：safety issues

居民出行：residents' travel

交通安全教育：traffic safety education

宣传：publicity

交通安全知识：traffic safety knowledge

交通安全演习：traffic safety drills

交通安全意识：awareness of traffic safety

交通规则：traffic rules

交通安全教育课程：traffic safety education courses

道路运输设施：road transportation facilities

道路容量：road capacity

道路安全：road safety

道路设施维护：road facilities maintenance

交通标志和标线：traffic markings and signs

非机动车道：non-motorized lanes

行人和非机动车辆安全：pedestrian and non-motorized vehicle safety

交通执法：traffic law enforcement

交警部门：Traffic Police Department

交通违规行为：traffic violations

酒后驾驶：drunk driving

超速行驶：speeding

交通秩序：traffic order

智能交通技术：intelligent transportation technology

信息化和智能化建设：informatization and intelligent construction

现代技术：modern technology

交通管理效率：traffic management efficiency

智能交通信号系统：intelligent traffic signal systems

协调控制：coordinated control

实时监测和分析：real-time monitoring and analysis

交通流量：traffic flow

交通事故：traffic accidents

交通违规行为数据：traffic violations data

科学依据：scientific basis

交通管理决策：traffic management decision-making

绿色出行：green travel

公共交通和骑行：public transportation and cycling

低碳和环保的出行方式：low-carbon and environmentally friendly travel methods

机动车尾气排放的监管：regulation of motor vehicle exhaust emissions

新能源汽车的推广：promotion of the use of new energy vehicles

环境污染：environmental pollution

综合科学保障：comprehensively and scientifically guaranteed

原文

随着崇明岛交通基础设施的快速发展，交通安全问题也逐渐浮现出来。为了确保居民的出行安全，崇明区政府采取了一系列有效的措施。

首先，加强交通安全宣传教育。通过举办交通安全知识讲座、开展交通安全演练等活动，增强居民的交通安全意识。例如，在学校开展交通安全教育课程，教育学生从小养成遵守交通规则的良好习惯。此外，崇明区政府还在社区、企业等场所开展交通安全宣传活动，让更多的人了解交通安全知识。

其次，完善交通设施。崇明区政府不断投资改善道路交通设施，提升道路通行能力和安全性。例如，加强道路设施维护，设置交通标线、标志等，确保道路畅通无阻。在此基础上，崇明区政府还加强了交通设施的更新和改造，例如，增加了人行道和非机动车道，提高了行人和非机动车的交通安全。

再次，加大交通执法力度。崇明区交警部门加强对交通违法行为的查处，营造良好的交通秩序。例如，严查酒驾、超速等交通违法行为，切实保障道路交通安全。在加强交通执法力度的同时，崇明区政府还加强了对交通违法行为的宣传，让更多人了解交通违法行为的危害性，自觉遵守交通规则。

此外，崇明区政府还推广了智能交通技术，积极推动交通信息化、智能化建设，利用现代科技手段提高交通管理效率。例如，安装智能交通信号系统，实现车辆与信号灯的协同控制，提高通行效率。还有，崇明区政府还建设了交通管理中心，实现了对交通流量、交通事故、交通违法行为等数据的实时监控和分析，为交通管理决策提供科学依据。

通过上述措施，崇明区政府在交通安全方面取得了显著的成效。据统计，崇明岛的道路交通事故率已连续多年保持下降趋势。未来，崇明区政府将继续关注交通安全问题，不断完善交通管理策略，打造绿色生态的交通体系。

在实现交通安全的同时，崇明区政府还注重绿色出行的推广。例如，崇明区政府大力推广公共交通和自行车出行，鼓励居民采取低碳、环保的出行方式。此外，崇明区政府还加强了对机动车尾气排放的监管，推广新能源汽车的使用，减少交通对环境的污染。

综上所述，交通安全是崇明岛发展的重要问题。崇明区政府将继续加强交通安全宣传教育、完善交通设施、加大交通执法力度、推广智能交通技术等措施，为居民提供安全、便捷的出行环境。同时，崇明区政府还注重绿色出行的推广，为实现可持续发展作出贡献。相信在崇明区政府的不断努力下，崇明岛的交通安全和出行环境将会得到更加全面、更加科学的保障。

译文

With the rapid development of transportation infrastructure on Chongming Island, traffic safety issues have gradually emerged. In order to ensure the safety of residents' travel, the Chongming District Government has taken a series of effective measures.

Firstly, strengthening traffic safety education and publicity. By organizing lectures on traffic safety knowledge and conducting traffic safety drills, residents' awareness of traffic safety is enhanced. For example, traffic safety education courses are conducted in schools to educate students to develop good habits of obeying traffic rules from an early age. In addition, the Chongming District Government also carries out traffic safety publicity activities in communities, enterprises, and other places to increase people's understanding of traffic safety knowledge.

Secondly, improving transportation facilities. The Chongming District Government continues to invest in improving road transportation facilities to enhance road capacity and safety. For example, road facilities maintenance is strengthened, and traffic markings and signs are installed to ensure smooth traffic flow. Based on this, the Chongming District Government has also strengthened the renovation and upgrading of transportation facilities, such as adding sidewalks and non-motorized lanes, improving pedestrian and non-motorized vehicle safety.

Thirdly, increasing traffic law enforcement efforts. The Chongming District Traffic Police Department strengthens the investigation and handling of traffic violations to create a good traffic order. For example, strict enforcement against drunk driving, speeding, and other traffic violations to effectively ensure road traffic safety. While strengthening traffic law enforcement, the Chongming District Government also enhances the publicity of traffic violations, allowing more people to understand the harm of traffic violations and consciously abide by traffic rules.

In addition, the Chongming District Government also promotes intelligent transportation technology and actively promotes the informatization and intelligent construction of transportation, using modern technology to improve traffic management efficiency. For example, installing intelligent traffic signal systems to achieve coordinated control between vehicles and traffic lights, improving traffic efficiency. In addition, the Chongming District Government has also established a traffic management center to realize real-time monitoring and analysis of traffic flow, traffic accidents, traffic violations, and other data, providing scientific basis for traffic management decision-making.

Through the above measures, the Chongming District Government（CDG）has achieved significant results in traffic safety. According to statistics, the road traffic accident rate on Chongming Island has continued to decline for many years. In the future, CDG will continue to focus on traffic safety issues, continuously improve traffic management strategies, and create a green and ecological transportation system.

While ensuring traffic safety, CDG also pays attention to promoting green travel. For example, CDG vigorously promotes public transportation and cycling, encouraging residents to adopt low-carbon and environmentally friendly travel methods. In addition, CDG has strengthened the regulation of motor vehicle exhaust emissions, promoted the use of new energy vehicles, and reduced the environmental pollution caused by transportation.

In summary, traffic safety is an important issue for the development of Chongming Island. CDG will continue to strengthen traffic safety education and publicity, improve transportation facilities, increase traffic law enforcement efforts, promote intelligent transportation technology, and provide residents with a safe and convenient travel environment. At the same time, CDG also emphasizes the promotion of green travel and contributes to sustainable development. It is believed that with the continuous efforts of CDG, the traffic safety and travel environment on Chongming Island will be comprehensively and scientifically guaranteed.

例句赏析

例1:

原文：在加强交通执法力度的同时，崇明区政府还加强了对交通违法行为的宣传，让更多人了解交通违法行为的危害性，自觉遵守交通规则。

译文：While strengthening traffic law enforcement, the Chongming District Government also enhances the publicity of traffic violations, allowing more people to understand the harm of traffic violations and consciously abide by traffic rules.

赏析：在翻译该段原文时，原文中"加强交通执法力度"和"加强了对交通违法行为的宣传"两个动作是并列的，而译者使用了"while"这个连词来连接两个动作，表示这两个动作是同时进行的。此外，在翻译"让更多人了解交通违法行为的危害性，自觉遵守交通规则"时，译者采用了"allowing more people to"这个结构，使得英文句子更加流畅自然。

例2:

原文：未来，崇明区政府将继续关注交通安全问题，不断完善交通管理策略，打造绿色生态的交通体系。

译文：In the future，the Chongming District Government will continue to focus on traffic safety issues，continuously improve traffic management strategies，and create a green and ecological transportation system.

赏析：在翻译该段原文时，原文中"绿色生态的交通体系"译者使用了"green and ecological transportation system"这个表达方式来翻译，其中"green"表示环保、低碳、节能等含义，而"ecological"则表示生态、可持续等含义。这样的翻译方式使得译文句子更加贴近原意，同时也符合英文读者对于交通体系环保和可持续性的关注。在用词方面，原文和译文都使用了比较常见的词汇，较少使用过于复杂的词汇。句子结构方面，原文使用了简单的主谓宾结构，而译文则使用了更多的并列结构。语言风格方面，原文和译文都比较客观、正式。

例3：

原文：崇明区政府将继续加强交通安全宣传教育、完善交通设施、加大交通执法力度、推广智能交通技术等措施，为居民提供安全、便捷的出行环境。

译文：The Chongming District Government will continue to strengthen traffic safety education and publicity，improve transportation facilities，increase traffic law enforcement efforts，promote intelligent transportation technology，and provide residents with a safe and convenient travel environment.

赏析：在翻译该段原文时，译者采用了直译和意译相结合的方法，尽可能地传达原文的意思。译文中使用了"strengthen""improve""increase""promote"等动词，与原文中的动词相对应。同时，译文中还使用了"traffic safety education and publicity""transportation facilities""traffic law enforcement efforts""intelligent transportation technology"等短语，与原文中列举的措施相对应。再就是，译文还使用了"residents""travel environment"等词汇，突出了政府的服务对象和服务目标。总的来说，译文比较准确、简洁、通顺，符合翻译的基本原则和技巧，在用词、句子结构、语言风格等方面也体现了较高的水平。

☞ **练习**

(一)将下列短语翻译成英文。

1. 交通安全教育和宣传

2. 道路交通设施

3. 交通法律执法力度

4. 智能交通技术

5. 绿色出行

(二)将下列句子翻译成英文。

1. 为了保障居民出行安全,崇明区政府采取了一系列有效措施。

2. 崇明区政府继续投资于改善道路交通设施,以增强道路容量和安全性。

3. 崇明区交警部门加强对交通违法行为的调查和处理,以创造良好的交通秩序。

4. 崇明区政府还推广智能交通技术,积极推进交通的信息化和智能化建设,利用现代技术提高交通管理效率。

5. 崇明区政府在确保交通安全的同时,也注重推广绿色出行。

(三)将下面段落翻译成英文。

其次,完善交通设施。崇明区政府不断投资改善道路交通设施,提升道路通行能力和安全性。例如,加强道路设施维护,设置交通标线、标志等,确保道路畅通无阻。在此基础上,崇明区政府还加强了交通设施的更新和改造,例如,增加了人行道和非机动车道,提高了行人和非机动车的交通安全。

☞ 参考答案

(一)

1. traffic safety education and publicity

2. road traffic facilities

3. traffic law enforcement efforts

4. intelligent transportation technology

5. green travel

(二)

1. In order to ensure the safety of residents' travel, the Chongming District Government has taken a series of effective measures.

2. The Chongming District Government continues to invest in improving road traffic facilities to enhance road capacity and safety.

3. The Chongming District Traffic Police Department strengthens the investigation and handling of traffic violations to create a good traffic order.

4. The Chongming District Government also promotes intelligent transportation technology, actively promotes the informatization and intelligent construction of transportation, and uses modern technology to improve traffic management efficiency.

5. While ensuring traffic safety, the Chongming District Government also pays attention to promoting green travel.

（三）

Secondly, improving transportation facilities. The Chongming District Government continues to invest in improving road transportation facilities to enhance road capacity and safety. For example, road facilities maintenance is strengthened, traffic markings and signs are installed to ensure smooth traffic flow. Based on this, the Chongming District Government has also strengthened the renovation and upgrading of transportation facilities, such as adding sidewalks and non-motorized lanes, improving pedestrian and non-motorized vehicle safety.

第八章　崇明生态教育

一、崇明生态教育的历史沿革和发展规划

翻译简介

　　本文是一篇关于崇明生态教育的文章，英文翻译质量较高，翻译准确，符合英语表达习惯。整篇文章用词准确，简洁明了，尤其在科技术语和教育术语的使用上，翻译得到了很好的体现。句子结构清晰，语言风格流畅自然，符合英语表达的规范和要求。在翻译过程中，译者采用了一些常见的翻译技巧和策略，如意译、加词、减词等，使得翻译更加符合英语表达的规范和习惯。在翻译原则方面，译者注重准确传达原文的意思，同时也考虑到英语表达的习惯和规范。整篇文章修辞效果好，表达清晰明了，能够准确地传达出原文的主旨和意图。

词汇表

　　生态岛：ecological island

　　生态文明：ecological civilization

　　生态教育：ecological education

　　历史演变：historical evolution

　　发展计划：development plan

　　环境保护：environmental protection

　　宣传：publicity

　　讲座：lectures

　　课程改革：curriculum reform

　　实践教学：practical teaching

上海市政府：Shanghai Municipal Government

实践活动：practical activities

网络：Internet

信息技术：information technology

环境设计：environmental design

可持续发展：sustainable development

人才支持：talent support

责任感：sense of responsibility

跨学科：interdisciplinary

原文

崇明岛是中国生态岛的典型代表，也是国家生态文明建设的重点区域。在崇明岛的生态保护和建设中，生态教育起着重要的作用。本文将介绍崇明生态教育的历史沿革和发展规划。

生态教育的历史沿革

崇明生态教育起源于 20 世纪 80 年代。当时，崇明岛的农村教育普及率很低，农民对环境保护的意识也很薄弱。为了增强农民的环保意识，提高其生态文明素质，崇明岛开始推广生态教育。最初的生态教育主要是通过宣传、讲座等形式来普及环保知识，但效果不尽如人意。

随着时间的推移，崇明生态教育开始注重实践教学和课程设置。1997 年，上海市政府在崇明岛试行了"生态岛小学"计划。该计划通过改革课程设置和教学方法，将生态教育渗透到各个学科中去，并通过实践活动来培养学生的环保意识和实践能力。这一尝试得到了广泛认可，为崇明生态教育的发展奠定了基础。2001 年，崇明县成为上海市第一个被国家环保总局正式命名的国家级生态示范区。2002 年 11 月，崇明县编制《崇明岛域总体规划》。2005 年 5 月，国务院批复长兴、横沙两岛划归崇明县；7 月，上海市委批准"生态崇明"功能定位；10 月，上海市政府批准通过《崇明三岛总体规划》。

2007 年 4 月 12 日，时任上海市委书记习近平到崇明调研村镇工作，并指导社会主义新农村建设；是年，崇明创建国家级生态县启动。2008 年 4 月，崇明岛国家地质公园建成开园。2009 年 10 月 31 日，上海长江隧桥建成通车。2010 年 1 月，上海市政府公布《崇明生态岛建设纲要（2010—2020 年）》；9 月，崇明县被授予"中国长寿之乡"称号。2011 年 7

月，崇明县获得"国家绿色能源示范县"称号。

2016 年至 2018 年，在美丽乡村建设、创建卫生城市、全国农村振兴计划、创建国家级文明城区、迎接花博会召开等一系列专题工作与重大活动的带动下，崇明区努力建设清洁、优美、文明、宜居的生态岛行动不松懈、目标更坚定、品质持续提升，使崇明三岛真正成为崇德明礼、近悦远来的长江口生态明珠。

崇明生态教育的发展规划

近年来，随着生态文明建设的不断深入，崇明生态教育也在不断发展和完善。为了更好地推广生态文明理念，崇明岛制定了一系列生态教育发展规划：

1. 提高生态教育课程的质量和深度。崇明岛将加强生态教育课程的设置和教学质量，让学生更全面地了解生态环境和生态保护的重要性。

2. 推进生态教育与实践相结合。崇明岛将加强生态实践活动的组织和管理，提升学生的实践能力，增强其生态保护意识。

3. 建立生态教育网络。崇明岛将通过互联网和其他信息技术手段，推广生态教育理念和知识，让更多的人了解、关注并参与生态保护。

贤达学院的环境设计学院与崇明生态教育的关系

贤达学院的环境设计学院致力于培养具有生态保护意识和创新能力的环境设计人才。在学院教育中，学生将接触到许多环保和可持续发展的理念，学院也鼓励学生在各种项目中探索生态友好的设计方法。这与崇明生态教育的理念不谋而合，也为崇明生态教育的发展提供了人才支持。

崇明生态教育的历史沿革和发展规划表明，崇明岛已经将生态教育作为一项重要的工作来推进。通过不断改进和完善，崇明岛将生态教育融入各个方面，并取得了显著的成效。生态教育的重要性不仅在于增强人们的环保意识，更在于培养人们的实践能力和责任心，推动生态文明建设的不断发展。

贤达学院的环境设计学院与崇明生态教育的紧密联系也表明，生态教育已经成为一个跨学科、跨领域的领域。未来，我们需要更加注重生态教育的发展和传播，让更多的人了解、关注并参与生态保护，共同建设一个美丽的地球家园。

译文

As a typical Chinese ecological island, Chongming Island is a key area for national ecological civilization construction. Ecological education plays an important role in the ecological protection and construction of Chongming Island. This section will introduce the historical evolution and development plan of Chongming ecological education.

History of Ecological Education

Chongming ecological education originated in the 80s of the 20th century. At that time, the popularity of rural education on Chongming Island was at a low level, and most farmers did not realize the importance of environmental protection. In order to improve farmers' awareness of environmental protection and the quality of ecological civilization, Chongming Island began to promote ecological education. The initial ecological education was mainly through publicity, lectures and other forms to popularize environmental protection knowledge, but the effect was not satisfactory.

Over time, Chongming Ecological Education began to focus on practical teaching and curriculum. In 1997, the Shanghai Municipal Government piloted the "Eco-Island Primary School" program on Chongming Island. The program infiltrates ecological education into various disciplines by reforming the curriculum and teaching methods, and cultivates students' environmental awareness and practical ability through practical activities. This attempt has been widely recognized and laid the foundation for the development of ecological education in Chongming.

In 2001, Chongming County became the first national-level ecological demonstration zone in Shanghai, officially designated by the State Environmental Protection Administration. In November 2002, Chongming County formulated the "Chongming Island Master Plan". In May 2005, the State Council approved the incorporation of Changxing and Hengsha Islands into Chongming County. In July, the Shanghai Municipal Committee approved the functional positioning of "Ecological Chongming". In October, the Shanghai Municipal Government approved the Chongming Three Islands Master Plan.

On April 12, 2007, Xi Jinping, then Secretary of the Shanghai Municipal Committee, visited Chongming to investigate rural and township development and provided guidance on the construction of a new socialist countryside. That same year, Chongming initiated the process of establishing itself as a national-level ecological county. In April 2008, the Chongming Island National Geopark was officially opened. On October 31, 2009, the Shanghai Yangtze River Tunnel and Bridge were completed and opened to traffic. In January 2010, the Shanghai Municipal Government released the Chongming Eco-Island Construction Plan (2010−2020). In September of the same year, Chongming County was awarded the title of "China's Hometown of Longevity". In July 2011, Chongming County was designated as a "National Green Energy Demonstration County".

From 2016 to 2018, propelled by a series of major initiatives and key events—including the Beautiful Countryside Construction Program, the establishment of a Hygienic City, the National Rural Revitalization Plan, the development of a National Civilized District, and preparations for the China Flower Expo—Chongming District remained steadfast in its commitment to building a clean, beautiful, civilized, and livable ecological island. With unwavering determination and continuous improvement in quality, Chongming's three islands have truly become an ecological pearl at the mouth of the Yangtze River, a place of virtue and harmony that attracts visitors from near and far.

Development Plan for Chongming Ecological Education

In recent years, with the continuous deepening of ecological civilization construction, Chongming ecological education has also been continuously developing and improving. In order to better promote the concept of ecological civilization, Chongming Island has formulated a series of development plans for ecological education:

1. Improve the quality and depth of ecological education courses. Chongming Island will strengthen the setting and teaching quality of ecological education courses, allowing students to have a more comprehensive understanding of the importance of the ecological environment and ecological protection.

2. Promote the combination of ecological education and practice. Chongming Island will strengthen the organization and management of ecological practice activities, enhance students' practical abilities and ecological protection awareness.

3. Establish an ecological education network. Chongming Island will promote the concept and knowledge of ecological education through the Internet and other information technology means, allowing more people to understand, pay attention to, and participate in ecological protection.

The Relationship Between Xianda College's School of Environmental Design and Chongming Ecological Education

Xianda College's School of Environmental Design is committed to cultivating environmentally conscious and innovative environmental design talents. In the education of the college, students will be exposed to many concepts of environmental protection and sustainable development, and the college also encourages students to explore eco-friendly design methods in various projects. This coincides with the concept of Chongming Ecological Education and provides talent support for the development of Chongming Ecological Education.

The historical evolution and development plan of Chongming's ecological education indicate that Chongming Island has made ecological education a significant endeavor. Through continuous improvement and refinement, Chongming Island has integrated ecological education into various aspects and achieved remarkable results. The importance of ecological education lies not only in raising people's environmental awareness but also in cultivating their practical abilities and sense of responsibility, promoting the continuous development of ecological civilization.

The close connection between the Environmental Design College of Xianda College and Chongming's ecological education also demonstrates that ecological education has become an interdisciplinary and cross-disciplinary field. In the future, we need to pay more attention to the development and dissemination of ecological education, allowing more people to understand, care about, and participate in ecological conservation, and jointly build a beautiful home for the Earth.

例句赏析

例1：

原文：该计划通过改革课程设置和教学方法，将生态教育渗透到各个学科中去，并通过实践活动来培养学生的环保意识和实践能力。

译文：The program infiltrates ecological education into various disciplines by reforming the curriculum and teaching methods, and cultivates students' environmental awareness and practical ability through practical activities.

赏析：在翻译该段中文时，译者将原文中的"生态教育"和"环保意识"这两个概念译成了"ecological education"和"environmental awareness"，这两个翻译都比较准确地传达了原文的含义。此外，译者还使用了"infiltrates"这一词汇来表达"渗透"的意思，比较生动地展现了该计划将生态教育融入各个学科的过程。在翻译技巧与策略方面，译者尽可能地准确传达原文的含义，并且保持语言风格的一致性。此外，译者还需考虑句子结构和修辞手法，以确保翻译的流畅性和表达效果。

例2：

原文：崇明岛将通过互联网和其他信息技术手段，推广生态教育理念和知识，让更多的人了解、关注并参与生态保护。

译文：Chongming Island will promote the concept and knowledge of ecological education through the Internet and other information technology means, allowing more people to understand, pay attention to, and participate in ecological protection.

赏析：该段中文表达清晰、语言简洁。从用词、句子结构、语言风格等方面来看，原文使用了简单明了的句子结构和通俗易懂的词汇，使得整个句子易于理解。译文则采用了类似的句子结构和词汇，使得翻译后的句子与原文表达基本保持一致，没有明显的中英文化差异。从翻译技巧与策略、翻译原则等方面来看，译者主要采用直译和意译相结合的方法，保证了翻译的准确性和流畅度。从修辞、表达效果等方面来看，整个译文表达简洁明了，符合科技和生态环保的主题，既传递了信息，也具有一定的感染力。

例3：

原文：生态教育的重要性不仅在于增强人们的环保意识，更在于培养人们的实践能力和责任心，推动生态文明建设的不断发展。

译文：The importance of ecological education lies not only in raising people's environmental awareness but also in cultivating their practical abilities and sense of responsibility, promoting the continuous development of ecological civilization.

赏析：在翻译该段中文时，译者不仅需要理解原文的意思，还要对用词、句子结构、语言风格加以重视。在用词方面，译者需要根据原文的意思选择合适的英文词汇。例如，原文中的"生态教育""环保意识""实践能力"和"责任心"等词汇都需要被准确地翻译出来。在翻译过程中，译者还需注意一些修辞手法，如译文中使用"lies not only in…but also in…"这样的结构，来强调生态教育的重要性。在句子结构方面，译者需要根据英语语法规则来调整句子结构，以使得译文更加符合英语读者的阅读习惯。例如，原文中，"不仅在于……更在于……"这样的结构在英语中不太常见，因此译者需要重新组织句子结构，使得译文更加流畅。在语言风格方面，译者需要注意用语要简洁明了，还要符合英语表达的习惯。例如，原文中"推动生态文明建设的不断发展"可以被译为"promoting the continuous development of ecological civilization"，这样的表达方式更符合英语表达的习惯。总之，该段的翻译中需要考虑多个方面的问题，包括用词、句子结构、语言风格、中英文化的异同、翻译技巧与策略、翻译原则、修辞、表达效果等。这些都需要译者作出权衡取舍，以达到最佳的翻译效果。

☞ **练习**

（一）将下列短语翻译成英文。

1. 生态文明建设

2. 生态教育

3. 环境保护意识

4. 实践教学

5. 课程改革

6. 网络推广

7. 可持续发展

8. 环保设计

(二)将下列句子翻译成英文。

1. 崇明岛是中国生态岛的典型代表，也是国家生态文明建设的重点区域。

2. 在崇明岛的生态保护和建设中，生态教育起着重要的作用。

3. 最初的生态教育主要是通过宣传、讲座等形式来普及环保知识，但效果不尽如人意。

4. 该计划通过改革课程设置和教学方法，将生态教育渗透到各个学科中去，并通过实践活动来培养学生的环保意识和实践能力。

(三)将下面段落翻译成英文。

近年来，随着生态文明建设的不断深入，崇明生态教育也在不断发展和完善。为了更好地推广生态文明理念，崇明岛制定了一系列生态教育发展计划：

1. 提高生态教育课程的质量和深度。崇明岛将加强生态教育课程的设置和教学质量，让学生更全面地了解生态环境和生态保护的重要性。

2. 推广生态教育与实践相结合。崇明岛将加强生态实践活动的组织和管理，增强学生的实践能力和环境保护意识。

3. 建立生态教育网络。崇明岛将通过互联网和其他信息技术手段推广生态教育的理念和知识，让更多的人了解、关注和参与生态保护。

☞ 参考答案

(一)

1. ecological civilization construction

2. ecological education

3. environmental protection awareness

4. practical teaching

5. curriculum reform

6. network promotion

7. sustainable development

8. environmental design

（二）

1. As a typical Chinese ecological island, Chongming Island is a key area for national ecological civilization construction.

2. Ecological education plays an important role in the ecological protection and construction of Chongming Island.

3. The initial ecological education was mainly through publicity, lectures and other forms to popularize environmental protection knowledge, but the effect was not satisfactory.

4. The program infiltrates ecological education into various disciplines by reforming the curriculum and teaching methods, and cultivates students' environmental awareness and practical ability through practical activities.

（三）

In recent years, with the continuous deepening of ecological civilization construction, Chongming ecological education has also been continuously developing and improving. In order to better promote the concept of ecological civilization, Chongming Island has formulated a series of development plans for ecological education:

1. Improve the quality and depth of ecological education courses. Chongming Island will strengthen the setting and teaching quality of ecological education courses, allowing students to have a more comprehensive understanding of the importance of the ecological environment and ecological protection.

2. Promote the combination of ecological education and practice. Chongming Island will strengthen the organization and management of ecological practice activities, enhance students' practical abilities and ecological protection awareness.

3. Establish an ecological education network. Chongming Island will promote the concept and knowledge of ecological education through the Internet and other information technology means, allowing more people to understand, pay attention to, and participate in ecological protection.

二、崇明的生态教育理念和课程设置

翻译简介

本文的翻译整体质量较高，符合中英文化的表达。在用词方面，译文使用了一些专业术语，如"ecological environmental protection""ecology""environmental science""ecological economy"等，使得翻译更加准确。在句子结构方面，译文采用了与原文相似的结构，使得翻译具有较高的可读性。在语言风格方面，译文使用了较为正式的语言风格，符合文章所描述的高等学府的形象。在翻译技巧与策略方面，译者采用了一些常用的翻译技巧，如同义词替换、重复使用某些关键词等，使得翻译更加准确、流畅。

词汇表

生态环境保护：ecological environmental protection

复合型人才：compound talents

教育理念：educational philosophy

人文性：humanistic nature

国际性：international nature

实践性：practical nature

生态学：ecology

环境科学：environmental science

生态经济：ecological economy

生态观念：ecological concept

分析和解决生态环境问题的能力：ability to analyze and solve ecological environmental problems

实践教学：practical teaching

课程实验：curriculum experiments

社会责任感：sense of social responsibility

生态示范区：ecological demonstration area

自然环境：natural environment

生态资源：ecological resources

实地考察：field trip

生态系统运作：ecosystem operation

植物的生长规律：growth laws of plants

环保科技实践课程：practical course on environmental protection technology

环保意识：environmental awareness

科技创新能力：technological innovation ability

环保志愿者组织：environmental volunteer organization

原文

生态环境保护是当今社会面临的重要问题之一，而贤达学院作为一所具有全球视野、创新思维和社会责任感的高等学府，一直致力于培养具有生态环保意识和能力的复合型人才。在教育理念上，贤达学院强调教育的人文性、国际性和实践性，以适应社会发展的需求。

在生态教育方面，贤达学院开设了一系列与生态环境保护相关的课程，例如生态学、环境科学、生态经济等，以帮助学生树立正确的生态观念，并培养他们分析和解决生态环境问题的能力。此外，学院还通过实践教学、课程实验等方式，让学生亲身参与生态环境保护项目，从而提高他们的实践能力和社会责任感。

崇明岛作为上海市的一个生态示范区，其独特的自然环境和丰富的生态资源成为贤达学院生态教育的重要场所之一。每年，学院都会组织学生前往崇明生态岛进行为期一周的实地考察，让学生了解生态岛的保护措施、生态系统运作等方面的知识。这种实践教学模式既增强了学生对生态教育的兴趣，也提高了他们的实际操作能力。

除了大学生，崇明岛的生态教育也涵盖了中小学生。崇明岛的大、中、小学在生态教育方面也有着丰富的经验和成果。例如，崇明岛第一小学开设了"绿色课堂"项目，通过种植、观察等方式，让学生了解植物的生长规律和生态系统的基本知识；崇明岛实验中学则在课程设置上增设了环保科技实践课程，让学生通过实践探究环保科技的原理和应用，提高他们的环保意识和科技创新能力。裕安中学地处崇明岛最东端的陈家镇，濒临崇明东滩鸟类国家级自然保护区，是一所普通的农村初级中学。该校始终坚守着崇明东滩湿地这一片教育的沃土，将东滩湿地作为培养"小生态人"的重要平台。

此外，崇明岛的生态教育还与社会各界密切合作，推动生态环保理念的普及和实践。例如，崇明岛的环保志愿者经常组织"绿色崇明"的成员到各个学校进行环保宣传和教育活动，让学生从小学习环保知识、形成环保习惯。

总之，崇明岛作为一个生态示范区，其丰富的生态资源和生态保护经验，成为贤达学院生态教育的重要场所之一。在崇明岛的实践教学和中小学的生态教育中，学生不仅能够获取生态知识，还能够提高实践能力和社会责任感，为未来的生态环保事业作出贡献。

译文

Ecological environmental protection is one of the important issues facing today's society, and Xianda College, as an institution of higher learning with global vision, innovative thinking and social responsibility, has been committed to cultivating compound talents with ecological environmental awareness and ability. In terms of educational philosophy, Xianda College emphasizes the humanistic, international and practical nature of education to meet the needs of social development.

In terms of ecological education, Xianda College offers a series of courses related to ecological environmental protection, such as ecology, environmental science, ecological economy, etc. , to help students establish correct ecological concepts and cultivate their ability to analyze and solve ecological environmental problems. In addition, the college also allows students to participate in ecological environmental protection projects through practical teaching, curriculum experiments, etc. , so as to improve their practical ability and sense of social responsibility.

As an ecological demonstration area in Shanghai, Chongming Island has become one of the important places for ecological education of Xianda College with its unique natural environment and rich ecological resources. Every year, the college organizes students to go to Chongming Eco-Island for a week-long field trip to let students understand the protection measures and ecosystem operation of the Eco-Island. This practical teaching mode not only enhances students' interest in ecological education, but also improves their practical ability.

In addition to college students, ecological education on Chongming Island also covers primary and secondary school students. Chongming Island's universities, middle schools and primary schools also have rich experience and achievements in ecological education. For example, Chongming Island No. 1 Primary School has set up a "green classroom" project, which allows students to understand the growth laws of plants and the basic knowledge of the ecosystem through planting and observation. Chongming Island Experimental Middle School has added a practical course on environmental protection technology to the curriculum, allowing students to explore the principles and applications of environmental protection technology through practice, so as to enhance their environmental awareness and technological innovation ability. Yu'an Middle School is located at the easternmost end of Chenjia Town on Chongming Island, adjacent to the Chongming East Beach National Nature Reserve for Birds. It is an ordinary rural junior high school. The school has always adhered to the rich educational soil of the East Beach Wetland, using it as an important platform for nurturing "little ecologists".

In addition, ecological education on Chongming Island also works closely with all sectors of society to promote the popularization and practice of ecological environmental protection concepts. For example, members of Chongming Island's environmental volunteer organization

Green Chongming often go to schools to carry out environmental protection publicity and education activities, so that students can learn environmental protection knowledge and form environmental habits from an early age.

In short, as an ecological demonstration area, Chongming Island has become one of the important places for ecological education of Xianda College with its rich ecological resources and ecological protection experience. In the practical teaching of Chongming Island and the ecological education of primary and secondary schools, students can not only acquire ecological knowledge, but also improve their practical ability and sense of social responsibility, and contribute to the future cause of ecological environmental protection.

例句赏析

例 1：

原文：在生态教育方面，贤达学院开设了一系列与生态环境保护相关的课程，例如生态学、环境科学、生态经济等，以帮助学生树立正确的生态观念，并培养他们分析和解决生态环境问题的能力。

译文：In terms of ecological education, Xianda College offers a series of courses related to ecological environmental protection, such as ecology, environmental science, ecological economy, etc., to help students establish correct ecological concepts and cultivate their ability to analyze and solve ecological environmental problems.

赏析：该段中文主要介绍了贤达学院开设的一系列与生态环境保护相关的课程，以及开设这些课程的目的和作用。在翻译该段原文时，译者使用了比较准确的词汇和句子结构，使得译文的表达效果比较清晰、简洁。同时，译者采用了一些翻译技巧和策略，如将"例如"翻译为"such as"，使得翻译更加符合英语表达习惯。在语言风格方面，译文比较符合英语的表达规范。例如，在中文中"生态经济"这个词汇可能比较常见，但是英文不太常用。因此，在翻译时，译者需要根据不同语言的表达习惯和文化背景作出适当的调整。

例 2：

原文：此外，学院还通过实践教学、课程实验等方式，让学生亲身参与生态环境保护项目，从而提高他们的实践能力和社会责任感。

译文：In addition, the college also allows students to participate in ecological environmental protection projects through practical teaching, curriculum experiments, etc., so as to improve their practical ability and sense of social responsibility.

　　赏析：该段文字是一句简单的陈述句，主要介绍学院通过实践教学和课程实验等方式，让学生亲身参与生态环境保护项目，从而提高他们的实践能力和社会责任感。翻译时，译者比较准确地传达了原文的意思，如"通过""实践教学""课程实验""生态环境保护项目""实践能力和社会责任感"等词都能被准确地翻译出来。译文的语言风格也比较清晰简洁，符合科技文献的风格。在翻译技巧和策略方面，译者使用了并列结构，将实践教学、课程实验等方式列举出来，使得句子更加清晰明了。在翻译原则方面，译者尽量保持了原文的语气和意思，几乎没有出现过误差。在修辞方面，译者通过列举方式，使得句子更加生动形象。

　　例 3：

　　原文：在崇明岛的实践教学和中小学的生态教育中，学生不仅能够获取生态知识，还能够提高实践能力和社会责任感，为未来的生态环保事业作出贡献。

　　译文：In the practical teaching of Chongming Island and the ecological education of primary and secondary schools, students can not only acquire ecological knowledge, but also improve their practical ability and sense of social responsibility, and contribute to the future cause of ecological environmental protection.

　　赏析：该段中文是一个较长的句子，翻译时，译者采用了比较精准的翻译方式，保留了原文的信息量和语言风格。在翻译过程中，译者首先把原文分解成三个并列部分，分别是"在崇明岛的实践教学和中小学的生态教育中""学生不仅能够获取生态知识，还能够提高实践能力和社会责任感""为未来的生态环保事业作出贡献"。这种翻译方式符合英文表达习惯，也更清晰地传达了原文的意思。在用词方面，译者运用了一些较为高级的词汇，如 practical，ecological，contribute 等，这些词汇恰当地表达了原文的含义。另外，译者还采用了一些翻译技巧和策略，如将"生态环保事业"译为"cause of ecological environmental protection"，强调了该事业的重要性和正义性。总体来说，该段文字的翻译比较精准、恰当，符合英文表达习惯，也保留了原文的语言风格和信息量。

☞ **练习**

　　(一)将下列短语翻译成英文。

　　1. 生态环保

　　2. 全球视野

　　3. 人文教育

　　4. 实践教学

5. 生态知识

6. 社会责任感

7. 环保科技

8. 生态资源

9. 环保宣传

(二)将下列句子翻译成英文。

1. 生态环保是当今社会面临的重要问题之一，而贤达学院作为具有全球视野、创新思维和社会责任感的高等教育机构，一直致力于培养具有生态环境意识和能力的复合型人才。

2. 贤达学院在教育理念上强调教育的人文性、国际性和实践性，以满足社会发展的需求。

3. 贤达学院提供了一系列与生态环境保护相关的课程，如生态学、环境科学、生态经济等，以帮助学生树立正确的生态观念，并培养他们分析和解决生态环境问题的能力。

4. 贤达学院允许学生通过实践教学、课程实验等参与生态环境保护项目，以提高他们的实践能力和社会责任感。

5. 作为上海的一个生态示范区，崇明岛以其独特的自然环境和丰富的生态资源成为先达学院生态教育的重要地点之一。

(三)将下面段落翻译成英文。

崇明岛作为上海市的一个生态示范区，其独特的自然环境和丰富的生态资源成为了贤达学院生态教育的重要场所之一。每年，学院都会组织学生前往崇明生态岛进行为期一周的实地考察，让学生了解生态岛的保护措施、生态系统运作等方面的知识。这种实践教学模式既增强了学生对生态教育的兴趣，也提高了他们的实际操作能力。

除了大学生，崇明岛的生态教育也涵盖了中小学生。崇明岛的大、中、小学在生态教育方面也有着丰富的经验和成果。例如，崇明岛第一小学开设了"绿色课堂"项目，通过种植、观察等方式，让学生了解植物的生长规律和生态系统的基本知识；崇明岛实验中学则在课程设置上增设了环保科技实践课程，让学生通过实践探究环保科技的原理和应用，提高他们的环保意识和科技创新能力。

☞ 参考答案

(一)

1. ecological environmental protection

2. global vision

3. humanistic education

4. practical teaching

5. ecological knowledge

6. sense of social responsibility

7. environmental protection technology

8. ecological resources

9. environmental protection publicity

（二）

1. Ecological environmental protection is one of the important issues facing today's society, and Xianda College, as an institution of higher learning with global vision, innovative thinking and social responsibility, has been committed to cultivating compound talents with ecological environmental awareness and ability.

2. Xianda College emphasizes the humanistic, international and practical nature of education to meet the needs of social development.

3. Xianda College offers a series of courses related to ecological environmental protection, such as ecology, environmental science, ecological economy, etc., to help students establish correct ecological concepts and cultivate their ability to analyze and solve ecological environmental problems.

4. The college also allows students to participate in ecological environmental protection projects through practical teaching, curriculum experiments, etc., so as to improve their practical ability and sense of social responsibility.

5. As an ecological demonstration area in Shanghai, Chongming Island has become one of the important places for ecological education of Xianda College with its unique natural environment and rich ecological resources.

（三）

As an ecological demonstration area in Shanghai, Chongming Island has become one of the important places for ecological education of Xianda College with its unique natural environment and rich ecological resources. Every year, the college organizes students to go to Chongming Eco-Island for a week-long field trip to let students understand the protection measures and ecosystem operation of the Eco-Island. This practical teaching mode not only enhances students' interest in ecological education, but also improves their practical ability.

In addition to college students, ecological education on Chongming Island also covers primary and secondary school students. Chongming Island's universities, middle schools and primary schools also have rich experience and achievements in ecological education. For example, Chongming Island No. 1 Primary School has set up a "green classroom" project, which allows students to understand the growth laws of plants and the basic knowledge of the ecosystem through planting and observation. Chongming Island Experimental Middle School has added a practical course on environmental protection technology to the curriculum, allowing students to explore the principles and applications of environmental protection technology through practice, so as to enhance their environmental awareness and technological innovation ability.

三、崇明的师资力量和学术成果

翻译简介

本文是一篇关于环境设计学院的介绍，主要讲述了学院的师资力量、学术成果、参与的生态环境保护项目和专业特色等方面。在翻译原文的过程中，译者基本做到了准确传达原文的信息。在句子结构方面，译者采用了主谓宾的简单句和并列句等简洁明了的语言结构。在表达上也尽量保持了原文的逻辑关系和语言风格，使得译文更具可读性。同时，在关于一些专业术语和名词的翻译方面，译者能根据上下文和专业背景进行选择和转化，以确保译文的准确性和可读性。

词汇表

生态环境保护：ecological environment protection

师资力量：faculty strength

教师队伍：team of teachers

理论基础：theoretical foundation

生态环境保护和设计经验：ecological environment protection and design experience

国内外：domestically and internationally

学术成果：academic achievements

研究论文：research papers

生态系统评估：ecological system assessment

生态修复技术：ecological restoration technology

绿色建筑：green building

生态保护措施：ecological protection measures

生态岛：ecological island

生态大厦：ecological building

太阳能热水器：solar water heater

雨水收集系统：rainwater collection system

绿色墙壁：green wall

积极参与：actively participate in

生态教育：ecological education

基础知识：basic knowledge

保护方法：protection methods

实践机会：practical opportunities

可持续发展：sustainable development

原文

环境设计学院是贤达学院的重要学院之一，其专业特色是将生态环境保护与建筑设计相结合，致力于打造更加生态、环保的建筑环境。在师资力量方面，该学院拥有一支专业素质高、教学经验丰富的教师队伍。这些教师不仅具有扎实的理论基础，还拥有丰富的生态环境保护和设计经验，在国内外享有较高声誉。

在学术成果方面，环境设计学院的教师在生态环境领域取得了一系列显著的成就。近年来，学院教师发表了数十篇与生态环境保护相关的研究论文，其中一些论文在国际权威期刊上发表，受到业界的高度关注和认可。这些论文涉及生态系统评估、生态修复技术、绿色建筑等多个方面，为学院的教学和科研工作提供了重要的支撑和指导。

除了学术研究，环境设计学院还积极参与国内外的生态环境保护项目。例如，在崇明生态岛的保护与规划中，学院教师发挥了积极作用，提出了一系列切实可行的生态保护措施。这些保护措施既保障了崇明生态岛的生态环境，又将生态保护理念贯彻到了建筑设计中。

环境设计学院的专业特色是将生态环境保护与建筑设计相结合，致力于打造更加生态、环保的建筑环境。学院的教师和学生们在这一领域取得了许多重要成果。例如，学院的教师曾设计了一座名为"生态大厦"的建筑，该建筑采用了多种生态建筑技术，如太阳能热水器、雨水收集系统、绿色墙等，实现了建筑与环境的良性互动。这些生态建筑项目不仅体现了环境设计学院的专业特色，也为学生提供了宝贵的实践机会。

崇明岛的大、中、小学在生态教育方面也与环境设计学院有着紧密的联系。例如，崇明岛的实验中学在课程设置上增设了绿色建筑设计课程，让学生通过实践探究生态建筑的原理和应用，提高他们的环保意识和设计能力。崇明岛的小学也积极探索生态教育的方式和方法，通过采集、观察、实验等方式，让学生了解生态环境的基本知识和保护方法。这些生态教育项目既加强了学生对生态环境的认识，也为他们未来的学习和生活提供了有益的帮助。

总之，贤达学院环境设计学院的师资力量雄厚，学术成果丰硕，其在生态建筑的专业特色和贡献不容忽视。同时，崇明岛的大、中、小学也与环境设计学院有着密切的联系，在生态教育方面取得了不少成果。相信在生态保护和环境建设的道路上，贤达学院和崇明岛的师生们将继续努力，为推进可持续发展作出更多的贡献。

译文

The School of Environmental Design is one of the important schools of Xianda College. Its specialty is combining ecological environment protection with architectural design, aiming to create a more ecological and environmentally friendly building environment. In terms of faculty strength, the school has a team of highly qualified and experienced teachers. These teachers not only have a solid theoretical foundation but also have rich experience in ecological environment protection and design, enjoying a high reputation both domestically and internationally.

In terms of academic achievements, the teachers of the School of Environmental Design have made a series of significant achievements in the field of ecological environment. In recent years, the teachers of the school have published dozens of research papers related to ecological environment protection, some of which have been published in international authoritative journals and have received high attention and recognition from the industry. These papers cover various aspects such as ecological system assessment, ecological restoration technology, and green building, providing important support and guidance for the teaching and research of the school.

In addition to academic research, the School of Environmental Design actively participates in domestic and international ecological and environmental protection projects. For example, in the protection and planning of Chongming Ecological Island, the school's teachers played an active role and proposed a series of practical ecological protection measures. These protection measures not only safeguard the ecological environment of Chongming Ecological Island, but also incorporate ecological protection concepts into architectural design.

The professional feature of the School of Environmental Design is the combination of ecological environment protection and architectural design, dedicated to creating a more ecological and environmentally friendly building environment. The teachers and students of the school have achieved many important results in this field. For example, the teachers of the school have designed a building called "Ecological Building", which adopts various ecological building technologies such as solar water heaters, rainwater collection systems, and green walls, realizing a positive interaction between the building and the environment. These ecological building projects not only reflect the professional characteristics of the School of Environmental Design, but also provide valuable practical opportunities for students.

The primary, middle, and high schools on Chongming Island also have close ties with the School of Environmental Design at Xianda College in terms of ecological education. For example, Chongming Island Experimental High School has added a green building design course to its curriculum, allowing students to explore the principles and applications of ecological architecture through practice and improve their environmental awareness and design abilities. Chongming Island's primary schools also actively explore ways and methods of ecological education, allowing students to learn basic knowledge and protection methods of the ecological environment through methods such as collection, observation, and experimentation. These ecological education projects not only enhance students' understanding of the ecological environment but also provide useful help for their future learning and life.

In summary, the School of Environmental Design at Xianda College has strong teaching staff and fruitful academic achievements, and its professional characteristics and contributions in ecological architecture cannot be ignored. At the same time, the primary, middle, and high schools on Chongming Island also have close ties with the School of Environmental Design and have achieved many results in ecological education. It is believed that Xianda College and the teachers and students on Chongming Island will continue to work hard to make more contributions to promoting sustainable development on the road of ecological protection and environmental construction.

例句赏析

例1：

原文：这些论文涉及生态系统评估、生态修复技术、绿色建筑等多个方面，为学院的教学和科研工作提供了重要的支撑和指导。

译文：These papers cover various aspects such as ecological system assessment, ecological restoration technology, and green building, providing important support and guidance for the teaching and research of the school.

赏析：该译文对原文的翻译整体比较准确，符合中英文表达习惯。在用词上，译文中的"cover"恰当地表达了"涉及"的意思，而"various aspects"则与原文中的"多个方面"相对应。在句子结构上，译者使用了并列结构，使得句子更加简洁明了。在语言风格上，原文和译文都采用了比较正式的语言，符合学术研究的要求。在中英文化的异同方面，原文中的"生态系统评估""生态修复技术""绿色建筑"等词汇都是比较新近的学术名词，而翻译时采用了常见的英文表达方式，符合英语语境的表达要求。在翻译技巧与策略方面，译文采用了直译的方法，使得翻译更加准确。在翻译原则方面，译文保持了原文的信息量和语言风格，符合忠实传达原意的原则。在修辞方面，原文使用了"重要的支撑和指导"一词进行强调，而译文则使用了"providing important support and guidance"来表达这一意思。在表达效果方面，译文准确地传达了原文的信息，使得读者能够清晰地理解该句话所表达的意思。

例2：

原文：例如，学院的教师曾设计了一座名为"生态大厦"的建筑，该建筑采用了多种生态建筑技术，如太阳能热水器、雨水收集系统、绿色墙等，实现了建筑与环境的良性互动。

译文：For example, the teachers of the school have designed a building called "Ecological Building", which adopts various ecological building technologies such as solar water heaters, rainwater collection systems, and green walls, realizing a positive interaction between the building and the environment.

赏析：该段原文描述了一座名为"生态大厦"的建筑，该建筑采用了多种生态建筑技术，实现了建筑与环境的良性互动。从语言风格和修辞方面来看，原文使用了"名为""采用了""实现了"等动词来描述建筑和生态建筑技术之间的关系，这些动词都具有强调和修辞效果。在翻译该段原文时，译者保留了这些动词，使得翻译效果与原文在表达上更加一致。原文中还使用了"良性互动"这一修辞手法来描述建筑和环境之间的关系，译者也很好地将其传达了出来。从中英文化的异同来看，该段原文的"生态大厦"和"绿色墙"等词汇，译者则直接将其翻译成英文，没有进行拆词或注释。这种做法在一定程度上保留了原文的中文特色，同时也让英文读者更容易理解。

例3：

原文：这些生态教育项目既加强了学生对生态环境的认识，也为他们未来的学习和生活提供了有益的帮助。

译文：These ecological education projects not only enhance students' understanding of the ecological environment but also provide useful help for their future learning and life.

赏析：该段原文描述了生态教育项目对学生的影响，既加强了学生对生态环境的认识，也为他们未来的学习和生活提供了有益的帮助。在翻译该段原文时，译者非常准确地将原文的意思传达了出来，同时也采用了一些常见的翻译技巧和策略，如使用"not only...but also"这一并列结构来表达"既……又……"的意思，并使用"provide useful help"来表达"提供有益的帮助"。从语言风格和修辞方面来看，原文使用了"加强了""认识""未来的学习和生活"等词汇来描述生态教育项目对学生的影响，这些词汇都具有强调和修辞效果。在翻译过程中，译者也保留了这些词汇，使得翻译效果与原文在表达上更加一致。原文中还使用了"生态环境"等词汇来描述生态教育项目的主题，翻译时，译者使用了"ecological environment"这一表达方式来传达相同的意思。还有"生态教育项目"和"生态环境"等词汇译者也尽量采用比较通用的英文表达方式来传达相同的意思，使其与原文保持一致。

☞ 练习

（一）将下列短语翻译成英文。

1. 生态环境保护与建筑设计
2. 高素质有经验的教师队伍
3. 国内外享有很高声誉
4. 生态系统评估
5. 生态修复技术
6. 绿色建筑
7. 实用的生态保护措施
8. 积极参与国内外生态环境保护项目
9. 科学的生态环境教育

10. 环保意识和设计能力

(二)将下列句子翻译成英文。

1. 环境设计学院是西安大学的重要学院之一，专业是将生态环境保护与建筑设计相结合，旨在创造更加生态、环保的建筑环境。

2. 该学院拥有一支高素质有经验的教师队伍，这些教师不仅拥有扎实的理论基础，而且在生态环境保护和设计方面也拥有丰富的经验，在国内外享有很高声誉。

3. 环境设计学院的教师在生态环境领域取得了一系列重要成果。近年来，该学院的教师发表了数十篇与生态环境保护相关的研究论文，其中一些发表在国际权威期刊上，并受到了行业的高度关注和认可。

4. 除了学术研究外，环境设计学院还积极参与国内外的生态环境保护项目。例如，在崇明生态岛的保护和规划中，该学院的教师发挥了积极作用，并提出了一系列实用的生态保护措施。

5. 环境设计学院的专业特色是将生态环境保护与建筑设计相结合，致力于创造更加生态、环保的建筑环境。该学院的教师和学生在这一领域取得了许多重要成果。

(三)将下面段落翻译成英文。

除了学术研究，环境设计学院还积极参与国内外的生态环境保护项目。例如，在崇明生态岛的保护与规划中，学院教师发挥了积极作用，提出了一系列切实可行的生态保护措施。这些保护措施既保障了崇明生态岛的生态环境，又将生态保护理念贯彻到了建筑设计中。

环境设计学院的专业特色是将生态环境保护与建筑设计相结合，致力于打造更加生态、环保的建筑环境。学院的教师和学生们在这一领域取得了许多重要成果。例如，学院的教师曾设计了一座名为"生态大厦"的建筑，该建筑采用了多种生态建筑技术，如太阳能热水器、雨水收集系统、绿色墙等，实现了建筑与环境的良性互动。这些生态建筑项目不仅体现了环境设计学院的专业特色，也为学生提供了宝贵的实践机会。

☞ **参考答案**

(一)

1. ecological environment protection and architectural design

2. a team of highly qualified and experienced teachers

3. enjoy a high reputation both domestically and internationally

4. ecological system assessment

5. ecological restoration technology

6. green building

7. practical ecological protection measures

8. actively participate in domestic and international ecological and environmental protection projects

9. scientific ecological environment education

10. environmental awareness and design abilities

(二)

1. The School of Environmental Design is one of the important schools of Xianda College, and its specialty is combining ecological environment protection with architectural design, aiming to create a more ecological and environmentally friendly building environment.

2. The school has a team of highly qualified and experienced teachers, who not only have a solid theoretical foundation but also have rich experience in ecological environment protection and design, enjoying a high reputation both domestically and internationally.

3. The teachers of the School of Environmental Design have made a series of significant achievements in the field of ecological environment. In recent years, the teachers of the school have published dozens of research papers related to ecological environment protection, some of which have been published in international authoritative journals and have received high attention and recognition from the industry.

4. In addition to academic research, the School of Environmental Design actively participates in domestic and international ecological and environmental protection projects. For example, in the protection and planning of Chongming Ecological Island, the school's teachers played an active role and proposed a series of practical ecological protection measures.

5. The professional feature of the School of Environmental Design is the combination of ecological environment protection and architectural design, dedicated to creating a more ecological and environmentally friendly building environment. The teachers and students of the school have achieved many important results in this field.

(三)

In addition to academic research, the School of Environmental Design actively participates in domestic and international ecological and environmental protection projects. For example, in the protection and planning of Chongming Ecological Island, the school's teachers played an active role and proposed a series of practical ecological protection measures. These protection measures not only safeguard the ecological environment of Chongming Ecological Island, but also incorporate ecological protection concepts into architectural design.

The professional feature of the School of Environmental Design is the combination of ecological environment protection and architectural design, dedicated to creating a more ecological and environmentally friendly building environment. The teachers and students of the school have achieved many important results in this field. For example, the teachers of the school have designed a building called "Ecological Building", which adopts various ecological building technologies such as solar water heaters, rainwater collection systems, and green walls, realizing a positive interaction between the building and the environment. These ecological building projects not only reflect the professional characteristics of the School of Environmental Design, but also provide valuable practical opportunities for students.

第九章 崇明生态政策与建筑

一、上海市对崇明岛建设的政策支持与规划布局

翻译简介

本文的译文部分翻译质量较高，采用了准确、简洁、流畅的语言表达方式，准确地表达了原文的意思，符合翻译的基本原则和要求。从用词方面来看，翻译选用了准确、简洁的词汇，使得翻译文本易于理解。例如，将"政策支持和规划布局"译为"policy support and planning layout"，将"生态保护"译为"ecological protection"，都是准确的表达方式。从句子结构和语言风格方面来看，译者采用了符合英语语法规则的句子结构和流畅的语言风格，使得翻译文本易于阅读和理解。例如，将"政府要求所有在崇明岛上的建设项目必须符合环境保护要求，否则……"译为"The government requires that all construction projects on Chongming Island must meet environmental protection requirements, otherwise..."，句子结构清晰、表达准确。从中英文化的异同角度来看，翻译考虑到了中英文化的差异，采用了符合西方习惯的表达方式。例如，"农家乐"这一中文特有的词汇，在翻译中被翻译成"farm stay"，符合西方人对农村旅游的习惯表达方式。

词汇表

生态环境保护：ecological environmental protection

政策支持：policy support

规划布局：planning layout

土地保护：land conservation

集约利用：intensive use

建设用地：construction land

农村宅基地：rural homesteads

绿色产业：green industries

生态旅游：ecological tourism

财政支持：financial support

优惠政策：preferential policies

农业生态旅游：agricultural ecological tourism

乡村民宿：rural homestays

农产品销售：sale of agricultural products

生态保护系统：ecological protection system

环保要求：environmental protection requirements

绿色建筑技术：green building technologies

节能环保建筑设计：energy-saving and environmentally friendly architectural designs

财政补贴：financial subsidies

绿色交通：green transportation

公共交通：public transportation

自行车道：bicycle lanes

城市绿化建设：urban greening construction

生态系统保护和修复：protection and restoration of ecological systems

湖泊建设项目：artificial lake construction projects

水资源利用效率：water resource utilization efficiency

生态环境质量：ecological environment quality

原文

随着人们对生态环保的重视程度不断提高，上海市政府对崇明岛建设的政策支持和规划布局也日益完善。政府的政策和规划涉及土地使用、产业发展、生态保护、交通、基础设施、绿化等多个方面，为崇明岛的发展提供了重要的指导和支持。

在土地使用方面，上海市政府出台了一系列政策，鼓励土地节约利用和集约利用。政府规定崇明岛每年新增建设用地不得超过 40 公顷，同时要求新增建设用地必须符合生态保护和环境整治要求。此外，政府还规定，崇明岛上的农村宅基地不得转为建设用地，以保护农村土地资源。

在产业发展方面，政府鼓励崇明岛发展绿色产业和生态旅游业，为符合条件的企业和项目提供一定的财政支持和优惠政策，鼓励其在崇明岛投资兴业。例如，政府鼓励崇明岛发展农业生态旅游，推广乡村民宿和农产品销售等业态，提升崇明岛的知名度和吸引力。

　　崇明岛上的农家乐旅游产业是近年来获得发展的新兴产业。政府通过鼓励农村民宿和农产品销售等业态的发展，促进了农业向旅游业的转型。例如，位于崇明岛南部的横沙村，发展了以农家乐为主的旅游业，吸引了大量游客前来体验农村生活和品尝农家美食。另外，位于崇明岛北部的陈家镇，以发展生态农业为基础，推广农村民宿和乡村旅游，成了崇明岛上的旅游热点。还有其他村落如新河村、长兴岛等也积极开展农家乐旅游业，为崇明岛的旅游产业发展注入了新的活力。

　　在生态保护方面，上海市政府实行最严格的生态保护制度，加大对崇明岛的生态保护力度。全区生态保护红线共划定 506.72 平方公里，超过崇明行政区划面积 2494.5 平方公里的 20%，并实施了最严格的保护要求。比如崇明东滩鸟类国家级自然保护区，崇明和市直部门先后用 10 多年时间开展了退化湿地的生态修复和提升工程，使崇明东滩的湿地逐年增长，成为迁徙鸟类理想的栖息地，鸟类数量逐年递增。政府要求崇明岛上的所有建设项目必须符合环保要求，否则不予批准。同时，政府还鼓励采用绿色建筑技术和节能环保的建筑设计，对符合条件的项目给予一定的财政补贴。例如，政府在 2016 年出台了《上海市绿色建筑推广实施方案(2016—2020 年)》，鼓励在崇明岛等生态敏感区域建设绿色建筑。

　　在规划布局方面，上海市政府注重绿色出行和城市绿化建设。政府将加大对基础设施的投入，提升崇明岛的道路、桥梁、水利等设施的建设水平，同时注重发展公共交通和自行车道等绿色出行模式。政府还大力推进城市绿化建设，加强对崇明岛的森林、湿地等生态系统的保护和修复，提高崇明岛的生态环境质量。

　　除了政策和规划的支持外，上海市政府还在崇明岛上实行了多项人工湖建设项目，以提高水资源利用效率和生态环境质量。例如，2018 年，政府在崇明岛南部的横沙岛上建造了一个面积达到 234 亩的人工湖，该湖不仅可以储存雨水，还可以提供生态景观和游泳、垂钓等休闲娱乐功能。

译文

As people's attention to ecological environmental protection continues to increase, the policy support and planning layout for the construction of Chongming Island by the Shanghai municipal government is also becoming increasingly perfect. The government's policies and plans involve multiple aspects such as land use, industrial development, ecological protection, transportation, infrastructure, and greening, providing important guidance and support for the development of Chongming Island.

In terms of land use, the Shanghai government has issued a series of policies to encourage land conservation and intensive use. The government stipulates that the annual increase of construction land in Chongming Island shall not exceed 40 hectares, and requires that the new construction land must meet the requirements of ecological protection and environmental improvement. In addition, the government also stipulates that rural homesteads on Chongming Island cannot be converted into construction land to protect rural land resources.

In terms of industrial development, the Shanghai Municipal Government encourages Chongming Island to develop green industries and ecological tourism. The government provides certain financial support and preferential policies for eligible enterprises and projects, encouraging them to invest and start businesses on Chongming Island. For example, the government encourages the development of agricultural ecological tourism on Chongming Island, promotes rural homestays and the sale of agricultural products, and enhances the island's reputation and attractiveness.

The rural tourism industry in Chongming Island is a newly developed industry in recent years. The government has promoted the transformation of agriculture to tourism by encouraging the development of rural homestays and the sale of agricultural products. For example, Hengsha Village in the south of Chongming Island has developed a tourism industry mainly based on rural homestays, attracting a large number of tourists to experience rural life and taste local cuisine. In addition, Chenjia Town in the north of Chongming Island has promoted rural homestays and rural tourism based on the development of ecological agriculture, becoming a tourist hotspot on Chongming Island. Other villages such as Xinhe Village and Changxing Island have also actively developed rural tourism, injecting new vitality into the tourism industry of Chongming Island.

In terms of ecological protection, the Shanghai municipal government implements the strictest ecological protection system, increasing efforts to protect the ecology of Chongming Island. The total ecological protection red line in the district covers 506. 72 square kilometers, which is 20% of Chongming's administrative area of 2,494. 5 square kilometers, and the strictest protection requirements have been implemented. For example, the Chongming Dongtan National Bird Nature Reserve, where Chongming and municipal departments have carried out ecological restoration and improvement projects for degraded wetlands over more than 10 years. As a result, the wetlands in Dongtan have been growing year by year, becoming an ideal habitat for migratory birds, with the bird population increasing annually. The government requires that all construction projects on Chongming Island must meet environmental protection requirements, otherwise they will not be approved. At the same time, the government also encourages the use of green building technologies and energy-saving and environmentally friendly architectural designs, and provides certain financial subsidies for projects that meet the requirements. For example, in 2016, the government introduced the "Shanghai Green Building Promotion Implementation Plan (2016-2020)", which encourages the construction of green buildings in ecologically sensitive areas such as Chongming Island.

In terms of planning and layout, the Shanghai Municipal Government focuses on green transportation and urban greening construction. The government will increase investment in infrastructure, improve the construction level of roads, bridges, water conservancy facilities and other facilities on Chongming Island, and pay attention to the development of green transportation modes such as public transportation and bicycle lanes. The government also vigorously promotes urban greening construction, strengthens the protection and restoration of ecological systems such as forests and wetlands on Chongming Island, and improves the ecological environment quality of Chongming Island.

In addition to policy and planning support, the Shanghai Municipal Government has implemented multiple artificial lake construction projects on Chongming Island to improve water resource utilization efficiency and ecological environment quality. For example, in 2018, the government built a 234-acre artificial lake on Hengsha Island in the south of Chongming Island, which can not only store rainwater but also provide ecological landscapes and leisure activities such as swimming and fishing.

例句赏析

例1：

原文：政府规定崇明岛每年新增建设用地不得超过 40 公顷，同时要求新增建设用地必须符合生态保护和环境治理要求。

译文：The government stipulates that the annual increase of construction land in Chongming Island shall not exceed 40 hectares, and requires that the new construction land must meet the requirements of ecological protection and environmental improvement.

赏析：该段原文讲的是一条简洁明了的规定。译文准确传达了原文的意思，同时保持了相同的正式语气。例如使用被动语态来强调规定，添加"annual"一词来澄清限制的时间范围。在词汇选择方面，译者使用了适当的词汇来传达原文的含义。例如，采用"stipulates"以传达政府规定中的权威感。译者还在句子结构中使用了平行结构，这有助于强调对新建设用地的两个要求。总体而言，译文忠实于原文，做到了准确有效的表达。

例2：

原文：政府鼓励崇明岛发展绿色产业和生态旅游，为符合条件的企业和项目提供一定的财政支持和优惠政策，鼓励其在崇明岛投资兴业。

译文：The Shanghai Municipal Government encourages Chongming Island to develop green industries and ecological tourism. The government provides certain financial support and preferential policies for eligible enterprises and projects, encouraging them to invest and start businesses on Chongming Island.

赏析：译文结构简单明了，符合英语表达的习惯。句子中使用了并列结构，使得翻译更加清晰明了。该译文使用了正式、客观的语言风格，符合政府文件的语言特点。原文中没有提到"上海市"这个信息，而译文中加入了"Shanghai Municipal Government"的信息，这是为了更好地让英语读者理解这个政策是由上海市政府出台的。翻译策略方面，译者采用了直译和补充信息相结合的策略，使得翻译更加准确、完整。

例3：

原文：政府将加大对基础设施的投入，提升崇明岛道路、桥梁、水利等设施的建设水平，同时注重发展公共交通和自行车道等绿色出行模式。

译文：The government will increase investment in infrastructure, improve the construction level of roads, bridges, water conservancy facilities and other facilities on Chongming Island, and pay attention to the development of green transportation modes such as public transportation and bicycle lanes.

赏析：译文整体上比较准确地表达了原文的意思，但在表述上有一些细节方面的调整。例如，"设施建设水平"被译为了"construction level"，这样更符合英语表达习惯。此外，"注重发展"在译文中被翻译成了"pay attention to"，这也是一种常见的英语表达方式。整体而言，在翻译政策性文件时，准确传递信息至关重要，因此译者需要尽可能地避免歧义和模棱两可的表述，保持翻译的准确性和规范性。

例4：

原文：政府还大力推进城市绿化建设，加强对崇明岛的森林、湿地等生态系统的保护和修复，提高崇明岛的生态环境质量。

译文：The government also vigorously promotes urban greening construction, strengthens the protection and restoration of ecological systems such as forests and wetlands on Chongming Island, and improves the ecological environment quality of Chongming Island.

赏析：该段原文是关于政策性的表述，用词比较严谨，句子结构也相对简单明了。其中，"大力推进城市绿化建设""加强对崇明岛的森林、湿地等生态系统的保护和修复"，以及"提高崇明岛的生态环境质量"是三个并列的动作，中间用逗号隔开。整个句子的语言风格比较正式，符合政策性文件的要求。在翻译该段原文时，译者需要考虑到多方面的因素，包括用词、句子结构、语言风格、中英文化的异同、翻译技巧与策略、翻译原则、修辞、表达效果等。只有在综合考虑这些因素的基础上，才能够准确地传递原文的意思，并且使得翻译结果达到最佳的表达效果。

例5：

原文：上海市政府还在崇明岛上实施了多项人工湖建设项目，以提高水资源利用效率和生态环境质量。

译文：In addition to policy and planning support, the Shanghai Municipal Government has implemented multiple artificial lake construction projects on Chongming Island to improve water resource utilization efficiency and ecological environment quality.

赏析：在翻译该段原文中的"提高水资源利用效率和生态环境质量"时，译者使用了"improve water resource utilization efficiency and ecological environment quality"来翻译，比较准确地表达了原文的含义。此外，"人工湖建设项目"被译为"artificial lake construction projects"，较好表达了原文的意思。

☞ **练习**

(一)将下列短语翻译成英文。

1. 生态环境保护

2. 土地利用

3. 生态旅游

4. 农家乐

5. 绿色建筑

6. 城市绿化

7. 人工湖

8. 生态系统

(二)将下列句子翻译成英文。

1. 上海市政府鼓励崇明岛发展绿色产业和生态旅游。

2. 上海市政府已经实施了最严格的生态保护制度，增加了对崇明岛生态的保护力度。

3. 政府鼓励在崇明岛发展农业生态旅游，促进农家乐和农产品销售。

4. 上海市政府规定崇明岛的新增建设用地不得超过 40 公顷，且新建建设用地必须符合生态保护和环境改善要求。

5. 上海市政府将加大对基础设施的投资，提高崇明岛道路、桥梁、水利设施等设施的建设水平。

(三)将下面段落翻译成英文。

崇明岛上的农家乐旅游产业是近年来获得发展的新兴产业。政府通过鼓励农村民宿和农产品销售等业态的发展，促进了农业向旅游业的转型。例如，位于崇明岛南部的横沙村，发展了以农家乐为主的旅游业，吸引了大量游客前来体验农村生活和品尝农家美食。另外，位于崇明岛北部的陈家镇，以发展生态农业为基础，推广了农村民宿和乡村旅游，成为崇明岛上的旅游热点。还有其他村落如新河村、长兴岛等也积极开展农家乐旅游业，为崇明岛的旅游产业发展注入了新的活力。

☞ 参考答案

(一)

1. ecological environmental protection

2. land use

3. ecological tourism

4. rural homestay 或 agrifainment

5. green building

6. urban greening

7. artificial lake

8. ecological system

(二)

1. Shanghai Municipal Government encourages Chongming Island to develop green industries and ecological tourism.

2. The Shanghai Municipal Government has implemented the strictest ecological protection system and increased efforts to protect the ecology of Chongming Island.

3. The government encourages the development of agricultural ecological tourism on Chongming Island, promotes rural homestays and the sale of agricultural products.

4. The Shanghai Municipal Government stipulates that the annual increase of construction land in Chongming Island shall not exceed 40 hectares, and requires that the new construction

land must meet the requirements of ecological protection and environmental improvement.

5. The government will increase investment in infrastructure, improve the construction level of roads, bridges, water conservancy facilities and other facilities on Chongming Island.

（三）

The rural tourism industry in Chongming Island is a newly developed industry in recent years. The government has promoted the transformation of agriculture to tourism by encouraging the development of rural homestays and the sale of agricultural products. For example, Hengsha Village in the south of Chongming Island has developed a tourism industry mainly based on rural homestays, attracting a large number of tourists to experience rural life and taste local cuisine. In addition, Chenjia Town in the north of Chongming Island has promoted rural homestays and rural tourism based on the development of ecological agriculture, becoming a tourist hotspot on Chongming Island. Other villages such as Xinhe Village and Changxing Island have also actively developed rural tourism, injecting new vitality into the tourism industry of Chongming Island.

二、建筑设计中融入自然元素与环保理念

翻译简介

本文是一篇介绍上海外国语大学贤达学院环境设计专业优秀毕业生的文章，主要介绍了他们如何将自然元素和环保理念融入建筑和景观设计中。文章主要从以下五个方面进行了介绍："鲸之旅"设计项目；"绿野悠游"设计项目；"适意"青年旅舍改造设计；"洗铅花"——上海非遗土布文化主题展馆设计；"林幽涧"寻鹿之旅——自然环境与建筑的融合。从语言风格方面来看，本文采用的是中性、客观、简洁的语言风格，符合新闻报道的特点。在翻译该段原文时，译者采用了合适的翻译策略，较为准确、流畅地传达了原文的意思。译文遵循原文的行文特点，语言简洁明了，条理清晰，符合新闻报道的要求。

词汇表

环保：environmental protection

建筑领域：field of architecture

生态屏障：ecological barrier

自然资源：natural resources

生态环境：ecological environment

自然元素：natural elements

环保概念：environmental concepts

毕业生：graduates

环境设计学院：Environmental Design School

建筑和景观设计作品：architectural and landscape design works

水上乐园：water park

鲸鱼主题：whale-themed

建筑结构：building structure

海洋生物：marine creatures

水循环系统：water circulation system

绿色能源：green energy

节能减排：energy consumption and pollution emissions reduction

红熊猫宿舍：Red Panda Hostel

生态材料：ecological materials

爬行架和休息区：climbing frames and rest areas

观察窗口：observation windows

年轻旅行者：young travelers

环保材料：environmentally friendly materials

节能设备：energy-saving equipment

自然光线：natural light

绿色植物：green plants

非遗土布文化主题展馆：Shanghai Non-legacy Tu Bu Cultural Theme Exhibition Hall

生态照明系统：energy-saving lighting systems

传统文化：traditional culture

山区民宿：homestay in the mountainous area

原文

随着全球环保意识的不断增强，人们对于建筑领域的环保问题也越来越关注。在中国，崇明岛作为一个重要的生态屏障，自然资源丰富，生态环境优美，因此，崇明岛建筑设计中融入了自然元素与环保理念，成为一个热点话题。本文将介绍上海外国语大学贤达经济人文学院环境设计学院的优秀毕业生们，如何将自然元素与环保理念融入建筑、园林设计作品中。

鲸之旅——水上公园中的自然元素与环保理念融合

鲸之旅是一座以鲸鱼为主题的水上公园,建筑设计师巧妙地将鲸鱼的形象融入建筑结构中,使游客仿佛置身于海洋生物的世界。同时,公园还采用了水循环系统和绿色能源,减少了能源消耗和污染排放。如此的设计理念,不仅令游客们在玩耍中感受到自然元素的美妙,也为保护环境作出了实质性的贡献。

绿野悠游——上海动物园红熊猫旅舍设计:为动物提供舒适的生活环境

设计师将红熊猫的生活习性考虑在内,为它们打造了一个充满绿意的生活空间。旅舍内设有攀爬架、休息区以及观察窗,既满足了红熊猫的生活需求,又为游客提供了观赏的机会。同时,设计师还运用了生态材料和绿色能源,实现了环保建筑的目标。这样的设计不仅让游客们能够近距离观察红熊猫的生活,也给红熊猫们提供了一个舒适的生活空间。

"适意"青年旅社改造设计:为年轻旅客打造环保的休憩空间

这是一个位于市区的青年旅社,设计师通过改造,为年轻旅客打造了一个舒适、环保的休憩空间。设计中采用了环保材料、节能设备,同时充分利用了自然光线和绿植,营造出宜人的氛围。年轻人对于环保问题的关注度越来越高,这样的设计既符合他们的需求,也给他们提供了一个身心愉悦的环境。

"洗铅花"——上海非遗土布文化主题展厅设计:传统文化与环保相结合

这个展厅以传统土布文化为主题,设计师巧妙地运用了自然元素和生态材料,展示了土布的历史、工艺和文化特色。同时,展厅还采用了节能照明系统,降低了能源消耗。将传统文化与环保相结合,不仅传承了文化遗产,也让人们在欣赏文化的同时感受到环保的重要性。

"林幽涧"寻鹿之旅:自然环境与建筑的融合

这是一个位于山区的民宿,设计师在建筑设计中融入了自然元素,使建筑与周围的自然环境融为一体。设计中采用了当地材料,运用了自然光线和绿植,营造出宜人的氛围。同时,设计师还通过节能、水循环等手段,实现了环保建筑的目标。这样的设计不仅让旅客们能够享受到自然环境的美妙,也为环境保护作出了实质性的贡献。

以上是上海外国语大学贤达经济人文学院环境设计学院的优秀毕业生们的设计作品,

他们通过将自然元素和环保理念融入建筑、园林设计中，为环境保护作出了实质性的贡献，也让人们在生活中更加关注环保问题。

译文

With the increasing global awareness of environmental protection, people are paying more and more attention to environmental issues in the field of architecture. In China, Chongming Island, as an important ecological barrier, is rich in natural resources and has a beautiful ecological environment. Therefore, incorporating natural elements and environmental concepts into Chongming Island's architectural design has become a hot topic. This chapter will introduce the outstanding graduates of the Environmental Design School of Xinda College of Economics and Humanities, Shanghai International Studies University, and how they incorporate natural elements and environmental concepts into their architectural and landscape design works.

"Whale Journey": Integration of Natural Elements and Environmental Concepts in Water Parks

"Whale Journey" is a whale-themed water park, where the architects ingeniously incorporated the image of whales into the building structure, making visitors feel like they are in the world of marine creatures. At the same time, the park also uses a water circulation system and green energy to reduce energy consumption and pollution emissions. Such design concepts not only allow visitors to experience the beauty of natural elements while playing, but also make substantial contributions to environmental protection.

"Green Leisure": Design of Shanghai Zoo's Red Panda Hostel to Provide Comfortable Living Environment for Animals

The designer took into account the living habits of red pandas and created a green living space for them. The hostel is equipped with climbing frames, rest areas, and observation windows, which not only meet the living needs of red pandas but also provide visitors with the opportunity to observe them. At the same time, the designer also used ecological materials and green energy to achieve the goal of environmental protection in building construction. Such design not only allows visitors to observe the lives of red pandas up close, but also provides a comfortable living space for them.

"Cozy" Youth Hostel Renovation Design: Creating an Environmentally Friendly Resting Space for Young Travelers

This is a youth hostel located in the city. The designer transformed it into a comfortable and environmentally friendly resting space for young travelers. The design uses environmentally friendly materials and energy-saving equipment, while fully utilizing natural light and green plants to create a pleasant atmosphere. Young people are increasingly concerned about environmental issues, and this design not only meets their needs but also provides them with a pleasant environment for body and mind.

"Xi Qian Hua": Shanghai Museum of Local Textile Culture: Combining Traditional Culture with Environmental Protection

This exhibition hall is themed around traditional Tu Bu culture. The designer cleverly used natural elements and ecological materials to showcase the history, craftsmanship, and cultural characteristics of Tu Bu. At the same time, the exhibition hall also uses energy-saving lighting systems to reduce energy consumption. Combining traditional culture with environmental protection not only inherits cultural heritage but also allows people to appreciate the importance of environmental protection while enjoying culture.

"Lin You Jian"— Seeking Deer Cry: Integration of Natural Environment and Architecture

This is a homestay located in the mountainous area. The designer incorporated natural elements into the architectural design, making the building blend in with the surrounding natural environment. The design uses local materials, natural light, and green plants to create a pleasant atmosphere. At the same time, the designer also achieved the goal of environmental protection through energy-saving and water circulation methods. Such design not only allows travelers to enjoy the beauty of the natural environment but also makes substantial contributions to environmental protection.

The above are the design works of outstanding graduates from the Environmental Design School of Xianda College of Economics and Humanities, Shanghai International Studies University. They have made substantial contributions to environmental protection by incorporating natural elements and environmental concepts into their architectural and landscape design works, and have also made people pay more attention to environmental issues in their daily lives.

例句赏析

例1：

原文：将传统文化与环保相结合，不仅传承了文化遗产，也让人们在欣赏文化的同时感受到环保的重要性。

译文：Combining traditional culture with environmental protection not only inherits cultural heritage but also allows people to appreciate the importance of environmental protection while enjoying culture.

赏析：在翻译该段原文时，译者需要注意到中英文的文化差异和表达方式的不同。例如，中文中常常使用成语或者俗语来表达某种意思，而英文中则可能需要使用类似的习语或者表达方式来传达相同的意思。此外，翻译者还需要注意到修辞手法的运用，例如原句中的"将传统文化与环保相结合"就是一个比较典型的修辞手法，用来强调两者的紧密联系。

例2：

原文：这是一个位于山区的民宿，设计师在建筑设计中融入了自然元素，使建筑与周围的自然环境融为一体。

译文：This is a homestay located in the mountainous area. The designer incorporated natural elements into the architectural design, making the building blend in with the surrounding natural environment.

赏析：整个译文的表达效果比较清晰明了，用词简洁明了，没有出现歧义或者误解。在翻译过程中，翻译者需要注意到中英文的文化差异和表达方式的不同。这个句子的译文比较准确地传达原文的意思，并且在语言风格和句子结构上也与原文保持了一致性。

例3：

原文：设计中采用了当地材料，运用了自然光线和绿植，营造出宜人的氛围。同时，设计师还通过节能、水循环等手段，实现了环保建筑的目标。

译文：The design uses local materials, natural light, and green plants to create a pleasant atmosphere. At the same time, the designer also achieved the goal of environmental protection through energy-saving and water circulation methods.

赏析：该段原文是一个简单句，主语是"设计"，谓语是"采用"，中间是一个并列结构，分别是"当地材料""自然光线和绿植""节能、水循环等手段"。译文还使用了"uses""creates""achieved"等动词，准确地传达了原文的意思，还使用了"environmental protection"这个词组，准确地传达了"环保"的含义。此外，翻译中还使用了"through"这个介词，准确地表达了使用手段的作用。整体来说，整篇译文比较准确、简洁、清晰，符合翻译的基本原则和技巧。

例4：

原文： 他们通过将自然元素和环保理念融入建筑、园林设计中，为环境保护作出了实质性的贡献，也让人们在生活中更加关注环保问题。

译文： They have made substantial contributions to environmental protection by incorporating natural elements and environmental concepts into their architectural and landscape design works, and have also made people pay more attention to environmental issues in their daily lives.

赏析： 从用词和句子结构的角度来看，原文和译文的结构基本相同，但是译文使用了更加精准和专业的词汇，如"incorporating"和"landscape design works"，使得句子的表达更加准确和流畅。从语言风格和修辞的角度来看，原文和译文都采用了比较正式的语言风格，但是译文在表达"让人们在生活中更加关注环保问题"时使用了"pay more attention"这一形象生动的表达方式，增强了表达效果。此外，在翻译固定搭配和习惯用语时译者需要注意不同语言之间的差异，并采用适当的翻译技巧和策略，如意译、借词、换序等，以达到最佳的翻译效果。

☞ 练习

(一)将下列短语翻译成英文。

1. 环境保护意识

2. 生态屏障

3. 自然资源

4. 建筑设计

5. 建筑结构

6. 水循环系统

7. 绿色能源

8. 设计理念

9. 生态材料

10. 红熊猫

(二)将下列句子翻译成英文。

1. 随着全球环保意识的提高，人们在建筑领域越来越关注环境问题。

2. 作为一个重要的生态屏障，崇明岛拥有丰富的自然资源和美丽的生态环境。

3. 因此，在崇明岛的建筑设计中融入自然元素和环保理念已经成为一个热门话题。

4. "鲸之旅"是一个以鲸鱼为主题的水上乐园，建筑师们巧妙地将鲸鱼形象融入到建筑结构中，让游客感觉自己置身于海洋生物的世界中。

5. 同时，该乐园还采用了水循环系统和绿色能源来降低能源消耗和污染排放。

6. "绿野悠游"是上海动物园红熊猫旅舍的设计，为动物提供舒适的生活环境。

7. 设计师考虑到了红熊猫的生活习性，为它们创造了一个绿色的生活空间。

8. 这个旅馆配备了攀爬架、休息区和观察窗口，不仅满足了红熊猫的生活需要，还为游客提供了近距离观察它们的机会。

9. 同时，设计师还使用了生态材料和绿色能源来实现建筑施工中的环保目标。

10. 这样的设计不仅让游客近距离观察到红熊猫的生活，而且为它们提供了舒适的居住空间。

(三)将下面段落翻译成英文。

设计师将红熊猫的生活习性考虑在内，为它们打造了一个充满绿意的生活空间。旅舍内设有攀爬架、休息区以及观察窗，既满足了红熊猫的生活需求，又为游客提供了观赏的机会。同时，设计师还运用了生态材料和绿色能源，实现了环保建筑的目标。这样的设计不仅让游客们能够近距离观察红熊猫的生活，也给红熊猫们提供了一个舒适的生活空间。

☞ 参考答案

(一)

1. environmental protection awareness

2. ecological barrier

3. natural resources

4. architectural design

5. building structure

6. water circulation system

7. green energy

8. design concept

9. ecological materials

10. red panda

(二)

1. With the increasing global awareness of environmental protection, people are paying more and more attention to environmental issues in the field of architecture.

2. In China, Chongming Island, as an important ecological barrier, is rich in natural resources and has a beautiful ecological environment.

3. Therefore, incorporating natural elements and environmental concepts into Chongming Island's architectural design has become a hot topic.

4. "Whale Journey" is a whale-themed water park, where the architects ingeniously incorporated the image of whales into the building structure, making visitors feel like they are in the world of marine creatures.

5. At the same time, the park also uses a water circulation system and green energy to reduce energy consumption and pollution emissions.

6. "Green Leisure" is the design of Shanghai Zoo's Red Panda Hostel, which provides a comfortable living environment for animals.

7. The designer took into account the living habits of red pandas and created a green living space for them.

8. The hostel is equipped with climbing frames, rest areas, and observation windows, which not only meet the living needs of red pandas but also provide visitors with the opportunity to observe them.

9. At the same time, the designer also used ecological materials and green energy to achieve the goal of environmental protection in building construction.

10. Such design not only allows visitors to observe the lives of red pandas up close, but also provides a comfortable living space for them.

（三）

The designer took into account the living habits of red pandas and created a green living space for them. The hostel is equipped with climbing frames, rest areas, and observation windows, which not only meet the living needs of red pandas but also provide visitors with the opportunity to observe them. At the same time, the designer also used ecological materials and green energy to achieve the goal of environmental protection in building construction. Such design not only allows visitors to observe the lives of red pandas up close, but also provides a comfortable living space for them.

三、生态建筑的案例

翻译简介

本文主要介绍了建筑与生态概念之间的密切关系，以及如何通过建筑设计实现可持续发展。在翻译原文时，译者在尽可能保留原文意思的前提下，采用了简明易懂的语言风格，使翻译更加贴近读者的阅读习惯。在词汇选择上，译者使用了大量与生态相关的词汇，如"sustainable development""environmental protection""ecological landscape design"等，突出了文章的主题和重点。在句子结构方面，译者尽可能保持了原文的结构和语气，使翻译更加准确地表达了原文的意思。在翻译技巧和策略方面，译者采用了一些常用的翻译方法，如意译、借词等，使翻译更加通顺和自然。在表达效果方面，译者准确传达了原文的信息，使读者能够清晰地理解文章的主旨和内容。总之，本文的译文翻译质量较高，准确传达了原文的意思和表达效果。

词汇表

和谐共存：harmonious coexistence

可持续发展：sustainable development

环境保护：environmental protection

资源利用：use of resources

重要部分：important part

能源消耗：energy consumption

碳排放：carbon emissions

雨水收集系统：rainwater collection system

节水设备：water-saving equipment

自然光线：natural light

通风：ventilation

环境污染：environmental pollution

环保材料：environmentally friendly materials

废物处理：waste disposal

生物多样性保护：biodiversity protection

生态景观设计：ecological landscape design

室内空气质量：indoor air quality

噪音控制：noise control

温湿度调节：temperature and humidity regulation

社会责任：social responsibility

安全合理的空间：safe and functionally reasonable spaces

不同群体的需求和可达性：needs and accessibility of different groups

环境意识：environmental awareness

社会可持续发展：social sustainable development

具体体现：concrete manifestation

追求环保和可持续发展：pursuit of environmental protection and sustainable development

杰出的建筑和景观设计作品：outstanding architectural and landscape design works

创新和可持续性：innovation and sustainability

建筑师：architect

海洋生态系统：marine ecology

可再生能源：renewable energy

红熊猫栖息地和生活习惯：living habits and habitats of red pandas

原文

建筑和生态理念之间存在着密切的关系。生态理念强调人与自然的和谐共生，追求可持续发展和环境保护，而建筑作为人类活动的重要组成部分，对环境和资源的利用具有重要影响。下面将详细说明建筑和生态理念之间的关系。

可持续发展：生态理念强调满足当前需求而不损害未来世代的需求。在建筑领域，可持续发展的目标体现在建筑的设计、施工和运营过程中。例如，使用可再生材料、节能设备和技术，减少能源消耗和碳排放；采用雨水收集系统和节水设备，减少水资源的浪费；设计建筑物的布局和朝向，最大限度地利用自然光和通风等。通过这些措施，建筑可以实现对环境的最小化影响，实现可持续发展的目标。

环境保护：生态理念强调保护自然环境和生态系统的健康。建筑可以通过设计和使用环保材料、减少垃圾产生、合理处理废弃物等方式来减少对环境的污染。此外，建筑还可以通过生态景观设计、绿化植被的增加、保护野生动植物栖息地等方式来促进生物多样性的保护。通过将环境保护融入建筑设计和运营中，可以实现建筑与自然环境的和谐共生。

健康与舒适：生态理念关注人类的健康和舒适。建筑可以通过设计健康室内环境、提供良好的采光和通风条件、减少有害物质的使用等方式来提升居住和工作环境的质量。生态建筑注重室内空气质量、噪音控制、温湿度调节等方面，为居住者提供一个舒适、健康的生活空间。

社会责任：生态理念强调建筑对社会的责任。建筑应当满足人们的需求，提供安全、功能合理的空间，并考虑到不同群体的需求和可访问性。生态建筑还可以通过社区参与、教育宣传等方式，促进环境保护意识的提高，推动社会可持续发展。

综上所述，建筑和生态理念密切相关，建筑应当积极响应生态理念，通过可持续发展、环境保护、健康舒适和社会责任等方面的实践，促进人与自然的和谐共生。生态建筑的发展不仅可以改善人们的生活质量，还能够保护环境、促进可持续发展，为未来创造更美好的生活环境。

在崇明岛这片美丽的土地上，生态建筑成了人们对环境保护和可持续发展的追求的具体体现。本文将介绍一些环境设计学院优秀毕业生的建筑和园林设计作品，这些作品以其创新性和可持续性而闻名于世。

首先，让我们来看看"鲸之旅"，这是一座令人叹为观止的建筑作品。它以鲸鱼为灵感，巧妙地融入了自然环境中。建筑师运用环保材料和可再生能源，将建筑与周围的海洋生态相融合，为人们提供了一个与自然亲近的体验。

另一个令人惊叹的设计是"绿野悠游"——上海动物园红熊猫旅舍。这个设计以红熊猫的生活习性和栖息地为出发点，创造了一个舒适、可持续的居住环境。建筑师运用生态建筑技术和绿色材料，为红熊猫提供了一个安全、适宜的生活空间。

除了动物园旅舍，"适意"青年旅社改造设计也是一项引人注目的工程。这个项目将一座老旧建筑改造成一个现代化的青年旅社，注重舒适性和可持续性。设计师运用可再生能源和节能技术，打造了一个环保、时尚的旅游住宿场所，吸引了许多年轻人的关注。

此外，"洗铅花"是上海非遗土布文化主题展厅的设计，"林幽涧"是寻鹿鸣的别墅设计，"汐悦"是惠南镇荡湾街道儿童之家的设计，"绿动棠林"是上海外环健康绿地景观设计的作品，"橘子树下"是上海长兴岛服务区更新改造设计的项目，"溪清欢"是上海金山区五一村乡"美湖区"改造设计的案例。这些作品都体现了设计师对环境的关注和对可持续发展的追求。

除了建筑设计，崇明岛还有许多令人惊叹的自然景观。长江大桥连接了崇明岛与上海市区，成为两地交流的重要纽带。崇明岛人工湖是一个美丽的水域景观，吸引了许多游客前来观赏。天鹅苑是天鹅的家园，这里有各种各样的天鹅品种，给人们带来了无限的惊喜和欢乐。

此外，西沙明珠湖景区、学宫博物馆、花博文化园、东平国家森林公园、瀛东度假村、前哨当代艺术中心、寿安寺、金油桥、云舍居、东禾九谷、灶文化博物馆、广福寺、东滩湿地公园等地也是崇明岛上值得一游的景点。

崇明岛以其丰富的自然资源和独特的生态环境吸引着众多的游客和设计师。本文介绍了一些生态建筑的案例和岛上的自然景观，展示了人与自然和谐共生的理念。通过这些案例和景点的介绍，读者可以更深入地了解崇明岛的生态之美，以及人们对于环境保护和可持续发展的努力。

译文

There is a close relationship between architecture and ecological concepts. Ecological concepts emphasize the harmonious coexistence between humans and nature, pursuing sustainable development and environmental protection. As an important part of human activity, architecture has a significant impact on the use of the environment and resources. The following will explain in detail the relationship between architecture and ecological concepts.

Sustainable development: Ecological concepts emphasize meeting current needs without compromising the needs of future generations. In the field of architecture, the goal of sustainable development is reflected in the design, construction, and operation of buildings. For example, using renewable materials, energy-saving equipment and technology, reducing energy consumption and carbon emissions; adopting rainwater collection systems and water-saving equipment to reduce water waste; designing building layouts and orientations to maximize the use of natural light and ventilation, etc. Through these measures, buildings can minimize their impact on the environment and achieve the goal of sustainable development.

Environmental protection: Ecological concepts emphasize the protection of the natural environment and ecosystem health. Buildings can reduce environmental pollution through the design and use of environmentally friendly materials, reducing waste generation, and proper waste disposal. In addition, buildings can promote biodiversity protection through ecological landscape design, increasing green vegetation, and protecting wildlife habitats. By integrating environmental protection into building design and operation, buildings can achieve harmonious coexistence with the natural environment.

Health and comfort: Ecological concepts focus on human health and comfort. Buildings can enhance the quality of living and working environments by designing healthy indoor environments, providing good lighting and ventilation conditions, and reducing the use of harmful substances. Ecological buildings focus on indoor air quality, noise control, temperature and humidity regulation, etc. , providing residents with a comfortable and healthy living space.

Social responsibility: Ecological concepts emphasize the responsibility of buildings to society. Buildings should meet people's needs, provide safe and functionally reasonable spaces, and consider the needs and accessibility of different groups. Ecological buildings can also promote environmental awareness through community participation, education, and publicity, and promote social sustainable development.

In summary, architecture and ecological concepts are closely related. Buildings should actively respond to ecological concepts and promote harmonious coexistence between humans and nature through sustainable development, environmental protection, health and comfort, and social responsibility. The development of ecological buildings can not only improve people's quality of life but also protect the environment, promote sustainable development, and create a better living environment for the future.

On Chongming Island, ecological buildings have become a concrete manifestation of people's pursuit of environmental protection and sustainable development. This section will introduce some outstanding architectural and landscape design works of excellent graduates from the School of Environmental Design, which are famous for their innovation and sustainability.

First, let's take a look at the Whale Journey, an amazing architectural work. Inspired by whales, the architect cleverly integrated it into the natural environment. The architect used environmentally friendly materials and renewable energy to integrate the building with the surrounding marine ecology, providing people with a close experience with nature.

Another amazing design is the Green Leisure Shanghai Zoo Red Panda Hostel. This design takes the living habits and habitats of red pandas as a starting point, creating a comfortable and sustainable living environment. The architect used ecological building technology and green materials to provide a safe and suitable living space for red pandas.

In addition to the zoo hostel, the renovation design of the Yiyi Youth Hostel is also a remarkable project. This project transformed an old building into a modern youth hostel, emphasizing comfort and sustainability. The designer used renewable energy and energy-saving technology to create an environmentally friendly and stylish tourist accommodation, attracting the attention of many young people.

In addition, "Xi Qian Hua" is the design of the Shanghai Museum of Local Textile Culture, "Lin You Jian" is the villa design of Xun Luoming, "Xi Yue" is the design of the Huinan Town Dangwan Street Children's Home, "Lü Dong Tang Lin" is the landscape design of the Shanghai Outer Ring Healthy Green Space, "Under the Orange Tree" is the project of the Shanghai Changxing Island Service Area Renewal and Reconstruction Design, the "Xi Qinghuan" is the case of the reconstruction design for Mei Hu Area in Wuyi Village of Jinshan District. These works reflect the designer's attention to the environment and pursuit of sustainable development.

In addition to architectural design, Chongming Island also has many stunning natural landscapes. The Yangtze River Bridge connects Chongming Island with Shanghai's downtown, becoming an important link for communication between the two places. Chongming Island Artificial Lake is a beautiful water landscape that attracts many tourists to come and enjoy. The Swan Garden is the home of swans, where various swan species bring infinite surprises and joy to people.

In addition, Xisha Mingzhu Lake Scenic Area, Xuegong Museum, Flower Expo Cultural Park, Dongping National Forest Park, Yingdong Resort, Outpost Contemporary Art Center, Shou'an Temple, Jinyou Bridge, Yunsheju, Donghe Jiugu, Kitchen Culture Museum, Guangfu Temple, and Dongtan Wetland Park are all worth visiting on Chongming Island.

Chongming Island attracts many tourists and designers with its rich natural resources and unique ecological environment. This section introduces some cases of ecological buildings and natural landscapes on the island, demonstrating the concept of harmonious coexistence between humans and nature. Through the introduction of these cases and scenic spots, readers can have a deeper understanding of the ecological beauty of Chongming Island and people's efforts for environmental protection and sustainable development.

例句赏析

例1：

原文：此外，建筑还可以通过生态景观设计、绿化植被的增加、保护野生动植物栖息地等方式来促进生物多样性的保护。

译文：In addition, buildings can promote biodiversity protection through ecological landscape design, increasing green vegetation, and protecting wildlife habitats.

赏析：在翻译该段原文时，译者首先需要理解原文的意思。原文中提到了建筑如何促进生物多样性的保护，主要有三种方式：生态景观设计、绿化植被的增加和保护野生动植物栖息地。因此，在翻译时，译者需要准确地表达这三种方式。本文译文使用了并列结构，将三种方式并列在一起，使得整个句子更加清晰明了。同时，在翻译中使用了"ecological landscape design""green vegetation"和"wildlife habitats"等专业术语，使得翻译更加准确和专业。

例2：

原文：建筑应当满足人们的需求，提供安全、功能合理的空间，并考虑到不同群体的需求和可访问性。

译文：Buildings should meet people's needs, provide safe and functionally reasonable spaces, and consider the needs and accessibility of different groups.

赏析：在翻译该段原文时，需要注意几点：首先是用词方面，原文中使用了"需求""功能合理""空间""群体"和"可访问性"等词汇，译文中对应的是"needs""functionally reasonable spaces""different groups"和"accessibility"。这些翻译都比较准确，但在一些情况下，有些词汇的表达并不是最常见的选择。例如，"functionally reasonable spaces"中的"functionally"可以用"functional"代替，更符合英语表达习惯。其次是句子结构方面，原文中采用了主谓宾的结构，而译文则采用的是"主语+谓语+宾语"的结构。这种结构转换并不影响句子的表达效果，但需要注意语序的变化。另外，语言风格也需要考虑。原文使用的是比较正式的语言风格，而译文则更接近于日常用语。这种差异可以从目标读者的角度来考虑，如果目标读者是专业人士，则需要保持原文的正式风格；如果目标读者是普通大众，则可以采用更接近日常用语的翻译方式。

例3：

原文：设计师运用可再生能源和节能技术，打造了一个环保、时尚的旅游住宿场所，吸引了许多年轻人的关注。

译文：The designer used renewable energy and energy-saving technology to create an environmentally friendly and stylish tourist accommodation, attracting the attention of many young people.

赏析：该段的原文和译文的结构基本一致。在翻译该段原文时，译者对原文中的"可再生能源"和"节能技术"进行了准确的翻译。译者采用了简洁明了的表达方式，对原文进行了准确的翻译，没有出现明显的文化差异。在翻译技巧与策略方面，翻译者采用了准确翻译和意译相结合的策略，使得译文贴近原文的意思。在翻译原则方面，翻译者遵循了准确传达原意的原则。在修辞和表达效果方面，翻译者没有进行太多修辞手法的运用，使得句子表达简洁明了，符合翻译的要求。总的来说，整个译文翻译质量较高，符合翻译要求。

☞ **练习**

(一)将下列短语翻译成英文。

1. 生态建筑

2. 可再生材料

3. 节能设备

4. 碳排放

5. 雨水收集系统

6. 水资源节约

7. 自然采光

8. 生态景观设计

9. 绿色植被

10. 社会可持续发展

(二)将下列句子翻译成英文。

1. 生态概念强调人与自然的和谐共存，追求可持续发展和环境保护。

2. 建筑对环境和资源的利用有着重要的影响。

3. 可持续发展的目标体现在建筑的设计、施工和运营中。

4. 通过使用可再生材料、节能设备和技术，降低能耗和碳排放，建筑可以实现减少对环境的影响。

5. 生态建筑可以通过采用雨水收集系统和水资源节约设备来减少水浪费。

(三)将下面段落翻译成英文。

环境保护：生态理念强调保护自然环境和生态系统的健康。建筑可以通过设计和使用环保材料、减少垃圾产生、合理处理废弃物等方式来减少对环境的污染。此外，建筑还可以通过生态景观设计、绿化植被的增加、保护野生动植物栖息地等方式来促进生物多样性的保护。通过将环境保护融入建筑设计和运营中，可以实现建筑与自然环境的和谐共生。

健康与舒适：生态理念关注人类的健康和舒适。建筑可以通过设计健康室内环境、提供良好的采光和通风条件、减少有害物质的使用等方式来提升居住和工作环境的质量。生态建筑注重室内空气质量、噪音控制、温湿度调节等方面，为居住者提供一个舒适、健康的生活空间。

☞ 参考答案

(一)

1. ecological architecture

2. renewable materials

3. energy-saving equipment

4. carbon emissions

5. rainwater collection system

6. water resource conservation

7. natural lighting

8. ecological landscape design

9. green vegetation

10. social sustainable development

(二)

1. Ecological concepts emphasize the harmonious coexistence between humans and nature, pursuing sustainable development and environmental protection.

2. Architecture has a significant impact on the use of the environment and resources.

3. The goal of sustainable development is reflected in the design, construction, and operation of buildings.

4. By using renewable materials, energy-saving equipment and technology, buildings can minimize their impact on the environment.

5. Buildings can reduce water waste by adopting rainwater collection systems and water-saving equipment.

(三)

Environmental protection: Ecological concepts emphasize the protection of the natural environment and ecosystem health. Buildings can reduce environmental pollution through the design and use of environmentally friendly materials, reducing waste generation, and proper waste disposal. In addition, buildings can promote biodiversity protection through ecological landscape design, increasing green vegetation, and protecting wildlife habitats. By integrating environmental protection into building design and operation, buildings can achieve harmonious coexistence with the natural environment.

Health and comfort: Ecological concepts focus on human health and comfort. Buildings can enhance the quality of living and working environments by designing healthy indoor environments, providing good lighting and ventilation conditions, and reducing the use of harmful substances. Ecological buildings focus on indoor air quality, noise control, temperature and humidity regulation, etc., providing residents with a comfortable and healthy living space.

参 考 文 献

［1］ 长江口民俗文化．崇明［EB/OL］.（2021-09-01）［2023-09-04］. https：//www.
bslib. org/cjkms/chongming/msgj. htm

［2］ 陈家宽．长江河口滩涂湿地：上海崇明东滩鸟类国家级自然保护区第二次综合科学考
察报告［M］.上海：上海科学普及出版社，2022.

［3］ 崇明岛的绿色出行与交通规划［EB/OL］.（2025-01-26）［2025-02-06］. https：//
m. renrendoc. com/paper/383394737. html

［4］ 崇明生态岛发展模式与经验研究［EB/OL］.（2014-05-01）［2025-03-07］. https：//
sustainabledevelopment. un. org/content/documents/6008GSDR%20Brief%204CN. pdf

［5］ 崇明生态优势持续转化，东海瀛洲成"诗和远方"［EB/OL］.（2023-11-16）［2025-
02-06］. http：//mp. weixin. qq. com/s? __biz = MzU2MzY3NzIwNA == &mid =
2247500660&idx = 2&sn = cd8f7be5b67df34cbd028efd502f7a71&scene

［6］ 崇明县成为第二批国家级现代农业示范区［J］.上海农村经济，2012（5）：46.

［7］ 打造"崇明大米"地理标志，擦亮绿色农业"金字招牌"［EB/OL］.（2023-05-26）
［2025-02-06］. http：//m. toutiao. com/group/7237506309401149987/? upstream_biz =
doubao

［8］ 国家林业和草原局．上海崇明东滩保护区开展申遗宣传活动［EB/OL］.（2022-12-07）
［2023-09-04］. https：//www. forestry. gov. cn/search/30171

［9］ 江苏省地方志编纂委员会．江苏省志·地理志［M］.南京：江苏古籍出版社，1999：
132.

［10］ 立德树人视域下的"生态教育"——"五育融合"的崇明实践［EB/OL］.（2024-03-
01）［2025-02-10］. https：//m. sohu. com/a/761198711_121124210/1

［11］ 人民网．崇明东滩长期致力生态修复，如今有23种珍稀保护鸟类在那越冬栖息
［EB/OL］.（2021-03-18）［2023-09-04］. http：//sh. people. com. cn/n2/2021/0318/
c176739-34628551. html

［12］ 如何培养"小生态人"? 揭开崇明推进生态教育的"学校密码"［EB/OL］.（2020-
10-10）［2023-09-04］. https：//www. thepaper. cn/newsDetail_forward_9510590

［13］上海崇明东滩大都市里的"候鸟天堂"［EB/OL］.（2025-01-12）［2025-02-06］.
http：//m. toutiao. com/group/7458963682794406426/？upstream_biz=doubao

［14］上海崇明东滩鸟类国家级自然保护区［EB/OL］.（2025-01-20）［2025-02-14］.
https：//baike. baidu. com/item/%E5% B4% 87% E6% 98% 8E% E4% B8% 9C% E6%
BB%A9

［15］上海市崇明区人民政府网 . 崇明概况［EB/OL］.（2021-02-18）［2023-09-04］. https：//
www. shcm. gov. cn/zjcm/006001/20210218/1e56ed92-7cec-4b15-91c8-9782d7aec6a. html

［16］上海市崇明区人民政府网 . 崇明概况［EB/OL］.（2022-10-01）［2023-09-04］.
https：//www. shcm. gov. cn/zjcm/006001/enter. html

［17］上海市崇明区人民政府网 . 崇明概况——地理环境［EB/OL］.（2020-02-12）［2023-
09-07］. https：//www. shcm. gov. cn/zjcm/006001/enter. html#tap1

［18］上海市崇明区人民政府网 . 崇明区生态空间"十四五"规划［EB/OL］.（2022-03-
08）［2023-09-04］. https：//www. shcm. gov. cn/govxxgk/qlhsrj/2022-03-08/3dee677a
c24e-4201-88a0-21a91322ddc1. html

［19］上海市崇明区人民政府 . 视频丨崇明非遗［EB/OL］.（2023-06-15）［2023-09-07］.
https：//shcm. gov. cn/xwzx/002006/20230616/69dff031-3138-46d6-8003-ec803b2fe312.
html

［20］上海市崇明区人民政府 . 视频丨寻味崇明美食，打造乡村版"米其林"体验［EB/
OL］.（2021-12-24）［2023-09-08］. https：//www. shcm. gov. cn/xwzx/002006/
20211227/1416149d-732d-46a9-b50b-cdc330d07724. html

［21］上海市崇明区人民政府 ."生态+"，崇明课后服务提质增效更多彩［EB/OL］.
（2022-03-08）［2023-09-08］. https：//www. shcm. gov. cn/bmdp/019002/019002003/
20220308/25de0186-34af-40b2-a0cf-269a4fa05be7. html

［22］上海市人民政府 . 崇明区：推进落实 2035 发展纲要和第五轮三年行动计划，打造人
与自然和谐共生的世界级生态岛［EB/OL］.（2022-11-10）［2023-09-08］. https：//
www. shanghai. gov. cn/nw15343/20221111/c5353dc5e7f240ce891d556fa96e3501. html

［23］上海市人民政府 . 上海市对崇明岛建设的政策支持与规划布局［EB/OL］.（2022-01-
10）［2023-09-08］. https：//english. shanghai. gov. cn/nw12344/20220114/44da2dee
52e2474d8c5942da188e3426. html

［24］上海学前教育网 . 深化生态教育改革实践，培育未来"生态小主人"［EB/OL］.
（2020-12-04）［2023-09-08］. https：//www. age06. com/Age06Web3/Home/Mobile
ImgFontDetail？Id=c6d6a6ac-e482-458a-8490-eb89ca698b65

［25］上外贤达商学院与崇明生态旅游集团校企战略合作签约仪式成功举行［EB/OL］.

（2023-05-25）［2025-03-07］．https：//www.xdsisu.edu.cn/2023/0525/c905a40574/page.htm

［26］生态崇明岛构建现代化绿色农业体系［EB/OL］．（2025-01-24）［2025-02-06］．https：//m.book118.com/html/2025/0123/8141116023007025.shtm

［27］湿地公园的植物景观设计以上海崇明岛西沙湿地公园［EB/OL］．［2025-03-07］．http：//m.doc.xuehai.net/b2f7a201ad999d96361b83e13-2.html

［28］汪榕培．陶渊明诗歌英译比较研究［M］．北京：外语教学与研究出版社，2000.

［29］许渊冲．中国古诗选三百首［M］．北京：北京大学出版社，1996.

［30］杨宪益，戴乃迭．Poetry and Prose of the Tang and Song［M］．Beijing：Chinese Literature Press，1984.

［31］中国农业信息网．崇明田间养殖稻花鱼让"两无化"水稻增产增收［EB/OL］．（2018-09-19）［2023-09-07］．http：//www.agri.cn/Y20/ZX/q1xxlb_1/sh/201809/t20180919_6249342.htm

［32］中华人民共和国农业农村部．好水里养出"大个头"崇明清水蟹［EB/OL］．（2021-05-24）［2023-09-07］．https：//www.moa.gov.cn/xw/qg/202105/t20210524_6368239.htm.

［33］中华人民共和国生态环境部．美丽中国先锋榜（1）．上海崇明岛"+生态"到"生态+"的规划建设创新实践［EB/OL］．（2019-08-14）［2023-09-04］．https：//www.mee.gov.cn/xxgk2018/xxgk/xxgk15/201908/t20190814_728903.html.

［34］中国青年网．崇明："生态教育"培养未来"生态人"［EB/OL］．（2017-09-07）［2023-09-08］．http：//news.youth.cn/jsxw/201709/t20170907_10665325.htm.

［35］中国青年报．持续擦亮生态底色——上海崇明高标准建设世界级生态岛桥［EB/OL］．（2023-07-28）［2023-09-08］．https：//baijiahao.baidu.com/s?id=1772670233786519885&wfr=spider&for=pc.

［36］着力推广绿色建筑　助推崇明生态建设［EB/OL］．（2021-10-27）［2025-02-10］．https：//m.taodocs.com/p-544815444.html.

［37］张利钧．崇明县志［M］．北京：方志出版社，2013.

［38］朱鑫德．崇明年鉴［M］．上海：上海三联书店，2021.

［39］William Acker．T'ao the Hermit：Sixty Poems by T'ao Ch'ien（365-427）［M］．London：Thames and Hudson，1952.

［40］70年70个瞬间——崇明生态岛建设历程［EB/OL］．（2019-10-01）［2025-03-07］．https：//www.sohu.com/a/344948731_391450.